Spies

Books by Ernest Volkman

Legacy of Hate
Warriors of the Night
The Heist (*with John Cummings*)
Secret Intelligence
Goombata (*with John Cummings*)
Till Murder Do Us Part (*with John Cummings*)

Spies

THE
SECRET AGENTS
WHO CHANGED THE
COURSE OF
HISTORY

Ernest Volkman

John Wiley & Sons, Inc.

New York • Chichester • Brisbane • Toronto • Singapore

For Eric, Michelle, and Christopher

This text is printed on acid-free paper.

Copyright © 1994 by Ernest Volkman
Published by John Wiley & Sons, Inc.

Library of Congress Cataloging-in-Publication Data:

Volkman, Ernest.
    Spies : the secret agents who changed the course of history / Ernest Volkman.
        p.   cm.
    Includes index.
    ISBN 0-471-55714-5 (North & South America   Only)
    ISBN 0-471-02506-2 (Rest of World)
    1. Military intelligence—History—20th century. 2. Espionage—History—20th century.   I. Title.
    UB270.V65   1994
355.3'432'0904—dc20   93-13786

Printed in the United States of America

10 9 8 7 6 5 4 3 2 1

Contents

Introduction

"Espionage," former CIA Director Allen Dulles once remarked, "is not a game for archbishops."

Just so. The game of intelligence—to use the modern polite euphemism for spying—has been called "the world's second oldest profession," and it has much of the same tawdry reputation as its two historical contempories. According to historians, espionage was one of three primordial professions that emerged at the beginning of the human experience on this planet: shaman, harlot, and spy. Shamans ultimately became politicians and lawyers, while spies and harlots evolved into . . . well, spies and harlots.

It is a matter of opinion which profession has acquired the most odious reputation. There is no dispute, however, about which profession has the most ambiguous reputation. Spies are alternately reviled and honored, rewarded and ignored, praised and disowned. This is largely a matter of perspective. Nathan Hale, the American spy during the Revolutionary War, is honored by his countrymen for his famous statement ("I regret that I have but one life to give to my country") upon the occasion of his execution by the British. But the British view of Hale is very different, understandably considering the number of British soldiers who died as a result of the intelligence he provided to General Washington. Similarly, the great Soviet spy Richard Sorge was posthumously honored by a commemorative postage stamp issued by Moscow some 25 years after his execution by the Japanese. But Germany will never proffer such an honor, for thousands of its young men died in the snows around Moscow in the winter of 1941 at the hands of Siberian troops shifted west to defeat the German onslaught against Moscow—a deployment that took place after Sorge found out the Japanese had decided not to invade the Soviet Union.

Even today, in a time of vast national espionage establishments that has made the business of spying institutionalized, "spy" is still not a nice word. (Which is why espionage organizations prefer to call themselves "intelligence agencies," and their employees prefer the job title "intelligence officer.") However much modern political cynicism might concede the necessity of snooping on certain other people in a dangerous world, espionage is not a profession parents hope their children will enter.

Spying acquired its unsavory reputation at the moment of its birth, somewhere around 5,000 years ago in ancient Egypt, when King Thutmosis III hit upon the idea of concealing men inside flour sacks to spy on the besieged city of Jaffa. Thutmosis organized history's first official government state espionage apparatus, an innovation he later had chiseled among hieroglyphics recording the triumphs of his reign—although he was careful to categorize his espionage feats under the heading of "secret science." They represented a distinctly secondary note alongside such real accomplishments as the construction of cities and the filling of granaries that provided food for his people. Thutmosis may have been a great spymaster, but he sensed there was something not quite nice about snooping, even on his enemies, and it is clear that he much preferred to be remembered for other examples of his statecraft.

The Bible subsequently recorded Moses dispatching spies to "go spy the land," but it was not until the creation of great nation states three centuries ago that organized espionage—and spies—became an integral part of statecraft. At the same time, a distaste for spies and spying began to develop among the people of those great nation states. (James Bond is only the latest in a long line of fictional characters who never seem to dirty their hands in the real-life grubby world of the spy.)

In the twentieth century, entire armies of spies have been deployed during a period in history marked by almost continuous war. And where there is war, there are spies. To confront the more than 200,000 spies employed by the Soviet Union at the height of its power, and the slightly smaller espionage army of the United States is to understand how deeply spying has woven itself into the fabric of modern civilization.

This century has sometimes been called "the century of the spy," because the insatiable quest for information by modern industrialized states has created the vast armies of spies who have come to play such a critical role in the course of world history.

This book makes no attempt to consider all the men and women of those armies. Such a task would be impossible between the covers of any size book; literally millions of spies have practiced what is still known as the "black art." But there has been only a relatively small number whose work has had a dramatic impact on history. These are the men and women who have directly affected the fate of empires, of nations, of history itself.

Be warned, however; none of these people possess the stuff of greatness. They run the gamut of human beings, from the brave to the cowardly, from the wise to the foolish, from the intelligent to the appallingly stupid. Some are extraordnary people, some very ordinary, and others somewhere in between. There is no common thread that unites them, except that all of them have been governed by the Three Great Spy Commandmants:

I. Thou Shalt Not Get Caught

II. If Thou Ist Caught, We Have Never Heard of Thee

III. Given the Foregoing, No Other Commandments Are Necessary

This book grew out of some discussions with members of the American intelligence community—as they prefer to call themselves—who like to ruminate on the place of the spy in history. As those conversations developed, a gradual consensus emerged: among the many spies who have ever attired themselves in the metaphorical cloak and dagger, it is astonishing how many of them had no impact whatsoever. Which is to say either they failed, or the governments that hired them failed.

The exceptions to that general rule represent the core of this book. I should emphasize that the men and women ultimately selected for inclusion in this volume are the result of my own research and conclusions. I'm certain that a fair number of people in the intelligence community will object to the inclusion of some names, and argue for the addition of others. I take full responsibility for the final list in this book, along with my interpretations. Readers may find a few familiar names missing—along with a few surprises.

A word on methodology. The spies discussed in this book are slotted into a number of categories, including moles, defectors, legends, traitors, spymasters, and infamies, along with several people I categorize as "mysteries" and "curiosities." Because a number of espionage careers overlap, readers will find some names bold-faced; those names so highlighted are treated separately elsewhere in the book. The names in this virtual espionage hall of infamy—spydom's "greatest hits," if you will—are listed in no particular order, chronological or otherwise. Spying, as its adherents learned a long time ago, is an activity that resists easy categorization.

As usual, this book would not exist without the advice, support, and direction of every writer's dream of a literary agent, Victoria Pryor of Arcadia.

ERNEST VOLKMAN
Danbury, Connecticut
Winter, 1993

Glossary

Like many other fields of human endeavor, espionage has its own special language. Whenever possible, I have tried to avoid using the jargon in this book, but unavoidably, there are some unique terms that have no ordinary language equivalents:

AGENT: A spy in the pay of a nation's intelligence service on a regular, salaried basis, with the status of government employee.

AGENT OF INFLUENCE: An asset (a term to be defined subsequently), usually in an important government position, who is assigned the job of influencing policy, rather than collecting intelligence.

AGENT PROVOCATEUR: An asset, usually under control of a counterintelligence or police agency, assigned to infiltrate a political organization and instigate violent action designed to discredit that organization and justify extreme countermeasures.

ASSET: A foreigner enrolled by an intelligence service—either for pay or because of political conviction—to serve as an intelligence source.

BLACK BAG JOB: Break-in or burglary to gain access to secret papers, which are photographed and returned, customarily in the same operation. Such operations are carried out by highly trained teams to conceal any trace of their presence.

BLACK PROPAGANDA: Propaganda whose origin is completely disguised and takes the form of a "clandestine" operation by alleged political dissidents against the target country, most often by means of a "secret" radio station within the country's borders or just outside them. The station is actually created by agents of a hostile intelligence service trained in such techniques, and is designed to sow discord and confusion while boosting the political fortunes of an "exile" faction.

BLOWN: Agent or asset revealed to counterintelligence. Also called "burned."

BRUSH CONTACT: Rapid, apparently accidental, contact between an agent or asset and a case officer or control agent to exchange material, most often in a crowded public place to confuse surveillance.

CASE OFFICER: Agent assigned to supervise an agent or asset (or a network—"ring"—of them), in matters of pay, collection of intelligence, and other details. Also called "control agent."

CHIEF OF STATION: Agent assigned to head an overseas intelligence unit, normally part of an embassy. In Soviet intelligence parlance, such an agent is known as a *rezident.*

COVER: Organizational disguise under which an agent hides connection to an intelligence agency. In American intelligence parlance, cover can be "light" (diplomatic) or "deep" (commercial or other such organizational affiliation).

CRYPTANALYST: Trained analyst who works to break codes and ciphers by attempting to recover the "key" (specific method) used in encryption. Currently, such analysts tend to be mathematicians who work with super-computers to attack computer-generated codes.

DEAD DROP: Site where agents can leave and exchange messages with other agents or their control, most often in nooks and crevices in public areas (a hole in a wall is a particular favorite). Such a technique is designed to avoid any contact between those "filling" (inserting material) the dead drop and those "servicing" it (removing such material). Also known as *dubok,* from Soviet intelligence parlance.

DISCARD: Agent or asset deliberately sacrificed to deflect attention from other, more important, agents.

FRONT: Legitimate-appearing entity created by an intelligence to provide cover for agents and assets. It can take many forms, from a charitable foundation to a corporate entity.

ILLEGAL: In Soviet intelligence, agent operating in a foreign country under an assumed identity or cover job.

LEGAL: In Soviet intelligence, agent operating in a foreign country under diplomatic cover, providing diplomatic immunity in event of arrest.

LEGEND: Faked biography of an agent to conceal real identity.

LETTERBOX: Person used as a go-between (often called "cutout") to receive and pass on messages.

MOLE: Asset inserted into the political, intelligence or military structure of a target nation with the specific objective of rising to a key position, at which point the asset is "switched on" to provide high-level intelligence.

ONE-TIME PAD: Cipher device that uses a pad with sheets of random numbers that are used to encrypt messages once, then discarded. Since each sheet is readable only to someone on the other end with the same pad, the system is theoretically unbreakable.

PLAYBACK: The technique of using a captured agent's radio to feed misleading information to the agent's control. Also called *funkspiel* (radio game) in German intelligence parlance. Intelligence agencies attempt to forestall such techniques by training agents to insert a "warn key" in their transmissions if captured and forced to send messages (usually a specific word that warns a receiving station). They also learn to recognize an agent's "fist" (distinctive method of sending or touch) that is difficult to duplicate by someone else using the agent's radio.

SLEEPER: Agent planted in another country with orders to carry out a normal life and conduct no intelligence operations until ordered to do so—most often, in the event of hostilities.

STATION: Chief office of an intelligence agency in a foreign country, most often located in an embassy.

WALKIN: Asset who literally walks into the embassy or intelligence headquarters of a foreign country and volunteers information or offers to work as a spy, either for pay or for political motives. Intelligence agencies on occasion will deliberately send an agent posing as a walk-in in order to penetrate the other side and plant false intelligence. Such an agent is called a "dangle."

The Agencies

(an alphabetical listing)

Abwehr
Allamvedelmi Hatosag (AVH)
Bundesamt fur Verfassungsschutz (BfV)
Bundesnachrichtdienst (BND)
Central External Liaison Department (CELD)
Central Intelligence Agency (CIA)
Chrezuyehainaya Komissiya po Borbe s Kontrrevolutisnei i Sab-
    bottazhem (CHEKA)
Direction de la Surveillance du territoire (DST)
Direccion General de Intelligencia (DGI)
Direction General de Securitie Exterieure (DGSE)
Federal Bureau of Investigation (FBI)
Geheime Staatspolizei (Gestapo)
Government Code and Cipher School (GCCS)
Government Communications Headquarters (GCHQ)
Glavnoye Razvedyvatelnoye Upravleni (GRU)
Hauptverwaltung fur Aufklarung (HVA)
Komit Gosudarstvennoy Bezopasnosi (KGB)
Mossad Letafkidim Meyouch-hadim (Mossad)
Mukhabarat el-Aam (Mukhabarat)
National Security Agency (NSA)
Naval Intelligence Division (NID)
Office of Naval Intelligence (ONI)
Office of Strategic Services (OSS)
Secret Intelligence Service (MI6)
Security Service (MI5)
Service de Documentation Exterieure et de Contre-Espionage
    (SDECE)

Sicherheitsdienst (SD)
Sluzba Bezpieczenstwa (SB)
Staatssicherheitsdienst (SSD)
Statni Tajna Bezpecnost (STB)
U.S. Army Military Intelligence Division (MID)

THE MOLES

FRITZ KAUDERS
Triumph of the Schieber

Code Name: MAX
Alias: Richard Klatt
1903–?

With his ingratiating politeness, Viennese charm, and oily manner, the short, stocky man with wavy hair was that prototypical European type known in German as a *schieber* (roughly, con artist). By 1939, Fritz Kauders, a man who had lived by his wits for most of the 36 years of his life, was among the sharpest hustlers in all Europe. He was ready for the scam of his career, which turned out to be one of the most significant deceptions in the history of espionage.

In terms of background, Kauders seemed ideal for the Byzantine world of pre-World War II European espionage. Born in Vienna of a Jewish mother and a Catholic father (this fact would assume critical importance in his life later on), Kauders worked as a journalist as a young man during the 1920s. However, he soon found there was a lot more money to be made hustling: setting up various shady deals, selling identity papers, and arranging introductions (for a price) to the officials of a half-dozen European countries he had managed to charm or bribe into co-conspiracy. A man who regularly visited most of the capitals of Europe in the course of running his many business deals, Kauders soon had a network of government contacts from the Baltic to the Mediterranean.

It was only a matter of time before one intelligence service or another would seek to recruit this artful *schieber* as an asset. That moment came in 1939 when a mysterious character named

Andrei Turkhul recruited Kauders for his own network, a huge ring comprised primarily of White Russian exiles, which provided intelligence from all over Europe and even from inside the Soviet Union. Or so Turkhul claimed to his ostensible employer, the German intelligence agency, *Abwehr*. Actually, Turkhul's real loyalty was to Soviet intelligence, which had recruited him nearly 20 years before. Turkhul had been keeping Moscow informed of *Abwehr* operations, but the recruitment of Kauders gave the KGB the idea for an even bigger game, the hoodwinking of Nazi Germany.

This required an audacious and patient plan: over a period of years, Kauders would be developed into the *Abwehr*'s chief source on the Soviet Union. He would be provided with a steady diet of low-grade intelligence from Moscow, consistently building his credibility until, at just the right moment, he would pass on a major piece of doctored intelligence the *Abwehr* would find irresistible. Neither Turkhul nor Kauders could have guessed at that point how poisonous that doctored intelligence would prove.

Turkhul slowly developed Kauders—who operated under the alias of Richard Klatt, a businessman—and with assistance from Moscow, soon was feeding a steady stream of middle-grade intelligence to the *Abwehr*. Kauders enhanced his growing reputation with some operations he devised himself, including the feat of stealing sensitive diplomatic papers from the office of the American consul in Zagreb, Yugoslavia.

All the while, Kauders was drawing a handsome monthly stipend from the *Abwehr*, but as the Germans became aware, there was something else he wanted: a piece of paper that was beyond price. That paper was a so-called "Aryanization certificate," a document issued by the Nazi government that certified that its holder, a presumed Jew, had been investigated by "race relations experts" and found to be in fact "Aryan." To the offspring of a mixed marriage like Kauders, that piece of paper could be a lifesaver; without it, he could be picked up at any moment and shipped off to a death camp.

But this was no simple request. The Nazis took the business of deciding who was a Jew very seriously, and even the highest-ranking officers of the *Abwehr* had very little influence in such matters. The *Abwehr* could not get him a certificate, but it could protect him from the Gestapo, in the process violating one of Nazi Germany's sternest strictures: No Jew was allowed to serve in any German intelligence agency. Incredibly, Kauders was not only protected by the *Abwehr*, this Jewish spy was also protected by Germany's Nazi intelligence agency, the SD.

The reason was not hard to discern. Simply, Kauders was regarded as German intelligence's prime source on the Soviet Union, a source so valuable that the risk of employing a Jew—a capital offense in Nazi Germany—was well worth the result. Kauders' vaunting reputation had been stage-managed by Turkhul, who claimed to his *Abwehr* controllers that Kauders had a network of contacts inside the Soviet Union that extended into the Soviet military's high command. The timing of this bait could not have been better: the Germans had invaded the Soviet Union, and were desperate for any intelligence on the Soviet military. Kauders said he could get it, provided that he be set up with his own transmitter, serve as the exclusive go-between for his top sources and German intelligence, and never be required to reveal the identities of those sources.

The *Abwehr* happily assented to those conditions, and set up Kauders in Sofia, Bulgaria, with his own radio transmitter. Almost from the first moment, Kauders, code-named MAX, proved to be a spectacular asset. He gave his *Abwehr* case officers a gushing river of topflight reports on Soviet military dispositions, and to the delight of the Germans, the reports were unfailingly accurate, resulting in several spectacular tactical victories. By 1942, Kauders represented the single most important intelligence source for the Germans on the Soviet military. Such German intelligence sachems as Reinhard Gehlen, head of the German army's military intelligence organization, and Wilhelm Canaris of the *Abwehr* pronounced MAX pure gold.

But not all the Germans were so elated. The *Abwehr* case officers in Sofia were suspicious of Kauders from the outset, and their suspicions deepened as they considered his operation. Where was all this top-level information coming from? Kauders claimed that his sources included high-ranking officers assigned to the *Stavka*, the Soviet high command, and he also had sources close to Stalin himself. These sources radioed over a top secret transmitter to Kauders, often within minutes of hearing of decisions reached inside Stalin's war council.

For any *Abwehr* officer with experience in Stalin's police state, with its unprecedented internal security—especially in wartime—Kauders' claims rang hollow. Some *Abwehr* officers monitored Kauders' radio transmissions, and discovered that the amount of traffic bore no resemblance to the volume of intelligence Kauders claimed to be receiving. Moreover, the idea that traitors in the Soviet High Command would take the extraordinary risk of radioing their treason directly from the Kremlin strained credulity.

The *Abwehr* men in Sofia finally concluded that Kauders was a Soviet mole, planted in German intelligence for the express purpose of passing on high-level strategic deception. But despite their complaints to Berlin, the faith of German intelligence in Kauders remained unshaken. As even his worst critics in Sofia were compelled to admit, his information—whatever the source—was rock solid. Where was the deception?

The Germans did not know that the Russians were biding their time, waiting for the right moment. They had coldbloodedly sacrificed entire units to bolster MAX, willing to trade lives for the purpose of enhancing his bona fides. In the late winter of 1942, the Russians finally made their move: Kauders reported that his sources had told him of the plan to confront the German Sixth Army at Stalingrad, and Stalin's order that the city be held at all costs. He provided further details: the actual identity of the Soviet units assigned to the battle, the plan to ferry units across the Volga at night, and the names of the generals assigned the mission of evicting the Germans from the city.

The intelligence seemed nothing short of sensational, but as the *Abwehr* discovered, incomplete: Kauders somehow did not learn that the Soviet plan included a giant pincer movement to sweep west and east of the city against the weak flanks held by Hungarian and Roumanian forces allied with the Germans, and trap the entire 250,000-man German Sixth Army. Within a month, the Soviet offensive surrounded Stalingrad, forcing the surrender of what was left of the Sixth Army, a defeat from which Nazi Germany never recovered.

Despite this disaster, MAX was still regarded highly. But in 1944, an even more significant Soviet deception finally ended his career as Germany's super-spy. It concerned the decision by the Soviet *Stavka* to unleash a major military offensive designed finally to shatter German military power in the east. MAX revealed that the offensive was code-named Operation Bagration, and aimed at the southern Ukraine, with the eventual aim of capturing the Balkans. The Germans dutifully concentrated their thin resources in the south, but when the blow fell, it came on the central front, over 400 miles away. Nearly a half-million German troops perished in the onslaught, which did not end until the Russians smashed their way into Berlin some months later.

MAX now began to look frayed around the edges, at least to his control officers in Sofia. They had discovered that Kauders was running a number of private business operations on the side, in the process bribing the Bulgarian police to overlook some of his more shady operations. It bespoke a character defect which compelled them to review the entire MAX operation. Finally, there was no doubt: He was a mole.

Interestingly, there was one intelligence agency outside the Soviet Union which in 1943 had reached the same conclusion: the British MI6. Thanks to its ULTRA code-breaking operation, the British were reading the *Abwehr* traffic between Sofia and Berlin. Initially, the British were concerned, for the detail of Soviet military secrets in the traffic indicated that the Germans had a source (or sources) at very high levels in the Soviet military command structure who was feeding high-grade intelligence via radio to Sofia, where an *Abwehr* agent—known only as MAX in the radio traffic—was then conveying it to Berlin. Alarmed, MI6 officials told the Soviets about the leak, but Moscow indicated no interest whatsoever in the revelation. MI6 concluded, correctly, that the astonishing Soviet indifference could only mean that MAX was part of an elaborate Soviet deception.

The *Abwehr* did not have the advantage of ULTRA, but nevertheless concluded that MAX was working for the Russians. Under ordinary circumstances, that would have meant death for Kauders. For the moment, however, he was saved, because at this critical juncture, German intelligence was in turmoil. After the abortive plot to overthrow Hitler in July 1944—a plot in which Canaris was directly involved—the *Abwehr* was disbanded and its functions taken over by the SD. Curiously, the SD continued to believe that Kauders was genuine and was determined to save him. It transferred MAX to the Hungarian intelligence service as a means of evading the rule against any German intelligence service using Jewish agents, but even that subterfuge failed. Hitler, furious when he learned that his intelligence services had been using a Jewish agent, ordered Kauders taken to a concentration camp. It took the personal intervention of General Heinz Guderian, chief of the General Staff, to get the order rescinded, but Kauders was imprisoned in a German military prison to get him out of harm's way. In May 1945, as Nazi Germany was collapsing, he was released. He fled to Austria under Turkhul's protection, and a few weeks later, was arrested again, this time by the Americans, as a Nazi agent.

A lifetime of hustling had prepared Kauders for such eventualities, and within a year, he had not only gotten himself released, but also had convinced the OSS to enlist him as an asset to operate against Soviet intelligence in Austria. The Soviets were displeased by this sudden switch when Turkhul told them about it, and in February 1946, they attempted to kidnap him, using a team of agents dressed in American Army MP uniforms. Army intelligence agents balked the attempt, but Kauders got the message: He disappeared. In 1964, he reappeared in Vienna to offer his services to the CIA. Suspicious CIA officials rejected the offer, and Kauders disappeared again.

It was not until some years later, when captured German intelligence records were analyzed, that the Americans realized Kauders was the fabled MAX, the mole who had done so much to undermine German military operations on the Eastern front.

The disappearance of Kauders left unresolved many mysteries connected with the MAX operation. Chief among them was motive: Why had Kauders put his head in the lion's mouth to carry out a deception that he must have known would inevitably be discovered? There is no indication he ever had Communist leanings, so any political motive apparently didn't inspire him. Did he agree to help destroy Nazi Germany because he was a Jew, determined to avenge Hitler's Holocaust against his people? Possibly, although he was not religious, and always insisted he was Catholic. Money? Perhaps, although the lavish funds he received from the Germans represented scant compensation for the near certainty of a bullet in the head when they discovered the deception. Or the answer may be simply that Kauders, the lifelong *schieber*, could not resist the biggest scam he had ever seen.

Only MAX himself knows the answer—wherever he might be.

H. A. R. PHILBY
The Mole's Mole

Code Names: STANLEY, AGENT TOM
1912–1988

" To betray," Harold Adrian Russell (Kim) Philby once said near the end of his life, "one must first belong. I never belonged."

However enigmatic, this is the only explanation Philby ever offered to explain a career that amounts to the most incredible in the entire history of espionage. Philby was the quintessential mole, the man who on behalf of the Soviet KGB* infiltrated his country's intelligence service and betrayed its secrets for nearly 30 years. He came within a hair's breadth of becoming chief of that intelligence service, which would have represented the ultimate espionage fantasy: the chief of an intelligence service actually working for the opposition, with consequences that can only be dreamed. The Philby saga has served as the inspiration for countless works of fiction, along with a large pile of nonfiction works that have attempted to explain the Philby phenomenon.

Analysts of the Philby case have unfailingly concentrated on his early life for clues to what made him tick. Born in India just before World War I, Philby was the son of a British mother and

---

* The KGB has undergone a number of acronymic evolutions, beginning with GPU (1922–23), OGPU (1923–24), NKVD (1934–44), NKGB (1944–46), MGB (1946–53), KGB (1954–91), and FIS (1991 to date). To simplify matters, "KGB" will be used in this book to refer to the Soviet Union's main foreign intelligence service from 1922 onward.

The quintessential mole: H. A. R. (Kim) Philby in 1955, when he was already under suspicion as a KGB agent who had infiltrated British intelligence.

a curious figure in British history, the Arabist H. St. John Philby. A full-blown eccentric, Philby senior made his name in the Middle East, where he worked on behalf of British intelligence to stir up Arab revolution against Turkey. After the war, convinced that Britain had betrayed the Arabs, he moved to Saudi Arabia, where he became a Moslem, took an Arabian woman as his second wife, and warned his son never to trust the word of the British establishment.

Philby and his son were close, but the father had nothing to do with his son's political conversion to communism. That process began when Philby entered Cambridge in 1929, where he became close friends with Guy Burgess and Donald Maclean, who had already become full-fledged Marxists. They recruited Philby, who would likely have remained just another undergraduate Communist except for an experience that was to prove the seminal one of his life.

During his vacations, Philby liked to tour Europe, where the sight of early Nazi terror further hardened his transformation into an ardent Communist. But it was in Vienna during the summer of 1934 that Philby decided he would become a "soldier," as he later put it, in the struggle against fascism.

He arrived in the midst of political turmoil. The right-wing government was locked in a life-or-death struggle with its leftist opponents, and Philby enlisted as a volunteer with Socialist revolutionaries (supported by the Austrian Communists), working primarily as a courier between various anti-government outposts. Coincidentally, he met and fell in love with Alice Friedman. Known as "Litzi," Friedman was an Austrian Communist. She was deeply involved in the struggle convulsing the city, which was climaxed by the shelling by government forces of workers' housing, killing hundreds. The experience of seeing a government slaughter its own people radicalized Philby.

Fortuitously for Soviet intelligence, at that time there were two KGB operatives working in the city: Theodor Maly, a Hungarian ex-priest who had converted to communism, and **Gabor Peter,** another Hungarian Communist. Both recognized in Philby that rare combination of intelligence and blind devotion, and he was recruited to serve the "cause of world revolution." But he would no longer demonstrate his commitment to the Communist cause by smuggling messages past police checkpoints; from now on, he was told, he was to conceal his political convictions and infiltrate the British government, preferably its intelligence service, by boring from within.

Upon his return to Britain, Philby immediately moved to erase his Communist past, the essential first step in gaining entry into the British establishment. Publicly, his politics veered suddenly rightward, and he joined the Anglo-German Fellowship, a right-wing group that actively promoted the idea of an alliance with Nazi Germany. As a further move toward concealment, he divorced Alice Friedman.

His penetration of the establishment came in 1936, when he landed a job with the *London Times* as a correspondent on the Franco side in the Spanish Civil War. His blatantly pro-Franco dispatches further cemented the idea of a right-wing Philby, although he was already providing to the KGB low-grade intelligence he picked up from Franco's entourage. (His espionage career almost ended prematurely one day when he was picked up by suspicious Nationalist soldiers for questioning. At the time, he had several pieces of incriminating paper on him. Asked to produce his wallet, he deliberately skidded it across a table; when the soldiers dived for it, Philby used the diversion to swallow the papers).

In 1939, while still a *Times* correspondent, Philby got the break he was looking for. Thanks to the influence of fellow alumnus (and Communist comrade) Guy Burgess, who was working in Department D (sabotage and propaganda) of MI6, he was recruited to join the organization. As was the practice then in the establishment-oriented MI6, Philby's vetting was casual. His father, asked about his son's known Communist sympathies while at Cambridge, dismissed it with the comment, "Oh, just some youthful political rot," and that was the end of it.

With this astonishingly easy background check out of the way, Philby achieved the goal the KGB had set for him five years before: to infiltrate British intelligence. At first, however, this entry did not seem very promising. Department D was eliminated in 1941 and replaced by an agency called *SOE*, and MI6 did not quite know what to do with Philby. For one thing, he had a lifelong stutter, which obviated the idea of putting him into the field. The solution, finally, was to assign him as a desk officer in Section V (counterespionage in foreign countries) of MI6. The decision could not have been more perfect for Philby and the KGB, for as a desk officer, he would be privy to a wide range of intelligence reports, giving him a much better overview than any field agent.

Philby was a popular man in MI6. A hard drinker like many of his fellow agents, he had sufficient credentials to be trusted by the upper classes who dominated MI6's leadership, but was also considered sufficiently common to mix easily with the more "ordinary blokes" who made up MI6's lower ranks. Called "Kim" after the Rudyard Kipling character because of his birth in India, Philby was regarded as a talented intelligence officer, and was widely assumed to be a "comer," the kind of officer who might someday become chief of the entire service.

In late 1944 Philby received another astonishing stroke of luck: he was named to revive Section IX of MI6. The section, assigned to combat Soviet subversion and intelligence operations, remained virtually moribund while the Soviet Union was Britain's wartime ally. Nevertheless, as the end of the war neared and it was clear that the Soviet Union would be the West's next enemy, MI6 decided to recreate the section under Philby, with 100 intelligence agents assigned to him.

A more perfect location for a KGB mole cannot be imagined. Precisely what Philby betrayed to Moscow may never be

known for certain outside the KGB archives, but it is known that
Philby performed two vital services for the KGB during the war.
One was the systematic balking of efforts by the anti-Nazi German
underground to obtain British support for an overthrow of Hitler.
The underground represented Moscow's worst nightmare: a new
German government that almost certainly would seek a separate
peace with the West; with consequences that could be catastrophic for the Soviet Union if the Germans could bring their
full military might to bear in the East. To abort such an eventuality, Philby sidetracked reports by German anti-Nazis working for
MI6, denigrated the effectiveness of the anti-Hitler opposition,
and ensured that MI6 reports on the German opposition ranked
them as "ineffectual" and not worth dealing with.

Philby's second service was to keep the KGB informed of the
names of assets MI6 was recruiting in Eastern Europe (later, when
Moscow took control of the region, the assets were rounded up).
At the same time, Philby betrayed the very anti-Soviet networks
he was creating as head of Section IX; armed with this warning,
the KGB simply took over the networks and fed back misleading
intelligence that virtually blinded British intelligence for years.

In 1945, Philby was suddenly confronted with a crisis that
threatened an end to his career. Almost simultaneously, two members of Soviet intelligence defected to the West. One, **Igor Gouzenko,** a code clerk at the Soviet embassy in Ottawa, Canada, had
fled with a batch of top-secret Soviet intelligence telegrams, along
with whatever knowledge was in his head. The second, Konstant-
sin Volkov, a senior KGB officer in Istanbul, had not yet actually
defected, but he had approached the British embassy with an
offer to defect, noting that he had intimate knowledge of KGB
infiltration of British intelligence. Volkov did not know the specific identities of the KGB moles, but he mentioned several clues,
among them one, which if fully investigated, would ultimately
have revealed Philby.

Philby consulted his control, Yuri Modin, the legendary KGB
agent-handler in London who oversaw the KGB's great prize, the
"Ring of Five" of KGB moles in Great Britain (Philby, Maclean,
Burgess, **Anthony Blunt,** and John Cairncross). In Modin's calculation, Philby could not handle both defections, so the KGB
was confronted with choosing the lesser of two evils. Either Gouzenko or Volkov might blow Philby—and others—but of the two,
the odds were that Volkov was the most dangerous. Gouzenko
worked for the GRU; thus, it could be assumed he might not

know of moles working for the KGB, an entirely separate intelligence agency. On the other hand, Volkov was a high-ranking KGB officer who apparently had picked up some clues about the KGB's penetration of British intelligence. Modin and Philby saw no option: Volkov was potentially the greatest danger, so as head of Section IX, Philby would offer to debrief Volkov personally. Gouzenko's debriefing, meanwhile, would be left to others—while Modin and Philby kept their fingers crossed.

Forewarned of Volkov's attempted defection, the KGB removed the threat while Philby took his sweet time getting to Istanbul. It has never been revealed what happened to Volkov, but witnesses saw a body, swathed head to toe in bandages, hustled aboard a Soviet airliner in Istanbul on the very same day that Volkov suddenly disappeared. Philby blamed Volkov's presumed capture on the Russian's "inattention to security."

As it turned out, Gouzenko had no real insight into KGB operations in Great Britain, so with the disappearance of Volkov, Philby was home free. At the end of the war, his star rose steadily brighter in MI6, which had no idea that he was betraying to the KGB a huge MI6 operation to infiltrate anti-Communist guerrillas into the Baltic states. A number of other such operations elsewhere in Eastern Europe also went sour, but no one associated Philby with the grim roster of intelligence disasters. Not yet, anyway.

There was talk around MI6 of Philby eventually succeeding his chief, Stewart Menzies, a career track confirmed in 1949 when Philby was named to one of MI6's most important posts, chief of station in Washington, D.C. There his duties included serving as liaison between MI6 and American intelligence. The KGB could hardly have wished for a more opportune posting, for Philby was now in a position not only to betray MI6's secrets, but the CIA's secrets, as well.

Philby had no sooner taken up residence in Washington when he learned of America's biggest secret. Code-named VENONA, it was a code-breaking operation directed against the huge backlog of Soviet intelligence radio traffic during the war from London, New York, and Washington. Both the Americans and British suspected, correctly, that the high volume was due to Moscow cranking up all its assets to provide intelligence at a time of greatest peril to the Communist regime. The operation had begun with the recovery of a partially-burned Soviet codebook in Finland, which provided several vital keys toward unlocking the

Soviet intelligence ciphers. It was a long, tedious process (the eventual operation took more than 30 years to complete), but the early indications were alarming: the Russians apparently had hundreds of assets in the United States and Great Britain.

The assets were identified only by code names, but the codebreakers were able to match those code names with other clues contained in various messages. They concentrated on the most significant ones, especially an asset who had provided information about the atomic bomb project (he turned out to be **Klaus Fuchs** and, more ominously from Philby's standpoint, a highly placed British asset code-named HOMER who was leaking high-level intelligence from the British Foreign Office. A careless clue contained in one message—that HOMER had travelled to New York from Washington at one point to see his pregnant and ill wife—pointed directly to a British diplomat serving at the British embassy in Washington: Donald Maclean.

As the British intelligence liaison in Washington, Philby was part of the intelligence team that monitored the progress of the VENONA decrypts, and so was able to warn the KGB that by 1951, the codebreakers had nailed Maclean. With that warning, Yuri Modin decided that Maclean, close to a nervous breakdown over the strain of his double life, would have to be exfiltrated to Moscow before he cracked under the strain of interrogation by British counterintelligence. Modin managed that exfiltration skillfully enough, but in the process an event he could not have anticipated brought Philby's usefulness to an end.

Modin assigned one of his prime assets, Guy Burgess, the task of getting Maclean out of Great Britain. Burgess was a close friend of Maclean, but he was also a close friend of Philby, and lived in Philby's house for a brief period when Philby was first assigned to Washington. That connection was bad enough, but when Burgess suddenly and mysteriously decided he would accompany Maclean on his flight eastward, that served to focus suspicion on Philby as the presumed "third man" who warned Maclean of imminent arrest.

From the KGB's standpoint, it was an unmitigated disaster. Just at the very moment when Philby occupied a critical intelligence post and was tantalizingly close to becoming the chief of MI6, Burgess' curious action ruined everything. Within months, CIA Director Walter Bedell Smith sent a curt note to MI6 Director Stewart Menzies: "Recall Philby or we break off the intelligence relationship."

And with that, Philby's real service to the KGB was at an end. MI6 kept him on, but under a cloud of suspicion, he was no longer in a position to provide the kind of intelligence the KGB had come to expect. Additionally, he was coming under attack by British and American counterintelligence, which suspected he was the top-level spy code-named STANLEY mentioned in the VENONA traffic decrypts. To make matters worse, several Soviet defectors were providing accumulating clues about him. By 1961, it was clear that the net was drawing tighter. **George Blake,** another prize KGB mole inside British intelligence, had been caught and made a full confession, in which he mentioned some clues that pointed toward Philby.

Modin now went into action. Tipped off about a pending MI6 plan to confront Philby and offer immunity in return for a full confession (who imparted this vital intelligence to Modin remains unknown), the KGB agent-runner sped to Beirut, where Philby was working under cover for MI6 as a newspaper correspondent. Modin's plan was for Philby to submit to MI6 interrogation to find out just how much hard information MI6 had on him, then flee to Moscow as soon as his interrogators showed their high cards. Philby duly gave his limited confession—he admitted only what he sensed MI6 already knew—and on January 23, 1963, he slipped out of a dinner party and disappeared. Six weeks later, Moscow announced that he had been granted political asylum.

If Philby thought this most sensational defection in the history of espionage would lead to some sort of senior position in the KGB, he was to receive a rude awakening. The Russians were prepared to provide a large apartment and plenty of money to live on, but they had no intention of using Philby in any intelligence operation. The simple fact was they did not trust him fully. In the KGB's calculation, there was no guarantee that he not been turned by the other side and was not now in the process of attempting to duplicate for the West what he had accomplished for Moscow. Accordingly, Philby became a frustrated English exile, wandering around Moscow with his copy of the *London Times* (another KGB benefit that allowed Philby to keep current with his consuming passion, English cricket). He was a witty, rumpled alcoholic who occasionally granted tantalizing interviews to visiting British newspapermen, and basked in the glow of the elaborate respect with which all Soviet officials treated him. He kept up a bustling correspondence with some of his old British friends, notably the novelist (and ex-MI6 colleague) **Graham Greene,** who made the thinly-disguised Philby the central character in his novel, *The Human Factor.*

Philby's arms-length relationship with the KGB did not change until 1980, when KGB chief Yuri Andropov invited him to serve as a consultant on operations in Great Britain. What advice Philby was able to render is not known, but the chance of getting back into the intelligence game appeared to reinvigorate him, albeit briefly. Philby was a sick man, and never appeared anywhere without a pair of white gloves to protect his hands from a virulent skin allergy. It was among a number of ailments that gradually sapped his strength, and in May 1988, he died.

The Soviets spared no effort to honor the greatest intelligence asset in their history. There was a funeral service attended by virtually every important political and intelligence official in the Soviet hierarchy, followed by an elaborate graveside service with full military honors (Andropov had promoted him to full general in the KGB). Philby insisted on being buried in Soviet soil, and his coffin was lowered into the ground with medals across his chest, Russian-style.

Prominent among them was the Order of Lenin, the Soviet Union's highest decoration. In his last years, Philby was fond of showing off the medal, but like the Englishman he remained to his death, he sniffed it was not as prestigious as a knighthood.

ANTHONY BLUNT
"The Pope Wants You!"

Code Name: JOHNSON
1908–1983

It would be difficult to find a more rock-solid example of the British establishment than Anthony Blunt, whose father was a clergyman and at one time chaplain to the British embassy in Paris, and whose mother was related to the Queen Mother. This made his recruitment as a KGB mole all the more mysterious.

Like the other members of the "ring of five" (the KGB's term for its major network of British assets), Blunt attended Cambridge in the *angst* of postwar Great Britain, a time of shattered illusions and bleak futures in which Marxist ideology was nurtured and flourished. Like many other Cambridge students, Blunt joined the Communist party, but unlike most of the others, he took the momentous step from political conviction to espionage.

Although Blunt himself never told, it is believed that he was recruited by the KGB in 1933 while a fellow at Cambridge, and he is therefore ranked as "the first man" in the "ring of five." It was Blunt who challenged younger Marxists to "do something" about the perceived drift of Britain and the capitalist system toward disaster, and stressed the urgent need to aid what he claimed was the beacon of the world's salvation: the Soviet Union.

Blunt's first recruit was Guy Burgess, a flamboyant homosexual (Blunt, also homosexual, was his lover), followed by others, notably Donald Maclean, and Michael Straight, an American student who would turn out to be a much more significant recruit

17

Anthony Blunt, a prominent art historian and art adviser to the Queen, in 1979 after his role as a Soviet spy was publicly revealed. (*AP/Wide World*)

than Blunt could have imagined. There was an ugly edge to Blunt's role as a talent spotter: he often used sexual blackmail to keep new recruits in line, threatening to expose their homosexuality. In the days when homosexuality was a serious crime in Britain, this was no idle threat.

At first glance, the KGB's effort in recruiting an obscure Cambridge fellow and art historian, along with the equally obscure men he in turn recruited, seems foolish. What could such assets possibly provide the KGB? But appearances were deceiving, for in fact the KGB had chosen shrewdly and well. It was from Cambridge and Oxford that the British government drew its future political leaders, civil servants—and intelligence agents. By investing early, and convincing their seedlings to subsume their Marxist convictions in favor of infiltrating the establishment they were so eager to destroy in the name of the proletariat, the KGB had in effect implanted cancer cells into the British body politic.

There was another reason for recruiting Blunt. He was an important figure in the British homosexual *demimonde*, giving him a priceless network of contacts that extended up and down the entire British ruling establishment. As the KGB was aware, one of Blunt's close friends—and presumed lover—was a man named Guy Liddell, a top official in MI5, who actively worked to recruit and protect fellow homosexuals. The KGB was patient enough not to bother attempting to blackmail Liddell, for he would serve more important functions: easing the entry of homosexual assets into British intelligence, while protecting such men from any awkward questions about their Marxist pasts or sexual proclivities.

At the KGB's urging, Blunt lobbied to enter British intelligence at the outbreak of World War II. He joined Field Security of army intelligence, but was discharged when security investigators uncovered his Communist background. Undaunted, Blunt then turned to his friend Liddell, who got him into MI5. At about the same time, Burgess had managed to join MI6. He later brought in **H. A. R. Philby,** which meant that the KGB had managed to plant three assets in British intelligence. Maclean, meanwhile, had joined the Foreign Office, so the KGB recruitments years before had now borne fruit.

Blunt paid immediate dividends. He was put in charge of an operation that surreptitiously opened diplomatic bags from neutral embassies in London, mostly by means of seducing the couriers with a stable of young men and women he had on the payroll. MI5 was delighted at the haul of secret papers Blunt photographed from those bags—and so was the KGB, which got its own copies. At the same time, Blunt kept Moscow informed about the activities of a number of exile governments in London in which the Soviets had a particular interest—especially Poland and Czechoslovakia.

In 1944, Blunt was named MI5 liaison with the Supreme Headquarters Allied Expeditionary Force (SHAEF) the Allied high command in Europe, a crucial crossroads that not only gave him access to ULTRA, the top-secret British codebreaking operation that cracked German codes, but also to high-level operational plans (including the Normandy invasion). It is not known what other services Blunt was able to perform for the KGB, but toward the end of the war, he carried out an operation that had nothing to do with either the war or the KGB, but one that put the Royal Family in his debt.

Throughout the 1930s, the British were worried about the Duke of Windsor, who was a blatant pro-Nazi. He had been pressured into abdicating the throne of England after a brief reign because of his refusal to break off his relationship with Mrs. Wallace Simpson, an American divorcee. In 1937 British intelligence learned that the Duke, while visiting Germany, had met with Hitler and expressed such fervently pro-Nazi sentiments that *Der Fuehrer* planned to install him as head of a puppet government once the Germans had conquered England. Later in the war, the British moved the Duke out of temptation's way, naming him governor-general of Bermuda after learning there was at least a reasonable possibility he was prepared to defect to the Germans.

The British government had managed to keep all this secret, but they were aware of a potentially damaging cache of papers in Germany, much of it correspondence from the Duke expressing his fervent hopes for a victory by Nazi Germany. At all costs, this cache had to be retrieved. Blunt successfully carried out the assignment, and a grateful Royal Family rewarded him with a job offer: Surveyor and Keeper of the Royal Pictures. (He was knighted in 1956).

Although Blunt officially resigned from MI5 at war's end, he was still of value to the KGB. Through the old boy network, he stayed in contact with ex-colleagues, and a weekly dinner with senior MI5 officers often produced enough interesting tidbits for passing on to the KGB. Blunt was also of value when MI5 became involved in the first wave of postwar spy cases. In 1951, when Burgess fled with Maclean to Moscow*, Blunt made things that much more difficult for MI5 by sneaking into Burgess' apartment before counterintelligence agents arrived and removing several incriminating papers. Among them were notes in the handwriting of one of the "ring of five," John Cairncross, and some passionate love lettters written by Burgess to one of his favorite male lovers: Anthony Blunt.

Nevertheless, as a known friend of Burgess, the cloud of suspicion fell on Blunt. Yuri Modin, his KGB handler, offered to get him out of Britain and to safety in the Soviet Union, but Blunt refused. Over the next several years, he was interrogated 11 times

---

* Burgess, who never learned Russian, had a bad time in exile. With his drinking nearly out of control, the KGB arranged for a small apartment, a menial job in a publishing house, and a young man to play with. He died in 1963, a toothless alcoholic. Philby, still angry at the precipitous flight that cut short his career as the KGB's greatest mole, pointedly did not attend the funeral. Maclean was given a job in a Soviet think tank, wrote articles under the alias S. P. Madzoevski, and scandalized his hosts by agitating for less control of Soviet society by the deadening hand of the Soviet Communist Party hierarchy. He died of cancer in 1983. Philby wasn't at that funeral, either, due to a certain awkward problem: he had seduced Maclean's wife after she fled to the Soviet Union to join her husband and married her.

by MI5, but there was no solid evidence against him, and any case against him languished.

In 1963, however, one of Blunt's recruits, the American Michael Straight, decided to apply for a federal job. Concerned that the required FBI background check would uncover his secret past, Straight volunteered that he had been recruited for the KGB by Blunt and performed some minor espionage tasks before deciding to break with the Communist party. Armed with that clinching piece of evidence, MI5 confronted Blunt and offered a deal: tell all in exchange for immunity. Blunt agreed to the deal, although there remains some question how enlightening he was to his interrogators; a number of MI5 officials suspected that in line with standard KGB practice, he revealed only what he was quite certain MI5 already knew. However, Blunt did offer a few nuggets. He revealed that Leo Long, a fellow MI5 officer during the war, had been recruited for the KGB as a source (Long later confessed under the same immunity arrangement that Blunt received). He also confirmed MI5 suspicions that John Cairncross was the fifth man in the "ring of five." (Cairncross also subsequently confessed). Blunt also identified the KGB case officers with whom he had worked, particularly Yuri Modin*, considered the KGB's leading specialist in the handling of homosexual agents. Given the fact that these Russians had long since departed Britain, the revelations were of limited value.

British intelligence intended its arrangement with Blunt to remain secret, but in 1979, some MI5 officers, outraged over what they considered to be favorable treatment of a pillar of the British establishment, leaked details of the deal to author Anthony Boyle, whose book on the case, *The Fourth Man*, set off a public storm. Prime Minister Margaret Thatcher was compelled to admit publicly that such a deal had been struck. There remains an ongoing dispute over whether a man like Blunt should have received immunity, although the fact is that without his confession, there was not enough solid proof to make an espionage case in court.

---

* Modin was *rezident* in London in 1956, when he was reassigned to Moscow. Lionized by the KGB for his masterful direction of the British assets, he later arranged for Philby's escape to Moscow. Subsequently, he became the KGB's leading disinformation specialist. Later, when that role was publicly exposed by the CIA, he became a top KGB espionage instructor, training an entire generation of KGB agents in the techniques of handling foreign assets. In 1990, as the KGB's senior statesman, he gave TV and radio interviews to Western journalists on famous KGB operations, in many of which he had played a key role.

Nevertheless, Blunt paid a price. He was publicly reviled, shorn of his knighthood, and finally consigned to a lonely retirement, hardly able to show his highly publicized face in public. He died in 1983, apparently unrepentant. When friends asked the man born into wealth and privilege why he had felt compelled to betray his country, he would answer with this historical anecdote: "The Florentine Army was fighting the Papal army and Benvenuto Cellini was on the Florentine side. During a lull in the battle, a voice came from the Papal lines: 'Benvenuto! The Pope wants you to work for him!' Cellini threw away his weapons, went over to the Papal Army and became a silversmith for the Pope. When he had finished his work, he returned to Florence where he was received with honor and rejoicing because he was a great artist."

Anyone hearing this anecdote could only wonder if the strange mind of Anthony Blunt actually saw a parallel between Cellini's betryal for art and his own treason.

OLEG PENKOVSKY
Soldier for Peace

Code Names: ALEX, CHALK, HERO, YOGA
1919–1963

On the evening of August 12, 1960, one of the most extraordinary chapters in Cold War espionage began on a bridge in Moscow when two American tourists were suddenly confronted by a stocky, red-haired man who thrust two envelopes into their hands. He told them to take the envelopes "to the CIA," then disappeared into the night.

The two young tourists were uncertain: they had been warned that the KGB occasionally sought to entrap tourists by just such a gambit—having someone put incriminating material into their hands, then arresting them for spying. After debating the matter a while, they finally decided to take the envelopes, unopened, to the American embassy.

At the embassy, the diplomat who opened the envelopes realized at once he was looking at something very undiplomatic. One letter, signed by "Colonel Oleg Penkovsky," offered to spy for the Americans, and listed a few items of military information. The second contained elaborate instructions for how the CIA station in Moscow could contact him.

Turned over to the CIA station in the embassy, the letters were regarded initially as an outright provocation, probably an attempt to plant a phony asset on the CIA. Certainly, an examination of Penkovsky's background indicated caution, for he represented a prototypical example of the career track of a dedicated Soviet functionary.

Colonel Oleg Penkovsky during his 1963 trial in Moscow on espionage charges
after he was caught passing intelligence to the CIA and MI6. (*AP/Wide World*)

Born 1919 in the Caucasus, the son of a mining engineer,
Penkovsky entered the Red Army in 1939, and as a Communist
party member with a clean record, was made a commissar. He
fought in the Russo-Finnish war of 1940, then served during
World War II in the artillery branch, suffering a severe wound in
June 1944. Two years later, Penkovsky, regarded as one of the
army's brighter officers, was recruited for the GRU. By 1955, he
was the GRU's *rezident* in Ankara, Turkey, under cover as military
attaché.

It seemed inconceivable that a man with this sort of record
of impeccable devotion to the Soviet cause would want to become
a spy for the CIA. Accordingly, the agency proceeded cautiously,
but all early doubts were cleared away when Penkovsky began
gushing forth an ocean of intelligence. Saying he wanted to be a
"soldier for peace," Penkovsky not only photographed every top-
secret document he encountered, he added his own intimate
knowledge of Soviet military technology. For good measure, he
provided insights into GRU cryptographic systems, and identified
hundreds of GRU officers serving throughout the world.

The Soviet SS-4 missile, seen on display in the 1962 May Day Parade in Moscow, was secretly deployed a short time later in Cuba by Nikita Khrushchev. Penkovsky revealed to the Americans the missile's deployment pattern, allowing U.S. intelligence to spot it. He also revealed the Soviet Union's greatest secret: the SS-4 was a technological white elephant, giving President Kennedy a fifth ace in the Cuban missile crisis. (*ITAR-TASS/ SOVFOTO*)

The scope of Penkovsky's revelations was so vast, the CIA operation became a joint one with MI6, which offered the services of one of its assets, a British businessman named Greville Wynne, to serve as cutout for Penkovsky's voluminous material.

"The answer to a prayer," Maurice Oldfield, the MI6 station chief in Washington, D.C., said of Penkovsky, and he was only exaggerating slightly. The appearance of Penkovsky came at a critical moment in Western intelligence, which was encountering growing difficulties in taking the measure of the burgeoning Soviet military power. Despite the advances in overhead reconnaissance, there was ongoing debate about the size, scope, and significance of the Soviet military. The chief concern was the Soviet rocket program; Moscow's space spectaculars indicated advanced rocket designs of intercontinental range. As everyone understood, a rocket capable of putting a satellite or a man into space was just as capable of delivering a megaton-sized nuclear weapon thousands of miles away. Indeed, the perceived view of Soviet nuclear-tipped rockets, boosted by Soviet Premier Nikita Khrushchev's boasts that his rockets could "hit a fly in space," indicated a massive force, much more powerful and numerous than the American ICBM force. Charges of a "missile gap" had helped elect John F. Kennedy during the 1960 presidential campaign.

To the shock of his MI6 and CIA debriefers, among Penkovsky's first major revelations was the intelligence that the "missile gap" was a myth. In fact, Penkovsky revealed, the Soviet rocket force consisted of only a few rockets, and none of them worked anywhere near their design parameters. In Penkovksy's earthy Russian phrase, "They couldn't hit a bull in the backside with a *balalaika.*"

This astonishing insight into the true state of Soviet rockets took place in London, where Penkovsky had been sent in early 1961 as head of a Soviet trade delegation (in fact a collection of GRU operatives assigned to gather intelligence on British technology and industry). While MI6 operatives kept the delegation busy with an exhausting schedule of visits to British industrial sites during their six-day trip, Penkovsky each evening slipped away from the delegation and met in a hotel suite with MI6 and CIA debriefers. He would then spend hours unburdening himself of Moscow's most vital military secrets.

His debriefers had long before discounted the idea of Penkovsky as a deliberate plant, for no plant would have conveyed so much vital intelligence. That left the question of motive. As his debriefers soon discovered, for all his impeccable record, Penkovsky actually was in serious trouble.

It had begun quietly enough: as part of the exhaustive background check as Penkovsky rose in the GRU hierarchy, KGB counterintelligence agents had investigated his family background. To Penkovsky's dismay, they discovered that his father, who he assumed died in 1920 of typhus (or so his mother told him), in fact had died fighting in the White armies during the Russian Civil War in 1919. The perennially suspicious minds in the KGB reached two conclusions, neither one of them helpful to Penkovsky: one, the fact that his father was a proven anticommunist raised the possibility that Penkovsky was not a dedicated Communist, and perhaps of dubious loyalty; and two, the fact that the circumstances of his father's death had been concealed by Penkovsky indicated perhaps even more serious motives.

As a result of these suspicions, Penkovsky's career was stalled; his scheduled assignment to India had been cancelled, and he faced potentially even more serious consequences. Combined with his growing disillusion with the Soviet system, it instilled a white-hot hatred of the regime in Penkovsky, sufficient to impel him toward a dangerous plan of action. As he told his debriefers, he had become convinced that the Soviet government intended to prepare for an offensive war sometime in the future; that when the Soviets felt militarily ready, they would confront the West in a final Armageddon to decide whether communism or capitalism would rule the world.

The fervency with which Penkovsky believed this apocalyptic vision and his own perceived role in saving the world struck his listeners as just this side of megalomania. Penkovsky betrayed further symptoms: he demanded a meeting with Queen Elizabeth (denied, although he was permitted a brief meeting with the then head of MI6, Dick White), and a face-to-face meeting with President Kennedy (denied on the grounds of a busy schedule). As a sop, MI6 and CIA officers arranged for a tailor-made U.S. army colonel's uniform and a British colonel's uniform to be prepared for Penkovsky, in which he was photographed by his debriefers. Penkovsky actually signed a contract with the CIA and MI6, in which he agreed to become a "soldier of the free world" who would be extricated from the Soviet Union with his family in the event the KGB began to close in on him.

All this amounted to a small price to pay (the entire Penkovsky operation only cost $82,000) for the kind of intelligence Penkovsky was providing. But the very value of Penkovsky created an operational problem: his overseas travel was limited, so some means would have to be devised to get his information in Moscow, where he lived and worked.

The system MI6 and the CIA finally devised seemed secure. Among the MI6 officers serving in Moscow under diplomatic cover was Roderick Chisholm; his wife Janet, who had worked as an MI6 secretary, lived with him in Moscow. One day each week, Mrs. Chisholm would take her two small children to a park. At a certain time, Penkovsky would approach, compliment her on the beauty of the children, and offer them candy from a box. Mrs. Chisholm would take the candy, which was actually microfilm. On other occasions, Mrs. Chisholm and Penkovsky would exchange messages at a dead drop located behind the radiator on the first floor of a nearby apartment building. At the same time, Greville Wynne—under cover as a businessman trying to drum up trade with the Soviet Union—would be used as a letterbox whenever he visited Moscow.

From the "candy" handed to Mrs. Chisholm, MI6 and the CIA received a gold mine of intelligence on the status of the Soviet rocket forces, Penkovsky's particular specialty in the GRU. The information arrived at a crucial time, for unknown to Penkovsky and his handlers, Khrushchev had decided to install offensive missiles in Cuba. Early CIA intelligence that rocket sites were being constructed on the island encountered a Soviet cover story claiming the construction was for air defense missiles to protect Cuban military installations and a Soviet brigade operating in Cuba. But the story collapsed when Penkovsky's intelligence was matched against Soviet claims; Penkovsky had provided precise data on the unique construction and deployment patterns of the SS4, the main Soviet medium-range nuclear missile. The information from their man in Moscow left no doubt in the minds of MI6 and the CIA: the construction in Cuba was for offensive nuclear missiles.

That was only the first benefit of Penkovsky's intelligence. He also informed his handlers of the amount of time needed from construction to actual deployment for the SS4, which told the Americans precisely how much time they had to get those missiles removed. And above all, Penkovsky provided President Kennedy with the fifth ace in the game of international bluff that became the Cuban missile crisis. Aware that Khrushchev's ICBM force was a bluff, Kennedy knew he could force the Soviets to the brink of nuclear war with the assurance they would have to back down. The Soviets were in no shape to challenge the United States in a nuclear war, which would have incinerated the Soviet Union in a firestorm of massive American superiority.

But by the time the missile crisis was underway, Penkovsky's career as a mole was over. Toward the end of summer, 1962, he became aware the KGB was onto him. His access to the restricted GRU library—where he photographed many documents—was suddenly cut off, and during one contact with Janet Chisholm, he noticed a car with men watching him. On October 22, 1962, just as the Cuban missile crisis was reaching its climactic point, Penkovsky was arrested.

How had the KGB managed to detect him? The question was of paramount importance, because both the CIA and MI6 had taken extraordinary precautions to protect Penkovsky. Only a handful of officials on both sides of the Atlantic were aware of his specific identity, and only a slightly larger number had access to the intelligence he produced. The arrest of so precious a source indicated that worst of all intelligence nightmares: a mole at a high level of either MI6 or the CIA.

However, it turned out that Penkovsky had been caught through a combination of diligent KGB counterintelligence work, a drunken U.S. Army sergeant, and a bad operational mistake by MI6.

As early as 1961, the KGB became aware that top-grade Soviet military secrets were finding their way westward. They had managed to recruit an alcoholic U.S. Army sergeant named Jack W. Dunlap, a low-level recruitment that paid unexpectedly huge dividends when he was assigned as a courier-driver at the National Security Agency, the American code-breaking agency. Despite his lowly position, Dunlap managed to gain access to many of the documents entrusted to his care, which he sold to the KGB. (Dunlap later committed suicide when FBI agents began closing in).

The KGB was appalled when they got a look at some of Dunlap's documents, for there was no doubt that the most sensitive military information was reaching the West. The source was carefully concealed, but the KGB concluded that the CIA and/or MI6 had a high-level mole working somewhere at the top levels of the Soviet military. But who? By KGB reckoning, some 1,000 officials had access to the kind of information finding its way West, presenting a daunting task, for each one of the 1,000 people—a list which included Penkovsky—would have to be investigated.

At the same time, the KGB concluded that the information probably was being passed in Moscow, headquarters of the Soviet military establishment. And that meant a CIA or MI6 agent under diplomatic cover probably was receiving it. So the KGB instituted a massive surveillance of all known MI6 and CIA agents operating under diplomatic cover in Moscow. The operative word is "known," for not every Western agent in Moscow was known. But they did know that Roderick Chisholm was, because their mole inside MI6, **George Blake**—who had served with Chisholm in the MI6's Berlin station during the late 1950s—had provided the KGB with a complete roster of all MI6 agents in Berlin. Chisholm's later assignment in Moscow was a bad mistake, for MI6 was perfectly aware that he had been blown: Blake was arrested by MI5 early in 1961, and admitted revealing the names of MI6 agents he knew.

Thus, when the blanket KGB surveillance began in Moscow, among its targets were the Chisholms, for the KGB knew that Janet Chisholm worked as an MI6 secretary in Berlin. The rest was pure end game: the spotting of Mrs. Chisholm in conversation with a GRU colonel named Oleg Penkovsky, the very same Oleg Penkovsky rapidly entering and leaving a nearby apartment building (an obvious dead drop), and Penkovsky's abnormally frequent visits to the classified GRU library. To obtain final proof, KGB agents implanted poisoned wax on the seat of the chair Penkovsky used to sit in while working at his desk in his apartment. The poison hospitalized Penkovsky for a week; the KGB used the time to install a movie camera concealed in the chandelier above the desk. When Penkovsky returned home, the camera recorded him writing out classified information for later delivery to the dead drop.

In early 1963, Penkovsky was put on trial (along with Greville Wynne), a show meant as a propaganda exercise to demonstrate his perfidy. Penkovsky, aware of the inevitable outcome, calmly gave his public confession. Some months later, he was executed, reportedly by the method reserved for the Soviet Union's worst traitors: he was slowly fed into a live furnace, with some of his closest former colleagues forced to watch.

GEORGE BLAKE
The Manchurian Candidate

Code Name: DIAMOND
Alias: Max de Vries
1922–

The thin man in the padded Chinese overcoat, a mere shadow of his former stocky build, who stepped across the demarcation line that spring morning in 1953 looked as though he had just emerged from a nightmare. In a way, he had: Vice-Consul George Blake, along with his fellow British diplomats, had been finally released following nearly three years of captivity in North Korea and Manchuria.

Blake was met at the prisoner exchange point by, among others, two MI6 agents who took him in hand for an immediate debriefing. Blake's job as vice-consul was only cover; he was an MI6 agent who in 1948 went to Seoul to open MI6's first Korean station. In 1950, the North Korean invasion swept into Seoul; Blake and his fellow diplomats had no time to escape, and they were taken to the miseries of captivity in North Korea and later Manchuria.

MI6 had an urgent question they needed Blake to answer: had the Communists discovered his intelligence connections? No, Blake reassured them; throughout his entire captivity, the Communists assumed he was only Vice-Consul Blake. His fellow captives spoke admiringly of Blake, recounting that he had acted with "high standards of courage and fortitude," and served as an inspiration to the other captives. There were further MI6 debriefings while Blake relaxed and recuperated in Hong Kong, but MI6 did not know that Blake met one night with a representative of another intelligence service, the one to whom Blake owed his true allegiance: the KGB.

It seems unbelievable that Blake's loyalty to the Communist cause would have remained unshaken after the experience of captivity in Manchuria, but it is only one of several contradictions connected with the man who represents what is surely the strangest spy story of all time.

To understand Blake, it is first necessary to understand that he was born in 1922 as George Behar, son of one of the most ancient and distinguished Jewish families in Amsterdam. Behar's father died when the boy was 14, and in accordance with his dying father's wish, he was sent to attend the famed English School in Cairo. He lived with relatives, spending most of his time with his uncle, Henri Curiel, who was not only a major figure in the Egyptian Communist party, but a longtime asset for the KGB as well. Curiel recognized the potential as an agent in the very bright boy, but bided his time; meanwhile, he was content to indoctrinate his nephew in the intricacies of Communist theory.

By the time the young Behar returned to Amsterdam, he was a fledgling Communist. He was attending a high school in Rotterdam when the Germans overran the country in 1940. His mother and two sisters fled to England; Behar decided to stay behind. He became one of the first members of the Dutch resistance under the alias Max de Vries, but when the Gestapo got on his trail, he fled to London via Belgium, disguised as a Trappist monk. In England, he changed his name to Blake and volunteered for the Royal Navy, emphasizing his wish to get into intelligence work.

He got his wish, but to his frustration and disgust, he was assigned a desk job. But it was while working at the desk job that he underwent the seminal experience of his life. He fell madly in love with an MI6 secretary named Iris Peake (later Lady in Waiting to Queen Elizabeth), and following a whirlwind wartime courtship, they decided to get married. But Peake's family blocked the marriage; there was no way one of the most prominent British families was about to permit the marriage of their daughter to a Jew. She reluctantly bowed to pressure, and the relationship collapsed.

Blake was devastated, and in his rage and frustration, vowed revenge against the snobbish establishment that had caused the loss of the love of his life. His closest relative and confidant, uncle Henri Curiel, listened carefully to his nephew's rage, and pro-

posed a revenge: Blake would work for the "cause of world revolution." Translated, that meant Blake would infiltrate British
intelligence and at the proper moment, he would be in a position
to wreak his revenge.

It took a while for Blake to achieve his main goal, entry into
MI6. At the end of the war, still working for NID, he was posted
to Hamburg as head of a small unit that arrested U-boat commanders and debriefed them. A year later, MI6 reached out, and
by 1948, Blake was assigned his first major post, chief of the new
Seoul station.

It is a tribute to Blake's single-mindedness that his three-
year captivity did not diminish for a moment his determination
to injure the British establishment. That chance did not come
until 1955, when Blake, following two years of desk work at headquarters, won a key assignment: posting to one of MI6's more
important posts, Berlin.

There weren't many better postings than Berlin for a KGB
mole in 1955. Berlin was a virtual crossoads of East-West espionage, aswarm with agents of every description and a vital outpost
for at least a half-dozen intelligence agencies. Not only was Blake
assigned to this critical intelligence station, he worked as one of
the British representatives to a joint MI6-CIA committee that
oversaw various major intelligence operations in which both
agencies were involved.

Almost immediately upon his arrival in Berlin, Blake got his
first big opportunity. He learned that MI6 and the CIA were busy
working on Operation Gold, an audacious plan to dig a tunnel
under the border of East and West Berlin, and tap into the main
Russian communications lines through which virtually all military, diplomatic, and intelligence conversations passed. The Russians assumed those lines were safe, since all their phones had
scrambler devices. But CIA technicians had devised a brilliant
piece of technology that enabled them to pluck conversations
from scrambled signals. The new technology would be installed
in the tunnel and attached to voice-activated tape recorders that
would grab every signal over the Russian telephone lines.

Warned of this operation via a Berlin dead drop, Blake's
chief link with the Russians, the KGB played its end of the game
carefully, so as not to jeopardize their prize source in British intelligence. The KGB allowed the tunnel to be dug, but ensured
that nothing very sensitive or revealing was transmitted over the
tapped lines. Meanwhile, at a cost of millions, the CIA—which

had agreed to fund the costs of the operation—recruited battalions of translaters to handle the voluminous telephone traffic. The CIA regarded the tunnel operation as a success, although they began to wonder why there was so little of real use in all those interceptions. Before the CIA could wonder too much longer, the KGB closed down the tunnel by having some East German guards "accidentally" discover it.

Blake followed up his betrayal of the tunnel operation by blowing the names of all the MI6 and CIA assets he knew operating under control of the Berlin station. However beneficial to the KGB—MI6 and CIA operations behind the Iron Curtain became virtually paralyzed—this wholesale betrayal of Western intelligence assets inevitably focused attention on the possibility of a mole in the Berlin station. Blake managed to talk his way out of increasingly suspicious inquiries, even when Horst Eitner, a German asset of the Berlin station, revealed that he was working for the KGB and hinted that Blake might be, too. Blake explained that he sometimes pretended to be a KGB sympathizer so as to discover who among the station's German assets were also double agents for the KGB.

Feeling the heat, Blake applied for another assignment. At Curiel's suggestion, he told MI6 he wanted to work in the Middle East. MI6 agreed, and in 1960 sent him to Lebanon to study at the Middle East College for Arabic Studies to prepare for a job in MI6's Beirut station. Blake did not know it, but his world was about to collapse.

As Blake arrived in Lebanon, an official of the Polish UB who was also functioning as a KGB asset began sending top-grade intelligence to the CIA; among other revelations, he said that the CIA/MI6 station in Berlin had been penetrated via a mole named George Blake. In January 1961, the UB agent, who turned out to be Mikhail Goleniewski, defected to the CIA, and brought incontrovertible proof lifted from the KGB files: documents to which Blake had access had wound up in the KGB's hands.

Recalled to London on the excuse that MI6 officials wanted to discuss his next intelligence posting, an unsuspecting Blake arrived at MI6 headquarters and was confronted with the evidence against him. To the surprise of his interrogators, Blake immediately confessed. He laid out an appalling picture of the damage he had caused, including the blowing of at least 42 assets (all of whom were executed), the secret of the Berlin tunnel, and a long list of other operations. Among them was the sad case of Pyotr Popov.

In 1952, Popov, then a GRU colonel working in Vienna, threw a letter into the car of an American diplomat. The letter volunteered Popov's services to the CIA, which soon learned that Popov had become disillusioned by the Soviet system and was determined to destroy it. The son of peasants, he became enraged at the privileges enjoyed by Soviet officials while most Soviets still lived in near-poverty. (He only accepted one small payment for his services from the CIA, which he promptly turned over to his brother to buy a cow).

Popov's intelligence was nothing short of sensational, for he provided the first insights into the closed world of the Soviet military: new weapons, deployments of Soviet forces in Eastern Europe, and how the Soviets planned to fight a nuclear war in the event of hostilities with the West. In 1956, he had been shifted to the GRU station in East Berlin, which meant that operational control for him was handled out of the MI6/CIA Berlin station. The moment Blake became aware of Popov, he told the KGB.

Popov was recalled to Moscow for "consultations," and was arrested. But instead of executing him, the KGB sought to turn him; under threat of death for his family, he was ordered to wear a body recording device and meet the newly-assigned CIA agent who would be his CIA control in Moscow. At their first meeting in a men's room, Popov wordlessly ripped off some bandages covering one of his hands to reveal the word "torture" written in ink on his palm. He then made a circular motion with both hands, warning the CIA man that he was wearing a wire.

The CIA man's caution in subsequent meetings tipped off the KGB that Popov somehow had warned him of the trap. The KGB finally tired of the game, and when Popov and the CIA man had a brush contact on a Moscow bus one day in October 1959, both men were arrested. (But not before Popov was able to scribble a warning that the Soviet military had detected the high-altitude U2 flights and were determined to shoot down one of the planes). The CIA man, under diplomatic cover, was expelled from the country, but Popov suffered what had become the standard fate for GRU traitors: he was slowly fed into a live furnace while his colleagues watched.

The betrayal of Popov was only one act in a lengthy catalog that was presented when Britain's High Court justices convened to decide Blake's punishment. Their mood was hardly improved when they saw a defendant who seemed almost proud of the damage he had caused to an establishment he hated so much. Accordingly, the High Court sentenced Blake to 42 years in prison, a sentence of unprecedented severity in a peacetime espionage case.

This virtual lifetime sentence (he was 39 years old at the time) would appear to have been the final chapter in the Blake story, but there was to be one further amazing development. In 1967, after serving six years in prison, Blake escaped. Although it was assumed that the escape had been arranged by the KGB, in fact it was the work of an Irish Republican Army activist (and former fellow inmate of Blake) named Sean Bourke. He hid Blake for a few weeks while a nationwide manhunt was underway, then contacted the Russians, who smuggled him to Moscow. Bourke went to Moscow, too, but after a few months, depressed by the city's grimness, returned to his native Ireland. He insisted until his death some years later that he arranged for the escape of Blake strictly out of friendship with the convicted spy, with no involvement by the KGB. Very few people believed him, but if in fact Bourke was working for the KGB, he took that secret to the grave with him.

As for Blake, he was given a comfortable home by the KGB, where he read, with some amusement, the Richard Condon novel, *The Manchurian Candidate*, based on his case. He married a Russian woman (abandoning a wife and two children in Britain). In 1990, he was interviewed by Soviet television, during which he boasted of betraying 600 CIA and MI6 agents.

NIKOLAI AND NADJEDA SKOBLIN
Death and the Kursk Nightingale

1899–1938
1897–1940

It seemed like something out of a movie script: the beautiful female spy, tied to a stake, refusing a blindfold as she defiantly contemplates the firing squad about to end her life. The dashing young cavalry officer, moved by the sight of her beauty and courage, suddenly rides up and orders the firing squad not to fire. He has her untied, then released into his custody. He'll handle this matter himself.

However improbable, that is precisely how the youthful General Nikolai Skoblin first met Nadjeda Vassilievna early one spring morning in 1920 in southern Russia. And it was at that moment when he fell in love with her, with consequences that would ultimately result in the near-destruction of the Soviet Union and the deaths of over 30,000 men. Among the victims was Skoblin himself.

Both Skoblin and Vassilievna were like characters from some sort of Romanov grand opera. Born into aristrocracy, Skoblin was a Czarist cavalry officer during World War I, and after the Bolsheviks seized power in Russia, fought on the White side in the Russian Civil War. By 1920, he was fighting a losing battle against the Red armies in southern Russia, the same year of his fateful encounter with Nadjeda Vassilievna. She was also born to an aristocratic family, became an opera singer, and before the war was known as the "Kursk nightingale." Accustomed to the good life of parties, fancy homes, beautiful clothes and jewels, her world was shattered by the Bolshevik revolution, which had no time for such frivolities. Worse, she had married a penniless ballet master named Edmund Plevitsky; by the end of 1918, she was desperate for money at a time when admirers no longer showered her with cash and jewels for her concerts.

How the CHEKA, the Bolshevik intelligence agency, decided that this spoiled, money-hungry diva would be the ideal asset to use against the White forces remains unknown. In late 1918, apparently appealing to her love of money, the CHEKA enlisted her to penetrate the various White organizations threatening the new regime.

To a certain extent, Vassilievna was almost perfectly suited for her role. Traveling throughout the White-held areas, she entertained the troops at free concerts, at the same time ingratiating herself with anti-Bolshevik leaders who had long admired the "Kursk nightingale." In the process, she began to collect interesting intelligence tidbits from some of the more indiscreet Whites (including those she slept with to pry even more information).

By 1920, with the civil war moving into a climactic phase, suspicions about the possible relationship between Vassilievna's visits and a series of catastrophic military defeats began to harden. Early in 1920, having intercepted some of her messages to the CHEKA, the Whites had final proof. She was caught and ordered to be shot.

Enter Nikolai Skoblin. Totally smitten, he was willing to forgive her shocking confession that she had been working for the CHEKA, meaning that she was an agent for the hated Bolsheviks. Under ordinary circumstances, such a confession would have ended Vassilievna's usefulness as an agent, but the CHEKA now had another inspiration: why not recruit Nikolai Skoblin as an asset?

The idea seemed preposterous, but as much as the CHEKA understood Vassilievna's vulnerability, it also understood Skoblin's. He was obsessed with the idea of "Holy Russia," the mythical land that existed before the czars. A megalomaniac, Skoblin saw himself as the leader of a whole new movement that would some day recapture the land of Russia and recreate his vision of a country out of a fairy tale. Vassilievna worked on that vulnerability, and by the time in late 1920 when they retreated with the remnants of the White forces into Turkey and permanent exile, she had convinced him.

In Skoblin's mind, he was merely using the CHEKA to achieve his eventual aim. On behalf of the CHEKA, he would destroy the Russian exile movement and gain control; once he had achieved that aim, he would lead a great holy crusade that would march back into Russia and destroy the CHEKA—and everything else Bolshevik. (At the same time, Vassilievna noted, she and Skoblin would be paid handsomely, something like selling rope to the hangman).

This most curious couple now departed for Paris, international headquarters of the Russian exile movement, which, in 1921, amounted to a considerable threat against the weak Communist regime. With more than 300,000 armed followers devoted to the Czarist cause, and well-financed by contributions from over a million followers scattered throughout the world, its very being was a matter of abiding concern to the CHEKA, to which Lenin had assigned the task of neutralizing or eliminating the threat.

Skoblin would be the prime instrument to accomplish that task. He married Vassilievna (her apparently understanding husband was best man at the wedding), and set about infiltrating the exile movement. Given his background and military experience, with a proven record of actual combat against the Bolsheviks, no one seemed to doubt Skoblin's bona fides. By the early 1930s, he was a key leader in the ROVS organization, the main combat force of the exiles. From that vantage point, he was able to keep Moscow informed of which "combat fighters" had been smuggled across the border into Russia to organize anti-Bolshevik combat units. He also became aware of the exiles' extensive forgery operations (whose products included allegedly "authentic" documents from the files of OKHRANA, the Czarist secret police, "proving" that Stalin had been a police spy).

The very success of Skoblin's operation, however, caused periodic evaluations of the exile movement by its leaders. And what they found was not encouraging, for the record was uniformly bleak. All the teams of "combat fighters" dispatched to the Soviet Union had disappeared, never to be seen again. The KGB (successor to the CHEKA) seemed to anticipate every exile move. Exiles who had been enlisted as assets for various intelligence organizations were routinely betrayed. Some 15 years after leaving Russia, the exiles had not made the slightest dent in the Soviet Union.

Inevitably, exile leaders began to look inward: was it possible that someone high in the organization was betraying the cause to Moscow? In that kind of spotlight, Mr. and Mrs. Skoblin stood out in stark relief. Not only did they know everyone of importance in the exile movement, they seemed to spend an inordinate amount of time trying to find out about the movement's plans. True, Skoblin had some justification for seeking such information, since he was officially head of foreign counterespionage operations for ROVS, a job he had held since 1934. Still, there was the oddity of the Skoblins' opulent lifestyle. Skoblin had no visible means of support, yet he and his wife lived lavishly. Nadjeda Skoblin claimed an income from recitals, but the limited market for a Russian opera singer in France could not have generated much in the way of money.

For the moment, Skoblin was under suspicion, although there was no firm proof. If Skoblin was bothered by the gathering suspicion, he didn't show it, for in 1936, he carried out his biggest assignment yet from the KGB, one that would make him a major figure in espionage history.

The assignment began with an approach by Skoblin to the German SD. He offered his services, claiming that he wanted SD help in gaining control of the entire exile movement, which he would then turn over to SD control as a "spear of war" against the Soviet Union. Since the SD didn't have much to lose in such an arrangement, it jumped at the opportunity, enlisting Skoblin as its asset inside the exile movement. There was to be a subsidiary benefit: Skoblin claimed to have important sources in the Soviet Union who occasionally provided top-grade intelligence, which he was now willing to share with the SD.

With the SD hooked, Skoblin now moved to the next phase of the operation. It was a bombshell: Skoblin claimed to have documentary proof that the top echelon of the Soviet military was planning a coup against Stalin. Skoblin was careful to say he wanted $2 million for these documents, a clever twist: as the KGB calculated, if a man like Skoblin were to offer the documents for nothing, the SD would be suspicious. So high a price could only mean that the documents were genuine—or were the products of the exiles' well-known paper mills that turned out very good forgeries.

The irony in this little game was that **Reinhard Heydrich,** head of the SD, could care less if the documents were genuine. By extraordinary coincidence, Heydrich was just then planning his own forgery operation, hoping to plant forged documents incriminating senior Soviet leaders in a coup plot; the resulting reaction by a notoriously paranoid Stalin would tear the Soviet Union apart politically.

A meeting between Skoblin and Heydrich presented an even more bizarre irony. Heydrich quickly deduced that Skoblin was working for the KGB, which obviously had been directed by Stalin to produce "proof" of the "conspiracy" the dictator had created himself. For his part, Skoblin understood that the KGB's aims coincided perfectly with the SD's. All of this made for an extremely smooth negotiation, with Heydrich finally agreeing to buy Skoblin's documents. He straightfacedly claimed he had even more sensational "documents" obtained by German intelligence, and he planned on slipping them to Stalin via one of the few intermediaries Stalin trusted: Eduard Benes, president of Czechoslovakia.

The result was one of the worst bloodbaths in history. Claiming that there was a military putsch in the making, Stalin purged his armed forces, executing about 35,000 officers. When the purge was over, 90 percent of the Soviet Union's generals, 80 percent of its colonels, and more than half of all other officer ranks were dead. The Soviet military had not yet recovered from this slaughter several years later when the Germans invaded; a virtually leaderless military lost 7 million men within 24 months.

However delighted they may have been with the result, the Russian exile movement knew nothing of Skoblin's role in it. The exiles still had suspicions about him and his wife. Nevertheless, he might have remained the KGB's prize mole in the movement had not Moscow overreached itself, in the process exposing Skoblin.

For reasons that have never been made clear, Moscow decided that General Anton Miller, head of the military wing of the exile movement, was a dangerous man who had to be eliminated. The decision was made to kidnap him from his Paris headquarters, then bring him to the Soviet Union for final disposal. So radical a solution to the problem of the largely ineffectual Miller seemed pointless, but Skoblin was nevertheless ordered to set up the kidnapping. In September 1937, Skoblin invited Miller to lunch, ostensibly to discuss future strategy. Unfortunately for Skoblin, Miller was among the exile leaders who had become suspicious of him. He agreed to the meeting, but cautiously left behind in his office a note memorializing the appointment.

The note was to cost Skoblin his life. Miller arrived for his meeting, and was immediately set upon by a KGB goon squad.

The old general put up quite a fight, and the commotion attracted the attention of eyewitnesses. The KGB agents finally managed to bundle Miller into a car and speed off, but the alarm was up. The police couldn't find Miller (who was smuggled to the Soviet Union and disappeared), but they did find the note he left behind. Then they went looking for Skoblin, who had gone into hiding. Nadjeda Skoblin was arrested, and in a sensational public trial, was convicted of involvement with her husband in the Miller kidnapping. She was sentenced to 20 years in jail, and died in prison in 1940.

As for her husband, the KGB helpfully offered to aid his escape to the Soviet Union for what he assumed would be a comfortable life funded by a grateful Soviet government. The same naivete that had led to his seduction by Soviet intelligence 19 years before led him in 1937 to follow a KGB rescue team to the Soviet Union, blissfully unaware of an obvious fact: there was no way Stalin would let a man like Skoblin remain alive. Simply put, he knew too much.

Skoblin was last seen alive in Barcelona, Spain, being escorted aboard the Soviet ship *Kuban*. Offered something to drink, he took one sip and dropped dead from the poison concealed in the glass of wine. Upon arrival in the Soviet Union, his body was given to a medical school teaching laboratory.

ISRAEL BEER
The Man Who Never Was

Code Name: COMRADE KURT
1908–1966

In the summer of 1960, an American businessman on a trip to Israel sat down in a Tel Aviv restaurant one afternoon for lunch. A man of some intelligence background—he had served in the OSS and before the war fought in the Spanish Civil War— he still retained the spy's involuntary habit of carefully scanning all the people in a room the moment he entered it.

As he gazed around the small restaurant, his eyes suddenly fastened on a man seated at a corner table. He stared, and the memory came flooding back in vivid detail: the last time he had seen that man, it was 1936 in Madrid. He was in a detention cell and the man, considered one of the most sadistic torturers in the KGB unit assigned to root out spies in the International Brigade volunteers, was beating him, demanding he confess to being a spy. The American was spared further agony when others vouched for him, but he never forgot his tormentor: thin, with a cadaverous face that appeared to be nothing more than skull with a thin layer of skin stretched over it.

And now, 24 years later, there his tormentor sat, no more than 15 feet away, calmly eating lunch. More significantly, he was wearing the uniform of a colonel in the Israel Defense Forces. How had such an infamous KGB thug become a senior military officer in Israel? Alarmed, the American left the restaurant and headed for the nearby headquarters of *Mossad*.

To the American's surprise, *Mossad* officials did not seem especially shocked by what he told them, for he had simply confirmed what they already knew: There was something seriously wrong with Colonel Israel Beer.

The matter of Beer had been an ongoing obsession with *Mossad* chief Isser Harel for the past 10 years. Harel, the legendary spymaster who had built *Mossad* into one of the world's greatest intelligence organizations, was renowned for his emphasis on the human element in intelligence operations. He set great store on an instinctive "feel" about people: which ones make good spies—and which ones become traitors. Relying on that instinct, he was quite convinced that Israel Beer was a KGB mole.

However certain, Harel had to admit that he did not have a shred of proof. Indeed, before 1959, there had been nothing in Beer's background that suggested he was anything but a loyal citizen of Israel.

Like many of his contemporaries, Beer had emigrated to Israel in the 1930s to escape Hitler's persecution. According to Defense Ministry records, Beer had been born in Austria, and in 1934 joined the Socialists. Three years later, he fought in the Spanish Civil War on the side of the Loyalists. In 1938, he emigrated to Palestine, and began a meteoric career track in the Jewish underground.

Beer joined the Haganah, the Zionist underground army, for whom he volunteered his services to the German Department of the British Mandate intelligence organization trying to keep track of the Zionist leaders. The British, unaware of Beer's link with the Haganah, gave him virtually unlimited access to its records on German-speaking Zionist leaders; slipped to the Haganah, it enabled key leaders to avoid arrest. (At the same time, Beer was able to learn which Jews were providing information to the British.)

Among the leaders Beer aided was the leading Zionist in Palestine, David Ben-Gurion. The two men became close friends, a relationship that would play a crucial role in Beer's life. By 1945, Beer was chief of operations in the upper Galilee for the Haganah. During the 1948 War for Independence, Beer served at the headquarters of the Haganah general staff in Tel Aviv, where he was considered among the important architects of the new nation's victory.

After the war, Beer occupied a position high in the Israeli military and intelligence establishment by virtue of his close relationship with the nation's first Prime Minister, Ben-Gurion, for whom he became a sort of general factotum. Among other duties, he was put in charge of keeping Ben Gurion's diary, a job that exposed him to an astonishing range of secrets that the Prime Minister committed to paper, intending to use at least some of them as the basis for his eventual memoirs.

Ben-Gurion trusted Beer totally, but Isser Harel, one of the key officials in Israel's nascent intelligence service, did not. He had one of his "feelings" about Beer. Nothing specific, but as he told his men, there was something that did not "ring right" about Beer; Harel resolved to keep an eye on him.

Since Beer was close with the powerful Ben-Gurion, Harel had to move very carefully. In 1952, when Harel was named head of the new intelligence agency called *Mossad,* he got some confirmation of his suspicions when Beer suddenly resigned his army commission and went into politics, joining the *Mapam,* Israel's most leftist political party. Less than a year later, he was ousted for "leftist deviationism." Beer recanted his political views, and became head of the party's information department. This sort of expediency hardened Harel's suspicions. He successfully blocked Beer's attempt to rejoin the army on the grounds of "security risk," but Beer, drawing on his friendship with Ben-Gurion, got a job in the Defense Ministry to prepare an official history of the 1948 war and to work on strategic studies.

Harel was alarmed, for Beer now had wide access to classified material. He was convinced Beer was a KGB mole, but without the proverbial smoking gun, was reduced to warning Ben-Gurion about his suspicions. Ben-Gurion, unimpressed, demanded proof. The first real proof did not come until 1959, when Mikhail Goleniewski, the Polish UB agent and KGB asset, began revealing to the CIA information on KGB assets around the world. The CIA passed onto Harel one especially alarming revelation from Goleniewski: the KGB had a mole, code-named COMRADE KURT, "somewhere in the upper levels" of the Israeli Defense Ministry. Goleniewski did not know the mole's specific identity, but provided enough clues that pointed to Israel Beer.

Several months later, Harel received another clue. The West German BND told him that Beer, on a visit to West Germany for a lecture to German military officials, had slipped across the border to East Germany, and returned after several hours. Beer had told no one about this trip, nor had he noted it in his report on the trip. Why would an Israeli colonel take a secret trip to East

Germany? Then came the information from the American businessman, and Harel was positive: Beer was a mole. Armed with
the new information, he was able to convince Ben-Gurion to au-
thorize a full-scale surveillance of Beer (something the Prime
Minster had refused to sanction up to that point).

One evening in March 1961, *Mossad* surveillance teams
tracked Beer, carrying an attache case, to a nearly-deserted restaurant in Tel Aviv. He sat there for a while, then was joined by a
man carrying the same kind of attache case as Beer. The team
immediately identified him as a Soviet diplomat who was in fact
a senior KGB officer. Beer and the Russian conversed for a short
period, then got up, each reaching for the other's case, a classic
espionage exchange. The team pounced: inside the case Beer
had handed to the Russian was a stack of classified documents.
Some months later, Beer was convicted of espionage and sentenced to 10 years in prison.

That would appear to have been the end of it, but *Mossad*
discovered the mystery of Israel Beer was just beginning.

Beer refused to cooperate in any way with his captors, so
Mossad was required to work backwards. Their first unsettling discovery was that they had arrested a ghost: the man calling himself
Israel Beer did not exist. Detailed checking revealed that nearly
everything known about Beer's background was a lie. The man
sitting in an Israeli jail cell, although he spoke fluent German,
was not from Austria. He had not been a member of the Austrian
Socialists. He had been in Spain during the civil war, but had not
served in the International Brigade. He was not Jewish. He had
not emigrated to Palestine to escape Nazi persecution.

Who, then, was he? *Mossad* never did find out. Beer, who
remained mute, died in 1966 of heart failure. Eventually, *Mossad*
was to conclude that the man who called himself Israel Beer represented a classic KGB mole operation; he had been planted in
Palestine before World War II with the specific purpose of infiltrating the Zionist underground. The unexpected bonus came
when that underground ultimately became the government of
the new nation of Israel.

Eventually, *Mossad* was to conclude that the entire operation
involved two men. One was the real Israel Beer. He in fact had
been an activist in the Austrian Socialist movement, and later
fought in Spain. But, *Mossad* was convinced, the real Israel Beer
had never left Spain alive; as was common KGB practice during
the Spanish Civil War, it appropriated the passports and other

papers of men fighting in the International Brigade. When one of the fighters died, the KGB had a genuine set of papers it simply used for one its agents who took over the dead man's identity.

Who was the second man? His real identity was never discovered, but *Mossad* believed that he had been a fanatical Communist activist in Austria, joining the Communist party in 1928. In 1931, he was recruited by the KGB to spy on fellow party members, an assignment he carried out successfully. Marked for bigger and better things, he was recalled to Moscow in 1934 for intelligence training, and two years later was sent to Spain as head of a squad assigned the job of rooting out "deviationists" from the ranks of the volunteers fighting in the war. He apparently overstepped himself at some point, for in December 1936, he was recalled to Moscow to answer charges of "gross errors." Normally, that would have meant a death sentence in the purge era, but he was "rehabilitated" a few months later and was transformed into "Israel Beer" for work as a mole.

And the real Israel Beer? His fate remains a mystery.

VLADIMIR I. VETROV
The Murder of Line X

Code Name: FAREWELL
1928–1983

Murder was not a common occurrence in Moscow in that February of 1982, so when the police arrived in the park and saw the body of a man stabbed to death and the severely wounded woman, they realized they were confronting something unusual. The case instantly became even more unusual when they identified the dead man as a senior KGB officer and the woman as a KGB secretary.

In other words, it was a case now fraught with political complications. The police had barely absorbed this complexity when they were confronted with another: An hour after police arrived on the scene, already swarming with KGB agents, a 54-year-old KGB colonel named Vladimir I. Vetrov showed up. The wounded KGB secretary pointed to him and announced that he was the man who had stabbed the dead man and tried to kill her. Police seized him, and found a bloody knife still in his pocket.

It was one of those crimes of human passion that occasionally afflict even the KGB, and the agency worked hard to keep the case from public view. Vetrov gave a full confession, during which he admitted having an affair with the KGB secretary. One night, they parked in his car at the park drinking champagne. Suddenly, another KGB officer, who had been taking a walk in the park, knocked on the car window. He had recognized his co-workers and wanted to exchange friendly greetings—and perhaps also get a sip of that champagne. But for some odd reason, Vetrov

A Soviet MIG-25 in a training sortie. Vladimir Vetrov of the KGB, a mole working for French intelligence, revealed that its technology was the result of a top-priority KGB effort to steal Western military innovations. (*ITAR-TASS/ SOVFOTO*)

panicked; apparently assuming that the KGB man was about to arrest him, he pulled out a knife and stabbed him to death. When the KGB secretary bolted from the scene, Vetrov tracked her down and stabbed her repeatedly. Assuming she was dead, he left, but returned an hour later to make certain.

The suspicious minds of KGB counterintelligence pondered this scenario. Why had Vetrov come so unhinged at the sight of another KGB officer? The fact that the married Vetrov was conducting an affair with a KGB secretary was not exactly an unprecedented occurrence, and even if discovered by his superiors, would not have resulted in any severe sanctions. So what was really going on with this high-ranking KGB officer? What terrible pressure was he under?

For the moment, the KGB did not have an answer, but they resolved to keep a close watch on Vetrov. He was convicted of murder and was sentenced to prison for 12 years. A careful KGB watch on his movements and actions in prison, along with opening and reading his mail, finally produced a clue. In one letter

to his wife, Vetrov hinted that the murder case had forced him
to abandon "something big."

KGB counterintelligence now went to work on Vetrov.
Whether he was tortured is not known, but the result was a document Vetrov wrote out himself in longhand, which he defiantly
headlined, "Confessions of a Traitor." The document caused
grave shock to the KGB, for Vetrov revealed that he had been a
mole for French intelligence for several years. Worse, he had
blown the KGB's greatest secret, a revelation from which it never
recovered—nor did the Soviet Union.

The first shock was that Vetrov, considered among the more
dedicated and accomplished KGB officers, had betrayed his country. A brilliant engineer, he had been recruited for the KGB after
finishing his graduate studies. He was assigned the job of creating
the KGB's most secret unit, known as "Line X," whose mission
was nothing less than saving the Soviet Union.

By 1964, when Line X was created, the KGB and the Soviet
Politburo were acutely aware that they were losing the Cold War
to the West. The problem was technology: the creaky Soviet system was falling further and further behind the West in every area
of technology and science, especially military technology. (Soviet
computer experts told the Politburo their technology was at least
30 years behind the United States, a gap widening each passing
moment). The eventual outcome was inevitable: the Soviet Union
would fall so far behind, superior Western technology would gain
the upper hand and turn the Soviet Union into a paper tiger.

Given the weak Soviet economy and even weaker military-
industrial base, there was no hope the Soviets could catch up,
even with a crash program. The solution was a complete reorien-
tation of Soviet intelligence toward the goal of stealing every
piece of Western technology they could get their hands on. Line
X, in the lead of this new offensive, would recruit a whole new
army of intelligence agents: technicians, engineers, and scientists
who would know what to look for and how to get it.

Line X succeeded brilliantly. In just one year, the KGB stole
over 5,000 of what it euphemistically called "industrial samples"
from the United States and other Western nations. Western military experts were astonished at the speed by which the Soviets
seemed able to obtain the most advanced technology and immediately incorporate it into their own designs. And what Line
X and their GRU helpmates could not steal, they bought. Western
intelligence agencies gradually became aware of a massive tech-

nology transfer operation: networks of dummy companies to divert sensitive technology barred from export to the Eastern Bloc, elaborate operations to bribe engineers and scientists into turning over blueprints, and infiltration of government agencies to influence shipments of sensitive technology.

And yet, in the midst of this glittering success, Vetrov began to have his doubts. The son of landed gentry, he nevertheless was concerned about the average Soviet citizen. He had always hoped that technological progress would eventually better the life of the Russian people, but as Soviet space stations circled the earth and the massive Soviet military machine grew larger and larger, he saw that the people were not sharing in the progress. The Soviet Union, obsessed about its military power, was pouring every resource it could muster into arms. And while the mighty Soviet rockets were trundled each May Day past the Kremlin on parade, the people were still lining up for hours to buy a piece of bread.

Vetrov kept these doubts to himself, but in 1965, assigned to Paris to supervise Line X operations in Western Europe, he began to consider the contrast between the average French citizen and his own countrymen. Even the poorest French family, he realized, lived a life that could only be imagined by his countrymen. His doubts grew. French intelligence became aware of them through a curious encounter that was to prove momentous.

Vetrov one day was involved in a serious automobile accident. He was unhurt, but the Frenchman's car he had smashed into was a virtual wreck. The Frenchman magnanimously offered to pay for all the damage, and arranged for repairs. He and a grateful Vetrov struck up a close friendship, and the Russian began to talk openly about his doubts.

What Vetrov did not know at the time was that the Frenchman, whom Vetrov assumed was a businessman, also happened to be an asset for France's counterintelligence agency, the DST. The DST knew that Vetrov was not merely the low-ranking diplomat he claimed to be, so the question arose of how his dissatisfaction could be exploited. DST officials decided to proceed very cautiously, for their own surveillances on Vetrov convinced them that he was a high-ranking KGB officer, probably involved in technology theft operations. As the DST was aware, France at that time was hemorrhaging its most vital technological secrets Eastward, so a recruitment of Vetrov promised to staunch that flow.

In 1970, his tour of duty in France over, Vetrov was recalled to Moscow to work in KGB headquarters. His French business-man friend maintained friendly contact, but did not attempt to recruit him directly, content only to let him know in subtle ways that he had a friend in France, available at a moment's notice to help. The DST's patience paid off in 1980, when Vetrov wrote a carefully phrased letter to his French friend, requesting an "urgent meeting" in Moscow.

So Vetrov had made his move at last. A subsequent meeting in Moscow confirmed DST's supposition: Vetrov said he would serve as a mole inside the KGB. In subsequent meetings right under the Kremlin walls, Vetrov handed over copies of top-secret documents, all of them stamped with the warning, PHOTOCOPY FORBIDDEN.

The documents revealed everything there was to know about the Soviet intelligence technology-theft operations. At that point a senior officer in the KGB's Department T (technological espionage), Vetrov had an overview of the scope of the program. Concerned that the time Vetrov spent at the KGB photocopying machines might arouse suspicion, the DST equipped him with a special high-speed camera that allowed him to photograph entire file cabinets of documents.

The film cassettes that Vetrov turned over to his control officer, a DST officer serving under cover as a military attache at the French embassy, provided the French (and the other Western intelligence services invited to share the treasures) with a double benefit. They not only revealed what Moscow was seeking in the way of technology, but they also revealed precisely which areas of the Soviet military were most technologically deficient. Moreover, the identities of nearly 300 KGB and GRU agents involved in technology theft operations were exposed, along with leads to more than 100 assets in the West who were aiding those operations.

For the KGB, it was an intelligence disaster of the first magnitude. The disaster would have been all the greater had not Vetrov, by 1982 near the breaking point because of the strain of his double life, committed the murder in the park. Still, as soon as the French became aware that Vetrov had been arrested, they and the Western allies decided to roll up Line X: 47 KGB officers under diplomatic cover were expelled from France, and another 150 were expelled from other nations. The KGB hurriedly pulled out another 200 before they could be arrested or expelled. A number of assets were arrested.

With that, Line X operations virtually collapsed, leaving the Soviet Union most vulnerable just as the huge American military buildup began during the Reagan administration. The Soviets, forced temporarily to rely on their own resources, never did catch up; the effort wrecked the Soviet economy and was among the chief causes of the Soviet collapse several years later.

As for Vetrov, the KGB's fury at him can only be imagined; not since **Oleg Penkovsky** had a mole working for the West caused such terrible damage. Initially, the KGB had plans to put Vetrov on trial, the idea being that a public airing of his "degenerate" life style (to be blamed on his exposure to the dissolute West during his Paris posting) would serve as a civics lesson. But no matter the severity of the threats against him, Vetrov had no intention of participating in a show trial. If the KGB wanted a trial, he made it clear he would use it as a forum on the failures of the Soviet leadership. He also made it clear he was prepared to indict the KGB, which he said was dominated by "alcoholism, corruption and nepotism." To underscore his determination never to play the role of penitent traitor, he insisted on adding to his confession, "My only regret is that I was not able to cause more damage to the Soviet Union and render more service to France."

Hopeless, the KGB decided, so the man poignantly code-named FAREWELL was taken out of his cell one morning in the spring of 1983 and shot.

THE STORM PETRELS

AFANSY M. SHOROKHOV
Flight of the Football Fan

Aliases: Vladimir Petrov,
Proletarsky, Sven Allyson
1907–1991

To his fellow members of the Russian Club in Canberra, Australia, the man officially known as Vladimir Petrov, Third Secretary at the Soviet embassy, was a very odd fish indeed.

Oh, he was unmistakably Russian, all right, the kind of Russian who, like most of his countrymen, loved his vodka and those throbbing, Gypsy-like songs of sadness and unrequited love. Curiously, however, he also took special delight in all things Australian, which included a passion for Australian football. His depth of knowledge about the game's finer points rivalled any native expert. Unusually enough for a Russian in those Stalinist times of 1953, he seemed to have a real sense of humor. And unlike the usual run of dour Russians who tended to regard Australians as capitalist creatures just short of barbarians, Petrov seemed to genuinely like Australians and often talked about how much he admired the country.

Most members of the club did not know quite what to make of Petrov, but one member made it his business to begin a close friendship with the Soviet diplomat. This was no chance encounter, for Dr. Mikhail Bialogusky, a Polish immigrant, was an asset for the Australian Secret Intelligence Organization (ASIO). He had joined the Russian Club, a mecca for homesick Russian diplomats, trade officials (and even a few emigrés) with the specific assignment of scouting which Soviet official might be susceptible to blandishments by the ASIO.

In selecting Petrov, Bialogusky was after a big fish. As ASIO was aware, Petrov's real job in Canberra was KGB *rezident* for Australia. He had been there since 1951, and from the moment of his arrival, ASIO realized he was pure KGB. Then 44, Petrov—an alias for Afansy M. Shorokhov—had already served more than 20 years in overseas posts from Peking to Stockholm, invariably accompanied by his wife Evdokia, who worked as a KGB clerk. Petrov's forte was cipher work; he had joined the Soviet navy in his teens, become a cipher expert, and was recruited into the KGB on the strength of his ability to handle codes. Trained by the KGB in the espionage arts, Petrov became that rare agent able to function as his own code room.

Given his reputation as one of the top KGB agents, ASIO suspected, correctly, that Petrov had been assigned to Australia to revive a highly successful wartime network of assets, mostly Communists and assorted sympathizers. After the war, the assets began to crumble away in the face of Cold War anticommunist purges, and the KGB wanted a revival.

ASIO's plan was for Bialogusky to pose as a rabidly pro-Soviet emigré, engage Petrov in political discussions, and slowly draw him out about his own real political leanings. To Bialogusky's surprise, however, the last thing Petrov wanted to hear was anything pro-Soviet. As he drew closer to his newfound friend, Volodya—to use Petrov's favorite nickname—began to open up. In truth, Petrov was in the process of becoming a very disillusioned spy. He took the dangerous step of revealing his disillusionment to Bialogusky, at the same time telling him that his wife Evdokia also was disillusioned. The problem, Petrov noted drily, was that Moscow did not accept resignations.

Petrov was careful not to mention his actual job as KGB *rezident,* nor did he discuss the real source of his low morale. His problem was twofold. One, he had been given an impossible assignment. By 1951, KGB operations in Australia, in part thanks to ASIO vigilance, had fallen to a low ebb, with no prospect of any immediate improvement. Moscow was demanding quick results, but to rebuild networks on the order of the KGB's wartime success might require decades. Second, and more ominously, KGB chief **Laventri Beria** was executed in 1953 after attempting to take power in the Soviet Union in the wake of Stalin's death. The inevitable anti-Beria purge had begun in KGB ranks; as Petrov knew, KGB operatives all over the world were being summoned to Moscow, there to receive a bullet in the back of their heads. Petrov felt especially vulnerable: Beria had recognized his talents some years before, and had promoted his career up the KGB ranks. This sponsorship was now a death warrant, for Petrov would be regarded as one of "Beria's boys."

ASIO officials sensed the moment had come, and Bialgusky was instructed to broach the subject of defection with Petrov. Any doubt Petrov may have had about such a drastic step was removed in April 1954, when he received the dreaded summons to report to Moscow for "consultations." Forced to make an instant decision, Petrov elected to defect, with his wife scheduled to follow later. He contacted Bialgusky and successfully made it to safety, but the KGB, the moment it realized Petrov had fled the embassy, seized Evdokia before she could escape the building. Petrov, meanwhile, hid out in an ASIO safe house.

There now began one of the most astounding public chapters in the history of Cold War espionage. The KGB decided to fly Mrs. Petrov back to Moscow as quickly as possible; the idea was that holding her as a hostage in Moscow would tend to dampen her husband's enthusiasm for revealing too much to the ASIO. The KGB was acutely aware that Petrov, among its leading agents, had a great deal of damaging information stored away in his head; what he knew about KGB cipher systems alone could be catastrophic.

A plane was dispatched to Australia by the KGB to pick up Mrs. Petrov, along with a squad of KGB thugs ordered to bring her back by force, if necessary. Legally, there wasn't much Australia could do to halt Mrs. Petrov's repatriation, since she was a Soviet citizen. But ASIO came up with a plan that would not only rescue her, but also give the KGB a black eye in the process.

Aware that the return flight to Moscow would have to refuel at Darwin, Australia, ASIO officials notified the media. By the time the plane landed, the airport was crowded with reporters, photographers and television cameramen drawn to the irresistible story: loving wife of defecting Soviet diplomat forced against her will to return to Moscow.

Confused by the media circus, the KGB made several bad mistakes. The KGB guards were ordered by Australian immigration officials to leave the plane with Mrs. Petrov. They did so although there was no legal reason for them to heed such an order. Then, they meekly complied with an order to go into the terminal—where ASIO agents separated Mrs. Petrov from their care and pressed a telephone receiver to her ear. On the other end was her husband, who told her to seek political asylum. "I do not want to go back to Moscow," she announced, giving the Australians sufficient legal reason to remove her from control of her bodyguards.

The KGB guards then committed the final, and worst, mistake in the entire drama. Under orders to bring Mrs. Petrov back to Moscow regardless of circumstances, they seized her and tried to force her into the plane. The Australians intervened, and the KGB thugs and their plane were ordered out of the country.

All of this was memorialized by the attending media contingent, and the pictures of a distraught-looking Mrs. Petrov, in the grip of two squat KGB goons from Central Casting—complete with ill-fitting suits and thick-soled shoes—made the front pages of every newspaper in the world. It was a public relations disaster for the KGB, for at the very time the Soviet government was trying to convince the world of its "peaceful" intentions, here was vivid visual proof of the real face of Soviet communism. Infuriated KGB leaders had a half-dozen KGB agents connected with the disastrous operation shipped off to Siberian labor camps as punishment, but the damage had been done.

Once safely in Australian hands, the Petrovs damaged the KGB further. It turned out that Petrov had surreptitiously kept copies of his reports to Moscow since 1952. These revealed a number of mid-scale Australian assets who were promptly rounded up. More interesting were the insights the Petrovs provided into the KGB cipher systems, of immense aid to the American and British cryptographers trying to read the KGB's World War II traffic.

Petrov's debriefing turned up a few surprises. One was his revelation that Guy Burgess and Donald Maclean, the British diplomats who had defected to the Soviet Union in 1951, were in fact KGB moles who had been implanted nearly 20 years before. He also told his debriefers that **H. A. R. Philby,** then under suspicion, was considered by the KGB to be their prize mole in Britain, and had been recruited in 1934. It was the first link in a chain that eventually forced Philby to flee eastward.

When all the debriefings were finished and his usefulness to Western intelligence at an end, Petrov settled down to a very different life as an Australian citizen. Given a new identity as Sven Allyson, a Scandinavian immigrant, Petrov and his wife wrote a book on their experiences, then opened a small general store they ran until Evdokia's death in 1990 and her husband's in 1991.

And for all those years, Petrov's neighbors were unfailingly puzzled why the pleasant Mr. Allyson had developed this consuming passion for Australian football. Pretty odd, they concluded, for a bloke from Sweden, or Finland, or wherever he said he was from.

IGOR GOUZENKO
The First Man

Code Names: CORBY, KLARK
Alias: Richard Brown
1919–1982

The 26-year-old Russian, newly arrived in Canada, had never seen anything like it. He cut the small story out of the local Ottawa newspaper and showed the clipping to all his co-workers. Was this not, he asked them, the most incredible thing they had ever seen?

The story, reporting a routine enough occurrence in the city of Ottawa, concerned a Greek fruit merchant who was suing the city for constructing a road in such a way that it was destroying his business. Igor Gouzenko read the story repeatedly, and the more he read, the more astonished he became. For a faithful Soviet *apparatchik*, the idea that an ordinary citizen could actually sue the government was almost beyond belief.

The fruit merchant episode was the first of several lessons on life in the West that caused a profound change in Gouzenko. The contrast between the standard of living of the average citizen in Canada and the grim, grinding poverty of a Soviet citizen could not have been greater. And as Gouzenko saw more aspects of life in the West, he became steadily more disillusioned about the Soviet system.

Gouzenko was a GRU agent, assigned to the GRU station in the Soviet embassy in Ottawa, under cover as a civilian cipher clerk for the embassy's diplomatic communications system. Actually, Gouzenko was specifically assigned to handle only GRU and KGB traffic from the embassy. He arrived in Ottawa, his first

61

MI5 Director Roger Hollis, whose handling of Soviet defector Igor Gouzenko caused mole-hunters in British intelligence to suspect him of being a KGB mole. (*AP/Wide World*)

overseas assignment, in June, 1943, following espionage schooling in Moscow. He had been a young army soldier in 1941, working in radio communications, when his brilliant abilities in handling cipher work brought him to the attention of GRU recruiters.

As Gouzenko was to learn, Soviet intelligence had a desperate need for cipher experts; the German invasion of the Soviet Union had compelled the GRU and the KGB to crank up to maximum power. Wholesale recruitments of hundreds of assets—including Communists committed to the Soviet cause and noncommunists eager to help defeat Hitler—had GRU and KGB radios humming around the clock, transmitting intelligence to Moscow. The radios (and the cipher experts who enciphered the messages) were essential, for intelligence in the fast-moving modern world was perishable, and had to be sent to Moscow as quickly as possible.

In Ottawa, Gouzenko learned that the GRU station was a key outpost in the Western Hemisphere, with intelligence tentacles that reached throughout North America. It had 25 well-placed assets in Canada alone, and also handled some of the massive volume of traffic generated from the United States.

But Ottawa represented something else to Gouzenko, who was the son of poor parents. Like an orphan child entering a rich man's home, he could hardly fathom that such a fairyland as the Canadian city actually existed. Arriving in Ottawa from the near-starvation rations of wartime Moscow, he was astonished to see that even with wartime restrictions, people in Ottawa had plenty to eat. Moreover, they were free in a way that no citizen of Stalinist Russia could fathom: people freely spoke their minds in public, on occasion actually criticizing the government.

Gouzenko seemed to be only dimly aware that wandering around Ottawa to savor this refreshing breath of freedom—and then telling his co-workers about it—was an extremely dangerous thing to do. For one thing, Gouzenko was a cipher clerk, which meant he had access to virtually every secret that was transmitted in and out of the embassy. For another, typical Stalinist paranoia ruled both the GRU and KGB stations inside the embassy building; some of the more than 100 agents who worked there were assigned the specific job of watching other agents to detect even the slightest sign of disloyalty.

Almost certainly, somebody in the embassy finally informed on Gouzenko, for in September, 1944, he received the dreaded summons to return to Moscow for unspecified "discussions." He had been in the GRU long enough to know what that meant: he was in serious trouble, undoubtedly suspected of drifting toward "dangerous Western deviationism." There was an even greater worry. For some time, Gouzenko had been hearing whispers among his GRU colleagues that that there was something strange going on with GRU and KGB cipher clerks. According to those whispers, Moscow had a habit of summoning home cipher clerks who worked in especially sensitive embassies, following which they would disappear. Reputedly, those cipher clerks were disposed of at regular intervals (and then replaced by new ones) for the simple reason that they knew too much; Moscow did not want to take the chance of a clerk defecting or becoming turned by the opposition. (GRU and KGB cipher clerks, who saw all the intelligence traffic, knew virtually all Russian secrets: the identities of all legals attached to the embassy, the illegals working outside who were in contact with the embassy, and the assets under control of regular agents, to say nothing of ongoing operations.)

Whatever the truth about these rumors, Gouzenko was spared from finding out firsthand. He was saved by his superiors at the Ottawa station, who furiously objected to his recall, arguing that his skills were irreplaceable "at this critical moment." Moscow gave way—for the time being, at least.

"At this critical moment" was no exaggeration, for the GRU station in Ottawa had suddenly shifted gears. Soviet intelligence had learned that the United States and Great Britain were jointly working on a top-secret project to develop an atomic bomb, a secret they were keeping from the Russians. A maximum effort was ordered for both the GRU and KGB: at all costs, that project must be penetrated. Stalin was not about to let his allies develop a weapon that would allow them to dominate the postwar world.

The joint GRU-KGB effort, code-named Operation Candy, focused much of its energy on Canada, where a scientific team was trying to work out the problems of producing fissionable uranium. Gouzenko handled the quantum jump in cable traffic as the Soviets reoriented their assets toward obtaining any information they could find on the atomic bomb project. Some months later, he realized that the GRU had suceeded brilliantly: he began transmitting volumes of technical data apparently obtained directly from assets working in the atomic bomb program. The prize asset, Gouzenko concluded, was a man code-named ALEX, who apparently was one of the scientists working on the program.

In the early summer of 1945, Gouzenko transmitted a report from his superior, Colonel Nikolai Zabotin (code-named GRANT), that indicated the GRU had penetrated the American end of the program. Zabotin not only provided details of what was going on at Los Alamos, New Mexico, the main development center for the bomb, he also knew the scheduled date of the first test, technical details of how the bomb was constructed, and, most precious of all, he had actually obtained a sample of U-235 (enriched uranium) from ALEX. A special plane was detailed to fly from Moscow to pick up the sample and bring it back to the Soviet Union, where it was used to accelerate the Soviet nuclear weapons program.

Awards, honors, and promotions showered upon the GRU station in Ottawa for its brilliant espionage feat, but Igor Gouzenko was not among the celebrants. Still under suspicion for his perceived "deviationism," he realized it was only a matter of time before Moscow would re-issue the summons to return home—with the strong possibility of a bullet in his head.

Gouzenko resolved to defect, but concluded that since Canada and the Soviet Union were still allies, there was the possibility the Canadians might simply give him back to the Russians. A plan took shape: he would defect with as much documentary evidence as possible of the massive Soviet spying operations in Canada. Once the Canadians saw the depth of Soviet perfidy, there was no way they would hand him back.

On the evening of September 5, 1945, Gouzenko finished his regular tour of duty in the embassy code room and walked out of the embassy with 109 GRU and KGB telegrams stuffed in a briefcase. Given the tight security in the embassy, he knew it would be only a matter of hours before the Soviets discovered the missing cables, so he had only a limited amount of time to put his plan into effect.

To his dismay, Gouzenko discovered that he could not even make the Canadians understand what he was trying to accomplish. His first stop was at the offices of the *Ottawa Journal*, the newspaper where he had read about the Greek fruit merchant some years before. The newspaper's editors didn't seem to understand what he was talking about, and ordered him out of the building. (Their failure in turning away the biggest story in decades resulted in succeeding generations of *Journal* staffers required to listen respectfully to every nut who wandered into the place, even those claiming to be receiving orders from space aliens via steel plates in their heads).

Gouzenko next visited several government offices, which also turned him away as some sort of crank. Increasingly desperate, Gouzenko locked himself in his apartment with his wife and two-year-old son, hardly daring to breathe as he heard GRU and KGB agents banging on his front door, demanding he come out. In a desperate move, Gouzenko poured out his story to his next-door neighbor, a Royal Canadian Air Force sergeant who agreed to give him and his family shelter. Gouzenko moved just in time: he had just settled into the adjoining apartment when he heard four KGB agents smashing in the front door of the Gouzenko apartment and ransacking the place.

The KGB's rash act actually helped Gouzenko, for police, summoned to the apartment building, realized that he was no ordinary crank, and that he was being hunted by the Russians for those papers he was clutching. By further fortuitous circumstance, Canadian-born **William Stephenson,** the legendary MI6 spymaster in New York during the war, happened to be in Canada as word spread throughout the Canadian security apparatus that something very strange was going on at the Soviet embassy in Ottawa. When Stephenson heard some of the first details, he instantly realized what had happened; thanks to his high-level contacts, he was able to mobilize the Royal Canadian Mounted Police (RCMP) Security Service to take Gouzenko under its wing. Meanwhile, the Russians were demanding Gouzenko's return, claiming that he had stolen a large sum of money from the embassy and would be taken to Moscow to "face serious consequences."

The Canadians ignored the Soviet demand, for the initial conversations with Gouzenko—and the treasures from the GRU code room—made it clear that something very significant had fallen into their hands. Of immediate concern were the 25 Canadian citizens revealed in those papers as Soviet intelligence assets, but there were even bigger shock waves. President Truman was informed that the great American atomic bomb secret—which the Americans had hoped they could keep for at least another 20 years—had been compromised. The British were informed that at least one of their scientists (who turned out to be Dr. Allan Nunn May,* the man behind the code name ALEX) was working for the Russians.

When the Gouzenko case became public, it fell like a thunderclap across the Western world. The Cold War had not yet begun, and the Russians were still generally regarded as wartime allies who had sacrificed the most in the struggle to defeat Hitler. In terms of public opinion, the Gouzenko revelations shattered at once the predominant impression that the Soviet Union was an imperfect, but generally benign, dictatorship that had stood shoulder to shoulder with the democracies. The Russians could no longer preserve the myth that they had no aggressive intentions against the West, and that they could coexist in a postwar world with their political opposites. The perfidy was there for all to see during a long series of espionage trials that grew out of Gouzenko's revelations: the massive recruitment of citizens to be-

---

* May pleaded guilty to espionage charges in 1946, and was sentenced to 10 years in prison. He confessed that he was a Communist sympathizer, recruited by the GRU early in the war to provide information on British scientific developments. The GRU got an unexpected dividend when May was assigned to the British end of the atomic bomb project. He received a total of $700 and two bottles of whiskey from the GRU in appreciation of his efforts, one of the great bargains in espionage history.

tray their own country by a wartime ally. Judging by the indications contained in the telegrams Gouzenko brought with him,
the GRU and the KGB had recruited hundreds of assets to uncover virtually every single important secret in the United States,
Canada, and Great Britain.

The sheer scale of the effort was breathtaking, but to the counterintelligence agents of those three countries who now flocked to
Gouzenko, there was far more interest in some other things he
had to say.

Like all intelligence operatives in sensitive positions, Gouzenko had been exposed to the inevitable office gossip during the
years he worked in Moscow. Outsiders might be surprised to learn
that there are few real secrets inside the halls of the average intelligence agency; like human beings everywhere who work in
offices, intelligence agents like to exchange gossip about their
superiors, complain about their treatment, carp against their perceived rivals, and boast of their greatest accomplishments.

Even in the rigidly controlled Soviet intelligence system, office gossip and office politics ran rampant. Gouzenko recalled a
few choice tidbits he had heard in Moscow Center (as the headquarters of Soviet intelligence was known). Two of them were to
cause minor earthquakes in the espionage world.

For the representatives of American intelligence, Gouzenko
had very disturbing news: friends in Moscow Center had bragged
to him of an American asset they had recruited, described as
"high in the State Department." Since the Americans had already
been told by **Whittaker Chambers** that State Department official
Alger Hiss was working for the KGB, they concluded that Gouzenko probably was referring to Hiss. For the British, Gouzenko
had even more disturbing news: he had heard about an asset,
code-named ELLI, who he understood was a senior official "in
British counterintelligence." He had no other information to further pinpoint this vital source, but recalled some GRU officials
mention that there was "something Russian" in his background.
MI5 official Roger Hollis, assigned the task of debriefing Gouzenko, discounted this lead, since ELLI was also the code name
assigned to one of the GRU's Canadian assets. It was deemed
unlikely that the Soviets would assign the same code name to two
different assets.

Many years later, Gouzenko's revelation and its curt dis-
missal by Hollis would lead to suspicions that Hollis himself was
a KGB mole, but meanwhile Gouzenko settled into his new life

in Canada. Under RCMP 24-hour guard, he was given a new identity as a Czech immigrant named Richard Brown (to account for
his heavy Slavic accent). He wrote a book of reminiscences of his
life in Soviet intelligence and his subsequent defection, and a
highly praised novel about life in the Soviet Union, both under
his real name.

Relations between Gouzenko and the RCMP were not warm.
He complained endlessly about the size of the government pension he was awarded, and seemed intent on becoming a rich capitalist. An enigmatic, very complex man, Gouzenko's relentless
hunt for money (in later years, he would charge $1,000 to re-
porters for a brief interview) antagonized his RCMP handlers,
who liked to joke that the motto on the Gouzenko family's coat
of arms was "What's In It For Me?" Eventually, as Gouzenko felt
more secure, the RCMP removed their guards, and its prize defector was on his own. His value as an intelligence source long
had passed, and he decided he wanted to live life in the fast lane.
Gouzenko went deeply into debt, caused largely by the $500,000
home just outside Toronto in which he insisted on living. To raise
money, he hit upon the expedience of filing libel suits: any author
or television commentator who even mentioned the name Gouzenko could expect a libel suit from him, filed under Canada's
very restrictive libel laws.

The proceeds of these suits—most publishers settled out of
court—helped Gouzenko maintain a fairly comfortable life-style,
but they could not protect him from the ravages of time. He
began to go blind from an incurable eye ailment, a source of rage
and frustration. His frustration worsened in the 1970s when British investigators came to visit him. They were involved in reopen-
ing the whole matter of KGB penetration of British intelligence,
and busily reinvestigating what had happened when Gouzenko
first spoke to MI5 in 1945. Furious, he listened as British agents
read him the 1945 reports on the MI5 debriefing of him, for the
reports bore no relation to what he said—especially his warning
that MI5 had a high-ranking KGB mole. "You have been penetrated!" Gouzenko shouted at them, unable to believe that British
intelligence in 25 years had been unable (or unwilling) to find
the mole.

On that sad note, history passed by Gouzenko. He died in
June, 1982, his funeral attended only by a few close relatives. Fol-

lowing an old Russian custom, they lined up at the casket and one by one passed by, bending to kiss the corpse. During a non-denominational service, a clergyman delivered a brief eulogy, describing the deceased as "Mr. Brown, who comes to us from Prague."

ANATOLI GOLITSIN
Even a Paranoid Has Enemies

Code Names: KAGO, STONE,
AE/LADLE, MARTEL
Aliases: Anatole Klimov, John Stone
1921–

Like high-stakes poker players pushing their stacks of chips across the table toward a player they were convinced was probably bluffing, the counterintelligence officers shoved piles of paper before the bull-necked Russian. "Please go through these reports," KGB Major Anatoli Golitsin was instructed, "and tell us which ones came to your attention in Moscow."

The spy-hunters from Great Britain, the United States, and France sat silently as the man nicknamed "Tolka" began to read through the papers. As all the men in that room understood, this was a very important litmus test.

It was January, 1962. A few weeks earlier, Golitsin had defected to the CIA from his post as *rezident* in Helsinki, Finland. He claimed to possess an astounding amount of information on KGB operations worldwide, and wanted to be set up as a virtual one-man counterintelligence agency to root out the KGB moles he claimed infested every Western government and intelligence service, the CIA included. As a mere sample of his knowledge, he told his debriefers he had read top-secret NATO documents while stationed in Moscow several years before because the KGB moles regularly provided Moscow with virtually all top-level NATO decisions as soon as they were written.

If true, that meant the KGB's penetration was so extensive that NATO was an open book. To some of his listeners, such revelations smacked of self-aggrandizement, a not-uncommon tendency by defectors to exaggerate their own knowledge and importance in order to boost their credentials—and qualify for the kind of lavish payments grateful counterintelligence agencies can pay to useful sources.

To test Golitsin's claim about KGB penetration of NATO, it was decided to present him with several documents, in which a number of cleverly forged papers were included. If he really had the knowledge he claimed he had, he should be able to spot the difference. To the shock of his audience, Golitsin treated the test as though it were child's play. "Deception," he announced in his heavy Slavic accent as he put aside one of the forged documents. Within a half hour, Golitsin scanned his way through the documents; unerringly, he was able to spot the fake ones. Asked how he had managed this feat by only rapidly scanning the pile of papers, Golitsin replied simply, "Because, as I've told you, I've already read these documents in Moscow."

With that, Anatoli Golitsin passed into espionage legend. Over the next two years, he was to uncover scores of KGB agents and assets in the Western world, resulting in a roster of damage unequalled by any other KGB defector. But, as things turned out, the damage he caused was not limited to the KGB; he was also to cause grave damage within the very Western intelligence agencies he professed to aid.

There was nothing in Golitsin's background to indicate his eventual role as any kind of wrecker, much less against the KGB. Born in 1926 of Ukrainian peasants, his record showed a typical profile for a loyal KGB careerist: military school, member of the *Komsomol* (Communist party youth movement), army artillery school, Communist party membership, transfer to military counterintelligence, and recruitment by the KGB. Clearly, he was a man early on regarded as an up and comer, for the KGB sent him to its High Intelligence School—the agency's graduate school for future senior espionage executives—and then posted him in 1953 to one of its most important outposts, Vienna. After a two-year tour, he returned to Moscow Center to work as a case officer in one of the KGB's most sensitive areas, the Anglo-American Department (where he saw the top-secret NATO documents while learning of the KGB's extensive penetrations of their Western opponents). In 1961, he was sent to another key KGB post, Helsinki, where on a snowy evening that December, he showed up at the U.S. embassy with his wife and seven-year-old daughter and announced he wanted to defect.

Although Golitsin did not know it, the CIA was not entirely surprised by his defection. Seven years before, another KGB officer operating in Vienna, Peter Deriabin, had defected. During his debriefing, his CIA handlers took him through a standard exercise for defectors: an analysis of all the other KGB officers he knew at the Vienna station, noting which ones he thought were susceptible to eventual defection or possible turning by the CIA. Deriabin picked out fellow KGB officer Golitsin. Despite his unblemished record, Deriabin pointed out that Golitsin was in fact regarded by Moscow Center as a royal pain in the neck. Arrogant, with overweening ambition, Golitsin had a tendency to aggravate his superiors. Some years before, while in Moscow, he had actually proposed a plan to reorganize the entire Soviet intelligence structure—a plan that placed himself somewhere near the apex. Golitsin, Deriabin reported, was regarded as insufferable and also possibly dangerous. Deriabin predicted that Golitsin, with his ambitions thwarted, would at some point defect to the other side.

Deriabin turned out to be right. Golitsin, fundamentally, was an intelligence chameleon. He was in the intelligence game for the pure excitement and intrigue it offered; whether he was working for the KGB, the CIA, or MI6 was of little consequence, so long as he was playing a key role. In later years, this mindset would be of some significance, but at least in the early stages of his defection, Golitsin was nothing short of sensational.

Thanks to his work in the KGB's Anglo-American Department, Golitsin had an overview of many of the agency's assets in the West. Among them was **H. A. R. Philby,** whom Golitsin finally, and positively, identified as a long-term KGB mole. It was Golitsin's clinching evidence that led MI6 to a final confrontation with Philby, who understood he now faced evidence he could never refute, and he fled behind the Iron Curtain.

Of more immediate operational interest, Golitsin then began blowing other KGB assets. Three of the more interesting involved deep penetrations whose revelation caused dismay among Western counterintelligence agencies, since they had no clue that such hemorrhages were taking place.

One involved John Vassall, a homosexual clerk in the British Admiralty, who had been recruited in 1953 when he was posted to Moscow. He was caught in a classic so-called "honeytrap" operation: the KGB set him up with a male prostitute (known as a "raven" in Soviet intelligence parlance), photographed the result, then threatened to show the photographs to Vassall's superiors unless he agreed to work for the KGB. Vassall made available to the KGB a wide range of classified material that came across his desk, most productively when he worked in NID and saw reports of British Naval intelligence.

In a similar honeytrap operation, the KGB had ensnared John Watkins, a Canadian diplomat and homosexual who agreed to work for the KGB when he was posted to Moscow as Canada's ambassador in 1958. As an asset, he was almost perfectly placed, since he could provide top-level diplomatic messages from Canada and other countries. (A subsidiary, and possibly even more important, benefit was that access to such traffic enabled Soviet cryptanalysts to find "cribs" that helped them break Western diplomatic ciphers).

The third, and most damaging of all, involved Georges Paques*, French attache to NATO, a secret Communist who had been recruited in 1946. He passed on high-level material from both NATO headquarters and the French government.

By late 1963, Golitsin had divested himself of just about everything he knew concerning specific KGB penetrations in the West. He then moved to the second, and much more controversial, part of his postdefection career. It involved something for which he had no hard information, but sufficient suspicions to intrigue his counterintelligence hosts: KGB penetration of Western intelligence services.

Golitsin's first hints of KGB moles in Western intelligence had a particular resonance in Britain, where a coterie of MI5 officers, led by Peter Wright and Arthur Martin, had been convinced for quite some time that both MI5 and MI6 were penetrated by the KGB. Further, they believed that the penetration was at a very high level, a super-mole (or several super-moles) who had facilitated the KGB's "ring of five" and subsequently were responsible for the miserable record of British intelligence throughout the first two decades of the Cold War.

Golitsin was lent by the CIA to the British for what had become a large in-house investigation code-named FLUENCY. Notoriously tightfisted with money for intelligence operations, the

---

* Golitsin revealed that Paques was only one of a large ring of KGB moles who had infiltrated nearly every level of the French government. Golitisin's revelation on this score was so alarming, President Kennedy personally wrote to French President Charles de Gaulle to warn him of the operations of the ring, code-named SAPPHIRE by the KGB. The effort by French counterintelligence to track down the ring was the subject of the Leon Uris novel (and Alfred Hitchcock movie), *Topaz.*

British nevertheless paid Golitsin $28,000 a month to serve as "consultant" for FLUENCY. Basically, the job entailed review of British intelligence operations, detailed examination of leads revealed by defectors, and myriad other clues in an attempt to pinpoint which man (or men) had been systematically undermining British counterintelligence against the Soviet Union.

There was much for Golitsin to consider. More than 20 years before, a defecting senior GRU officer, Walter Krivitsky, had warned of KGB moles in British intelligence. Although he did not know their identities, he had a number of clues. For example, he had heard about a "Scotsman of good birth" who was working in the Foreign Office, and an "establishment figure" who was working as a newspaperman in Spain. Even a moderate effort would have tracked down the men behind these clues: Donald Maclean and **H. A. R. Philby,** but nothing was ever done. There was also the mysterious matter of how **Igor Gouzenko** had been handled by MI5, and how his warning of a KGB mole in MI5 was sidetracked. Additionally, there was the mystery of how such infamous KGB assets as **Klaus Fuchs** and Allan Nunn May had been cleared for top-secret work by MI5 despite their open Communist affiliations (Fuchs had been a member of the German Communist party and May was a leading activist in a notorious Communist-controlled association of scientists and technicians).*

A newspaper story reporting the FLUENCY probe and Golitsin's role prematurely ended his work in Britain. Returning to the United States, he passed into the control of the CIA's famed head of counterintelligence, the legendary James Angleton. At that point, for reasons Angleton never made clear, the counterintelligence chief became a devoted acolyte of Golitisin.

As he had claimed to British intelligence, Golitsin insisted that there was high-level KGB penetration of American intelligence as well, specifically in the CIA. According to Golitsin, this super-mole was code-named SASHA, who in turn was supporting a network of similar moles. Many of these moles were involved in Golitsin's crowning theory: a massive and cunning KGB disinformation campaign that had completely misled the West about Soviet capabilities and intentions. (As part of that theory, Golitsin

---

* The molehunt in MI6 and MI5 was to paralyze British intelligence throughout the 1970s, with little to show for it: **Anthony Blunt** confessed, naming two other assets, but the "big fish" were never found. Wright was convinced that MI5 Director Roger Hollis was the KGB's "super-mole," but Hollis was finally cleared by the FLUENCY investigation.

insisted that the Sino-Soviet split was in fact a large-scale deception.)

Angleton proceeded to tear the CIA apart looking for the super-mole, spurred by Golitsin's hints that no one in the agency's Soviet Division could be trusted, especially any who spoke Russian. As a result, CIA operations against the Soviet Union were paralyzed, while the careers of more than 100 CIA officers were blighted by suspicion. This mad hunt reached its nadir in 1964, when another defecting KGB officer, Yuri Nosenko, was illegally detained for nearly three years because Golitsin told Angleton that Nosenko was probably a KGB plant to sow disinformation. (Nosenko had told his debriefers that there was no KGB mole in the CIA, and that, contrary to hints by Golitsin, the KGB had no operational interest in Lee Harvey Oswald when the presidential assassin lived in the Soviet Union).

Golitsin's baleful influence ended in 1974, when Angleton was fired following public revelations of his role in an illegal CIA domestic spying operation. Still, Golitsin had his devotees in both British and American intelligence, and they were ready to help when he produced his *magnus opus*, a million-word manuscript for a book that turned the Western view of the world upside down. Golitsin wrote that nearly all assumptions about modern history were wrong, for the unbelievably cunning KGB disinformation operation had managed to fool just about everybody. He tried to find a professional writer to convert this mass into a readable book, but all the writers he approached decided not to participate, possibly deterred by his insistence on carrying his manuscript around in a briefcase chained to his wrist. Golitsin's devotees in MI5 and the CIA then sat down and extracted a book from the manuscript, called *New Lies for Old*. It was published commercially, but sunk without a trace.

Golitsin subsequently faded from the intelligence scene. Most of his supporters on both sides of the Atlantic, including Angleton, had either died or retired. In 1990, living in the U.S. under an assumed identity, Golitisin claimed that the collapse of communism in Eastern Europe was actually part of a long-term Soviet deception operation. No one, aside from his few remaining acolytes, paid any attention.

WHITTAKER CHAMBERS
The Man with Two Faces

Code Names: BOB, CARL, EUGENE
Aliases: George Crosley, Carl Carlson
1901–1961

On a spring morning in 1939, what would prove to be the most momentous meeting in modern espionage took place in a nondescript hotel room in New York City between two men who were determined to severely injure Soviet intelligence.

The contrast between the two men could not have been greater. One was a pudgy, slovenly man with bad teeth named Whittaker Chambers, an editor for *Time* magazine. The other was a former citizen of the Soviet Union, now alien resident in the United States, named Schmeka Ginsberg (although he had been using the operational alias Walter Krivitsky for some years). He was a small, dapper, and very precise man with a distinct touch of Old World courtliness.

Despite these contrasts, both men shared a common background: they were former spies. Chambers, then 38 years old, had been a devout American Communist who had joined the party in 1924 and eight years later was recruited for the party's underground apparatus. The apparatus recruited promising Communists who were officially stripped of party membership and assigned various espionage missions for the KGB and the GRU. In 1933, Chambers was secretly dispatched to Moscow for espionage training, and on his return was assigned work as a courier for several cells of Communists working in U.S. government positions who were providing information to the party. But increasingly disenchanted with communism, he quit both the party and his underground assignment in 1937.

Krivitsky, then 41, had joined the GRU in 1923, and by 1936, when he was transferred to the KGB, he was *rezident* in The Hague, responsible for coordinating Soviet intelligence operations in Western Europe. But in 1938, when his fellow KGB operative and lifelong friend Ignace Poretsky was killed in a Stalinist purge to eliminate Jewish agents, Krivitsky defected to the French. He later made his way to Canada, and then contacted the FBI, which gave him sanctuary in the United States. By that point, Krivitsky had become thoroughly disillusioned with communism, and was determined to wreak vengeance for his friend's death against the KGB.

Chambers shared Krivitsky's determination, and they jointly agreed that spring day to expose the depth of Soviet intelligence's penetration of the western democracies. Both men were soon to discover, however, that preconceptions about the Soviet Union would make this no easy task.

To a certain extent, the difficulties Chambers initially encountered were the result of his own curious approach. In late 1939, he contacted Assistant Secretary of State Adolph A. Berle and told him of KGB infiltration of the State Department, but he apparently wanted to protect the identities of the people he knew were members of Communist cells and working for the KGB. Without names, Chambers' assertions were vague, at best, and the Roosevelt White House decided to ignore the whole thing. In 1942, when Chambers approached the FBI, he was still hesitant about naming any assets.

But the FBI was already on the trail. They had been previously alerted by Krivitsky, who told them he had heard of a key KGB asset "high in the U.S. State Department," and that the Soviets had another 31 well-placed assets throughout the U.S. government. Additionally, Krivitisky said he had heard of another 61 KGB assets in Great Britain. The FBI dispatched him to London to talk with British intelligence. As a result, Krivitsky was able to pinpoint two important KGB assets: John Herbert King, a Foreign Office code clerk, and Tyler Kent, a U.S. State Department code clerk who was also providing material to the German *Abwehr.**

---

* Krivitsky was more concerned about exposing higher-level KGB moles operating in Britain. He had only clues to **H. A. R. Philby,** Donald Maclean, and others, but the British never followed up. Increasingly discouraged about the U.S. and British failure to investigate his leads, he committed suicide in 1941.

Whittaker Chambers, who set off the most explosive spy case in American history. (*AP/Wide World*)

The FBI was puzzled by Chambers' reluctance to name names. Since he admitted to serving as a courier for Sovet rings operating inside the U.S. government, and thus obviously knew the identities of those assets, the FBI suspected he was protecting a close friend.

That suspicion was not confirmed until August, 1948, when Chambers went before an executive session of the House Un-American Activities Committee and dropped a bombshell: one of the KGB assets from whom he received material was his former friend, Alger Hiss. The assertion was explosive. Hiss, a top official in the State Department's Far Eastern Division until 1944, and later president of the Carnegie Endowment, was a pillar of the American foreign policy establishment.

Informed of this allegation, Hiss demanded time from the committee for a public session to deny the charge, vehemently insisting that he did not even know Whittaker Chambers. The Hiss case ignited a public spy controversy that smolders to this day.

The committee was faced with a quandary: it seemed difficult to believe that Chambers would risk exposing himself to a charge of perjury by making up the allegation about Hiss, but on the other hand Hiss' denials had been so forthright and frank, it was difficult to believe this distinguished establishment figure was lying.

But however convincing Hiss appeared, one member of the committee, Congressman Richard Nixon of California, was certain he was a liar. To prove it, he had Chambers return in executive session and recount every detail he could remember about the time in the 1930s when he claimed to have known Hiss. Then Hiss was called for a similar session and asked details of his life during the same period. Almost all the details of both accounts meshed, so there was no doubt: Chambers had known Hiss very well. Hiss himself began to waver, and said he now recalled knowing a man named George Crosley, whom he said resembled Chambers.

That still left the problem of proof: Chambers claimed that Hiss gave him State Department documents for transmittal to the KGB. Chambers said he photographed and then returned the originals to Hiss, but his unsupported word amounted to insufficient evidence. Several months later, Chambers produced the proof, consisting of a cache of microfilms of State Department documents hidden in a dumbwaiter, and even more melodramatically, a further cache hidden inside a pumpkin on the Chambers farm. The cache included several notes in Hiss' own handwriting, along with material later proven to have been typed on an old typewriter once owned by Mrs. Hiss.

Hiss ultimately was convicted of perjury, but the importance of the case extended far beyond that. Aside from making Nixon's political career, the furious public controversy set off the first spasm in what came to be a nationwide anticommunist hysteria, finally climaxing in the excesses of Senator Joseph McCarthy.

Taken as a whole, it was not entirely the result Chambers intended, but no one could have foreseen the explosion he would set off the day he sat down with Walter Krivitsky. Until his death in 1961, Chambers remained content to have succeeded in his basic goal, exposing the multiple rings of American Communists who worked in the government. More than three dozen such assets ultimately were exposed. To this day, no one is quite certain the precise dimension of their services to Soviet intelligence, but it is known that at least three of them worked in the OSS during the war, and another, Lachlin Currie, served as an adviser to President Roosevelt.

More importantly, perhaps, Chambers can be regarded as the real father of the American conservative movement, for his lonely crusade was to inspire an entire generation of conservatives. Among them was the president of the Screen Actors Guild, who in 1950 moved to purge Communists from that organization. Thirty-six years later, the Guild chief, now President Ronald Reagan, arranged for the posthumous award of the Medal of Freedom, the nation's highest civilian award, to Whittaker Chambers, the man whom, Reagan noted, "history has proven right."

THE LEGENDS

LEIBA DOMB
The Red Orchestra

Code Names: UNCLE, OTTO
Aliases: Adam Mikler, Leopold Trepper,
Leopold de Winter, Jean Gilbert, V. I. Ivanoski
1906–1983

"I am a Communist because I am a Jew," Leiba Domb often said. This was a standard explanation by those Eastern European Jews who saw Marxism as their only salvation in the pervasive anti-Semitism of pre-world War II Europe, when Jews were always perched on the edge of a precipice. The sense of impending holocaust created in Domb a deeply committed revolutionary—and, as the intelligence agencies of a half-dozen countries were to find out, one of the most formidable spies of all time.

By the time he was 19 in 1925, Domb already was a revolutionary activist who had been fired from a leather factory in his native Poland, for agitating among its workers. In that year, Domb joined the Polish Communist Party, where his revolutionary ardor, high intelligence, and natural leadership abilities marked him as a man destined for greater things. Polish authorities also noticed him, and in 1928 arrested him for "revolutionary activities." He was ordered deported from the country in lieu of a jail sentence. Domb first went to Marseilles, France, and then emigrated to Palestine.

Once in Palestine, Domb went right to work organizing Communist cells, an activity that quickly brought him to the attention of British Mandate authorities. They deported him back to France, where he became a key figure in the Jewish immigrant labor section of the French Communist party. His drive and organizational skills caused him to be noticed by still another set of

Leiba Domb (Leopold Trepper), the fabled head of the Soviet "Red Orchestra" spy network during World War II, in Copenhagen in 1974. Beside him is his wife Liba. (The Great Game *by Leopold Trepper, McGraw Hill: 1977/Yivo Institute*)

governmental authorities, but before the French could act, the party decided to move him out of harm's way to Moscow, where he was to attend "higher party training" in the "university for national minorities" of the Comintern (Stalin's organization of international Communist parties that oversaw party activities throughout the world).

Translated, that meant Domb, considered among the party's brightest stars, was being trained and groomed for a future leadership role. But his future as a party leader never came to fruition, for Domb's abilities were noted by an organization that was to have the most profound effect on his life: the GRU.

The same qualities that had caused the Communist party leadership to look favorably on Domb—daring, drive, total commitment, high intelligence—were also attractive to **Jan Berzin**, head of the GRU. Noted for his ability to spot and recruit top-flight agents, Berzin saw in Domb that combination of attributes the GRU chief had decided were essential for good agents: "Cool head, warm heart, and nerves of steel."

Domb seemed to fit the prescription. A short, squat man, he radiated a powerful personal energy and an aggressiveness that created the impression of someone who would put his head through a wall, if necessary, to achieve what he wanted. He also projected an air of total fearlessness, and even in the rigid, doctrinaire world of the Communist party was known for his willingness to challenge people and doctrines he thought wrong.

Honed by years of clandestine underground party work, Domb demonstrated a real flair for espionage. After a brief period working with a small network in France during the early 1930s to perfect his espionage skills, Domb was deemed ready for the real role Berzin had in mind for him: *rezident*. In Berzin's calculation, the GRU urgently needed to prepare for the war he was certain would break out within just a few years. Germany was the key, but with the German Communist party and almost all Soviet intelligence networks in that country shattered by Hitler, it was essential to reconstruct an entirely new intelligence structure that would keep an eye on the Soviet Union's most dangerous enemy. Berzin's plan was to avoid the danger of attempting to build networks in the Nazi police state, and instead create a series of networks just outside German borders, the most important of which would be located in Belgium and France. Domb would be their creator.

In May 1939, Domb arrived in Brussels and went to work. He was to build a series of commercial covers throughout Europe whose tentacles would reach into Nazi Germany itself. Under his new identity as a Canadian-born businessman named Jean Gilbert, Domb created a commercial cover company called Simexco, and a year later, created the Simex Company in Paris. He energetically began recruiting assets, and by the outbreak of World War II, he had built a series of compartmentalized rings that consisted of professional agents, civilian assets, and local Communists. His rings extended from the North Sea to Switzerland, and even included a small ring inside Nazi Germany itself, consisting of a group of fanatical German Communists who had managed to conceal their political sympathies and obtained jobs in the Nazi government.

Most of Domb's nearly 200 assets were located at or near what he like to call "switch points," the crossroads of modern governmental bureaucracies where essential information came to be processed. Domb believed that vital intelligence could be found in even the most obscure government office—provided that his agents knew what they were looking for.

Domb demonstrated how that theory worked in France, where most of his best assets were located. After the German invasion, he discovered that the best way to obtain intelligence on German troop dispositions in France—a secret closely guarded by the Germans—was via a little-known agency known as the French Billeting Office, a Vichy agency that handled billeting arrangements for German occupation forces quartered in French army bases and civilian facilities. In the process, of course, it learned the identities and movements of all German units in the country. Similarly, a network of French railway officials, who worked as liaison with the Germans on movements of German military trains along the French system, knew precisely the levels of German logistics and military units being moved in and out of France. Yet another obscure government bureaucracy proved to be an intelligence gold mine. This one handled the payments under a French-German agreement that mandated that France pay the costs of its own occupation. The precise Germans were scrupulous about accounting for every penny, in the process revealing the exact numbers of their forces in France.

Even better was Domb's greatest inspiration: affiliating his cover company with the German Organization Todt, a huge German bureaucracy that handled all the military construction and other logistical details for the German war machine. Simex Company representatives, in the course of doing business with the organization, were given precious travel passes from the German military authorities that allowed them entry into restricted military areas. It was a spy's dream.

Throughout the first 18 months of the war, the Germans were unaware of the proliferating Domb networks all over occupied Europe. Domb was cautious; aware that the radios he used to transmit intelligence back to Moscow represented his weakest link—German "radio finder" teams were adept at tracking down clandestine radios—he made sure that the transmissions lasted only a short period, following which the radios were moved to new locations. The brevity of the transmissions (which did not allow the radio-finders sufficient time to triangulate the beams) kept his growing operation secure, but caused problems when he uncovered one of the great secrets of the war to that point.

Domb's careful monitoring of German troop movements in France and Belgium paid off in late 1940, when his assets detected the sudden shift of German military forces eastward. Since Poland was in no imminent danger of attack, Domb concluded, correctly, that Hitler, balked in the Battle of Britain, was about to turn his attention to the Soviet Union. Combined with other intelligence, Domb in December 1940, was able to transmit a huge volume of traffic in bits and pieces from his constantly shifting radios. He supplied an accurate outline of Operation Barbarossa, Hitler's plan to invade the Soviet Union sometime in the spring of 1941—including precisely which German units had been assigned to the operation, giving Moscow a complete order of battle.

It had required a supreme effort to send all this information in short transmissions, but Domb felt the work was worth it, since the Soviet Union was now warned of the danger. But to his dismay, Stalin refused to believe it. Convinced that the Germans would not invade the Soviet Union, he scrawled across a GRU report on Domb's intelligence, "Find out the author of this provocation and have him punished." (Fortunately for Domb, GRU head-quarters took the terrible risk of ignoring the order.)

Undeterred, Domb soldiered on, feeding Moscow a steady stream of intelligence about the German military buildup for the upcoming invasion—which Stalin continued to ignore. All that suddenly changed on the morning of June 22, 1941, when Germany invaded the Soviet Union. Proved right, Domb was now bombarded with demands from Moscow Center for every scrap of intelligence he could collect on the German military machine. In response, Domb's radios hummed nearly around the clock, pumping transmissions eastward. He provided an almost minute-by-minute stream of intelligence on German military disposi-tions, and he was able to warn of German plans for an attack on Moscow (which was checked by fresh Russian divisions that in-flicted the first defeat on the German *blitzkrieg* in the East). In November, Domb was able to learn details of the German plan for an offensive in the Caucasus, an offensive that ended at Sta-lingrad.

But by that point, Domb concluded that time was running out for his operation. As he was the first to realize, in the very success of his organization lay the seeds of its destruction; the longer his radios were on the air broadcasting reams of vital in-telligence to Moscow, the more likely that the German radio-find-ers would track them down. The dilemma was insoluble: at that critical hour, when the Soviet Union was desperate for the intel-ligence Domb was providing, he had no choice except to keep his radios on the air for hours at a time. Which meant, as his assets began reporting with more frequency, German radio-finder trucks with their distinctive aerials were drawing nearer to the transmitters.

The Germans were indeed drawing nearer. Since early 1941, their radio-intercept stations had been detecting coded transmissions beamed eastward from a number of transmitters in Western Europe. The messages proved unbreakable, so the Germans concluded that they had been enciphered by one-time pads—the almost certain indicator that the radios belonged to Soviet intelligence. Although the ciphers couldn't be broken, the Germans could track down the transmitters. A joint Gestapo-*Abwehr* counterintelligence operation went to work.

The Germans got a break in June 1941, when the transmitters suddenly began broadcasting for hours at a stretch, allowing the radio-finder teams that much more time to triangulate the signals. In the habit of using musical terms to describe clandestine transmitters, they decided to call this newly-discovered network of transmitters the "Red Orchestra," the name by which Domb's network finally became known in espionage legend.

As the Germans began to close in, Domb made arrangements to dismantle his network and escape. He erased his legends under various aliases, including the one he used most frequently, Jean Gilbert. "Monsieur Gilbert" suddenly died a natural death, and Domb actually had a fake tombstone in that name prepared for an empty grave in a Paris cemetery.

Domb hoped to complete his dismantlement by January 1942, but on December 13, 1941, the Germans tracked down one of Domb's more important transmitters in a Brussels house. A raid caught several members of the network and a radio operator in the middle of a transmission. Incredibly enough, Domb himself showed up at the house as the raid was underway; thinking fast, he was able to pass himself off as an itinerant rabbit-seller whom Gestapo agents sent on his way.

Torture of the captured agents quickly revealed the real identity of that rabbit-seller, and a continent-wide manhunt was soon underway. Meanwhile, the Germans began rolling up the entire Red Orchestra all over Europe, and by the middle of 1942, Domb's network was collapsing. But Domb was still at large; constantly on the move, he evaded capture until October 1942, when the Germans detected one of his many aliases and tracked him down to a dentist's office in Paris. They found him in the dental chair, waiting to have an aching tooth treated.

"Congratulations," Domb said in a professional's tribute to the professional *Abwehr* agents who grabbed him. "You have done very well."

What happened next remains a matter of dispute. According to the Germans, the *Abwehr* had an ambitious plan in mind. In their estimate, although Moscow knew the Red Orchestra was under assault, the Russians could not be certain which branches had been compromised, and certainly they did not yet know that Domb himself had been captured. The Abwehr plan was to use Domb in a *funkspiel,* as a means of feeding deception material to Moscow. The Germans claim that Domb not only readily agreed, but further agreed to betray the remaining components of the Red Orchestra, along with members of the French Resistance who had served as assets for his network. In Domb's later version of these events, however, he claims that he agreed to play along with the Germans for their little radio game, intending to warn Moscow at the first opportunity. He denies ever betraying any of the Red Orchestra assets.

In any event, using one of the captured Red Orchestra radio operators (who also agreed to cooperate), the Germans began transmitting to Moscow, signing the messages with Domb's name. The Soviet response seemed to indicate that Moscow had taken the bait, but in fact the GRU from the first moment, apparently alerted by the captured radio operator's secret signal, realized that Domb was now operating under *Abwehr* control. The Russians played out their end of the game, demanding more and more precise information from Domb on German military plans. By June, 1943, the *Abwehr* realized that the Russians were onto the game somehow, and the *funkspiel* ended.

Whatever revenge the Germans might have planned against Domb was obviated when he suddenly escaped from the *Abwehr's* loose confinement by the simple expedient of asking to be taken to a drug store for heart medicine, then walking out the back door while *Abwehr* agents watched the front door. He went underground in Paris, and did not emerge until liberation. A few months later, he was summoned to Moscow for unspecified "discussions."

Upon arrival in Moscow, Domb made the mistake of complaining how his intelligence on Operation Barbarossa was ignored, and how Moscow's insistence on keeping transmitters working too long caused the network's breakup by the Germans. He was promptly accused of betraying the Red Orchestra to the Germans, and sentenced to 10 years in prison. He was released following Stalin's death in 1953, and permitted to emigrate to his native Poland.

By now disillusioned with communism, Domb turned to a new cause: Zionism. He became the leader of the remnants of the Polish Jewish community, and his agitation on their behalf in the face of the Polish government's refusal to allow free emigration to Israel soon brought him into conflict with the authorities. Facing the threat of another prison sentence, Domb was saved, ironically enough, by Soviet intelligence. Embarked on a public relations campaign to rehabilitate their image, the KGB and the GRU began publicizing the feats of some of its most famous spies. Among them was Domb, now lionized by the very institution that had imprisoned him.

The sudden publicity saved Domb from prison in Poland, but the authorities still would not allow him to emigrate to Israel to live out his last years. Finally, under pressure from Moscow, in 1974 he was allowed to leave. He died in 1983 in Jerusalem.

WILHELM WASSMUSS
The German Lawrence

1880–1931

For a man who came to be called "the German Lawrence," Wilhelm Wassmuss did not look the part—certainly nothing like his famous English counterpart's image of flowing Arab robes and dashing rides through the desert. Short and corpulent, Wassmuss was bald, with a round face and narrow eyes behind large spectacles. He appeared to have all the glamour and excitement of an insurance agent.

Yet, this was the man who at one point had a $500,000 price on his head for his capture dead or alive, preoccupied an entire British army, was the virtual king of fierce hill tribes, and came within a hairsbreadth of changing history. Although he was never trained for it, he was espionage's first covert action agent: a spy who does not collect intelligence, but works to reorient an entire nation's politics in favor of his country. In years to come, the methods Wassmuss used would become familiar staples of Cold War espionage to destabilize nations: bribery, propaganda, and political manipulation.

Wassmuss had no idea of his future role when he was assigned as a German consular agent in Bushire, Persia, in 1909. Then 29, and considered among the brightest stars in the German diplomatic service, Wassmuss had arrived at an especially sensitive time in an equally sensitive place. Persia was the battleground between Germany and Great Britain for the glittering prize of Persian oil concessions. The prize was beyond price, for whichever country managed to win those concessions would be able to fuel its great industrial machine; the loser would be relegated to permanent second-class status. The kingdom of Persia, with a society that seemed to exist in the 12th century, was in no position to argue with either side. Weak, it was pressed between the Ottoman Empire in the west, Russia on the north, and the British Empire's crown jewel, India, on the south and southwest. Its ruler, the Shah, presided over a feudal court but his influence hardly extended a few miles outside Tehran; the rest of the country was in the hands of assorted hill tribe warlords.

Wassmuss' instructions were to promote German interests in this vital region. To that end, he had been equipped with a large cache of gold—the prevailing currency in that area—to buy the loyalty of the tribal leaders. Meanwhile, the British were also buying warlords, creating a thriving market for loyalty. This competition would have remained a simple influence-peddling operation, but in 1914, Germany and Great Britain went to war, instantly raising the stakes.

Like the other German diplomats in Bushire, Wassmuss could have left for Germany. After all, German prospects in Persia were now untenable: the country's location between Mesopotamia and India and proximity to Turkey made it a vital sphere of influence to the British, who began moving in military forces. Germany, without equivalent military power in the region, was in no position to argue.

But Wassmuss was not prepared to admit defeat. He informed his superiors in Berlin he would stay in Persia and fight the British occupation from the hills. At the same time, he informed German intelligence that he would function as their eyes in the region. Berlin accepted this offer, although they had to wonder what a single, obscure German diplomat could hope to accomplish in an area now firmly under British control.

Wassmuss, accompanied only by a consular assistant and a cache of 140,000 gold marks, soon demonstrated what one man of determination, energy, and organizational ability could accomplish. Fluent in Farsi and the Tangistani dialect, within months he had organized the hill tribes into an anti-British force; British troops found themselves under attack the moment they moved out of their coastal bases. He also organized a flourishing anti-British propaganda operation that extended throughout the entire Persian Gulf region, utilizing a vast network of ordinary Persian citizens to spread rumors about alleged British defilements of Islamic shrines. (Such propaganda was especially effective among the Persian Islamic establishment, including a young theological student named Khomeni).

By 1916, Wassmuss had become a full-fledged menace to the British. He had not only turned Persia into a hornet's nest, but also was busy as far afield as Afghanistan, where he was stirring up native tribes to attack the British. If all that weren't bad enough, the British learned that Wassmuss had become something of a demigod among the Persians, whose warrior castes admired this improbable chubby warrior who could barely ride a horse. But he was a man who had won their hearts and respect. The gold he paid from the steady stream of the precious metal that arrived from Berlin helped, but they also appreciated that Wassmuss had taken the trouble to become fluent in Farsi and the Tangistani dialect. Moreover, in what was strictly a marriage of statecraft, he had married the daughter of the most powerful Persian warlord; the wedding, to which Wassmuss had invited thousands of ordinary Persians as guests, was the talk of the hills for months. (Many of those guests had been enlisted for their host's sprawling spy network that he called "ten thousand eyes.")

The British decided to put Wassmuss out of action, but several armed expeditions failed because Wassmuss' spy network gave him plenty of warning of their approach. The same network, the British discovered, had become active in India, and there were indications that the Germans now had a complete picture of virtually all British military moves from Baghdad to Bombay. Desperate, the British offered a reward of $500,000 to anyone who could capture Wassmuss for them. No one took the offer.

Despite Wassmuss' extraordinary talents, he could not reverse the tide of war. By early 1917, as the war turned against Germany, the Persians began to examine their options: clearly, despite Wassmuss' claims, Germany was not about to defeat Great Britain, so perhaps it was time to strike a deal with the British. Possibly even more importantly, their German patron's gold supply was beginning to dry up, while the British seemed to have an inexhaustible supply. Wassmuss tried to head off this erosion with ever more virulent propaganda, including his claim that the Kaiser had converted to Islam.

But it was only a matter of time. By early 1918, the 100,000 troops and flotilla of warships the British detailed to stop Wassmuss began a major offensive to end the problem once and for all. Wassmuss slipped out of the trap and fled to Turkey, where the British tracked him down after the Armistice. Imprisoned, Wassmuss was an endless source of fascination to his British jailers who found it hard to believe that this plump character was the fabled "German Lawrence."

Released in 1920, Wassmuss returned to the poverty and turmoil of his native Germany, aware that Persia and its precious oil had fallen under the influence of his enemy, where it would remain for the next four decades. He tried to turn his talents to business, but the genius he demonstrated in the wild Persian hills was of no help in Germany's shattered economy. He died, bankrupt and sick, in 1931, virtually forgotten by his countrymen.

IAN FLEMING
Art Imitates Life

Code Name: 17F
1908–1964

Even for the broadminded men who ran wartime British intelligence, it was too much. Right there, in a London radio studio, the announcer was calling Winston Churchill "that fat, syphillitic Jew" in colloquial German, which somehow made it seem worse. Who was responsible for such an outrage?

They might have guessed: Ian Fleming. The naval intelligence officer always seemed to be behind these kinds of stunts; if there was something especially outrageous going on in any phase of British intelligence, it was an almost certain bet Fleming had dreamed it up.

Called on the carpet, Fleming took full responsibility and explained that in black propaganda operations, it was essential that the actual source be thoroughly concealed. In this case, he had dreamed up the idea for a black propaganda radio station targeted against the German military. Ostensibly based somewhere in Europe, the "clandestine" station actually operated from London. It used announcers, speaking colloquial German, posing as ex-German military men who had somehow obtained access to their own transmitter. They broadcast gossip about the German high command and other news of interest to German forces, interspersed with caustic comments about Allied leaders and policies.

As distasteful as the British government found this project, it had to admit that Fleming's black propaganda operation was

The "perpetual schoolboy," British agent Ian Fleming, whose World War II exploits paled beside his greater fame as the creator of James Bond. (*AP/Wide World*)

proving brilliantly successful. Captured Germans, especially U-boat crews, recounted how the broadcasts were not only highly popular, but credible, too; when they heard about General so-and-so buying a mink coat for his mistress while his troops in Russia were freezing to death, they believed it. The station's effect on German military morale was devastating.

And so still another wild Fleming operation was entered into the books as a success. There would be a string of them before the war was over, for Fleming's fertile—if somewhat odd—mind was constantly spinning out a stream of dirty tricks.

How Fleming had arrived at that point may have been inevitable. The son of wealthy parents, he early in life developed a reputation as a "perpetual schoolboy," the incorrigible hell-raiser who loved action, excitement, and constant motion. By the summer of 1939, he was a 31-year-old London dandy who had drifted into his family's stock brokerage business. He was totally bored, but in an encounter that would change his life, he met Admiral John Godfrey, then head of NID. Godfrey, certain that war was inevitable at any moment, was actively rebuilding NID for the coming struggle. He was looking for bright young men with brains and daring.

In Fleming, Godfrey found exactly what he was looking for. He gave the stockbroker naval officer rank and enrolled him as his "special assistant," meaning he would be the man who would come up with ideas. And, Godfrey made clear, the wilder, the better.

When war came, Fleming began spinning out ideas. Among the more interesting was his plan for a special commando unit that would include tainted, but talented, misfits suitable for "impossible missions" behind enemy lines. Called Assault Unit Number 30, it slipped into France as the country was being overrun by the Germans and retrieved a vital cache of advanced military equipment. The eventual basis for the novel and movie *The Dirty Dozen*, Assault Unit Number 30 was to perform a number of derring-do missions, including the 1944 capture of an entire German radar station—and its 300-man garrison.

But Assault Unit Number 30 was only one of Fleming's ideas. Another, and much more esoteric one, involved an audacious plan to sow dissension in the Nazi leadership by getting one of its most senior members to defect to the other side. The chosen target was Rudolph Hess, Hitler's deputy and oldest comrade-in-arms. The British knew that the superstitious Hess was a fanatic about astrology, so Fleming arranged for the recruitment of two Swiss astrologers known to be regularly consulted by the Nazi leader. By cleverly concocted astrological tables, prepared by Fleming, Hess was led to believe that his "hour of destiny" had arrived, and he flew alone to England to negotiate the peace between Britain and Germany that, according to his charts, would make him the greatest man of the century. Actually, he was probably the stupidest, and his flight served only to dramatically boost British morale. (Hess, imprisoned, was later charged as a war criminal. He died in prison in 1989.)

In 1941, Fleming was assigned to the MI6 station in New York, then busily at work trying to get the United States involved in the war. As part of that operation, a very close liason had been established between the head of the MI6 station, **William Stephenson,** and William Donovan, President Roosevelt's COI (Coordinator of Information). Donovan, later head of the OSS, was convinced by the British that the Americans needed a centralized, civilian intelligence agency. Fleming was detailed to help Donovan draw up a plan for such an agency, based on the British model. Roosevelt decided not to adopt the plan, but later it would serve as the template for the creation of the CIA.

Not a man to sit behind a desk for long, Fleming used part of his time in New York to personally conduct a black bag job at the Japanese Consulate General office. A team of safecrackers, recruited from the elite of the criminal ranks, opened a safe to allow Fleming to photograph code books. For good measure, he made impressions of all the keys he found in the place.

By the end of the war, Fleming had been involved in so many operations that ran across the entire intelligence spectrum, nobody had any real idea of precisely which ones had sprung from his brain. Fleming seemed to be everywhere: in North Africa, arranging for the theft of Italian naval records and ciphers; in France, running an operation that stole advanced aircraft engines; in Germany, at the end of the war, capturing the entire German naval archives section with records dating back to 1870; in Lisbon, running an operation to bankrupt the *Abwehr* chief of station at a gambling casino.

It all seemed to be the stuff of fiction, which is precisely what occurred to Fleming after the war was over. A restless man, a return to the staid world of stock brokerages quickly paled beside the life he had lived for seven years. There was no new world war to exercise his talents, but he could relive that life vicariously. Fleming became a novelist, and it was in that role that he is best known in espionage history.

His adventure tales, as Fleming was the first to admit, were meant merely as entertainment. The central character of his books, agent James Bond (code name 007), was a composite of several agents he had known or worked with (along with a dose of Fleming himself), and Bond's boss "M" was based on the real-life Maxwell Knight, a renowned spy-catcher who was a senior executive in MI5. Fleming never intended his words to have serious literary merit, but to his surprise, the James Bond series of action adventures became highly popular, especially as shown in films. Until his death in 1964, Fleming insisted he was not James Bond, but those who knew of his wartime feats had cause to wonder.

DUSKO POPOV
The Real James Bond

Code Names: TRICYCLE, SCOOT,
ND-63, IVAN
1912–1981

From the moment he walked into the majestic office of FBI Director J. Edgar Hoover that August day in 1941, Dusko Popov realized he was about as welcome as an attack of poison ivy. Hoover, glaring, didn't even bother to get up and greet him.

From Hoover's standpoint, the problem was not Popov's espionage credentials. Popov, a star double agent of MI5, had been sent by the British agency to Hoover for purposes of discussing a very interesting piece of microfilm he had been given by the *Abwehr* a few weeks before in Portugal. The *Abwehr*, under the illusion that Popov was their agent, had dispatched him to the United States with a spy's shopping list: a catalog of American military installations about which Popov was supposed to learn everything he could.

Hoover was willing to concede MI5's estimate of Popov as its star double agent, but ever the stern moralist, he had strong reservations about Popov personally. This antagonism was to have grave consequences.

Popov represented everything Hoover hated. A pure hedonist, he had been given the code name TRICYCLE by MI5 wags in tribute to his proclivity for taking two women to bed at once. That was only one of a number of vices Popov actively pursued in a life devoted to wine, women and song, although his ostensible avocation was commercial law. Born of a moderately wealthy family in Yugoslavia, Popov had studied law in Germany, and in 1939

Dusko Popov, the dashing double agent who convinced the Germans that the British were much stronger than they actually were in 1940. His work contributed to the abandonment of Operation Sea Lion—Hitler's plan to invade the British isles. (*UPI/Betteman*)

was hired by a consortium of Yugoslavian banks to represent their interests in Lisbon, Portugal.

Then a young 27-year-old lawyer, Popov settled in Lisbon, which as a neutral capital, was already the crossroads of international espionage. Given his fluency in several languages and his commercial contacts all over Europe, he was a natural recruit for any of the dozen espionage agencies then operating in the city. The *Abwehr* made the first approach; some of his old university classmates, now *Abwehr* officers, recruited him for the purpose of gathering political and economic intelligence on the British. They did not know that Popov had come to despise the Nazis; soon after his recruitment, he approached the British and volunteered to be a double agent.

As both sides were to discover, Popov was an expensive proposition. Economically comfortable in his own right, he nevertheless needed much more money to support his lifestyle of expensive restaurants, women, and nightclubs. Both sides happily underwrote such high living because to each, he was an espionage superstar. To the *Abwehr*, the asset they code-named IVAN was a treasure, a fountain of intelligence on everything from political events in London to military operational plans. (All of which were carefully devised—"cooked" in intelligence parlance—by British intelligence, a shrewdly-prepared mixture of genuine and fake material). To the British, he represented a pipeline into one of the more important *Abwehr* outstations. As a controlled source, he could be used to feed all kinds of deception into the *Abwehr* mainstream, while at the same time he was in a position to identify all the Abwehr operatives with whom he came in contact.

At this point, Popov passed into control of one of the most successful counterintelligence operations of all time, the so-called "double cross system" of MI5.

The operation sought to take advantage of British intelligence's greatest secret and its greatest strength: the cracking of the German Enigma machine codes. This unparalleled achievement, code-named ULTRA, enabled the British to read all the *Abwehr* traffic, providing a double benefit. One, the British knew from the decoded messages which agents and assets the Germans were dispatching to any given point. Second, the British could read the agent reports sent via Enigma back to headquarters in Berlin. In the event of a double agent like Popov, the British could monitor how well their deception material was playing in Berlin.

This second benefit gave birth to a brilliant idea: since the British could monitor the material going back to Berlin, why not attempt to turn captured German agents and assets instead of merely arresting and then executing them? So the double-cross system was born. MI5 was able to identify every single agent or asset dispatched from Germany. Those sent to British territory were rounded up and evaluated as possible doubles; those who either refused or did not seem suitable for the task were executed.*

---

* Two star doubles were Wulf Schmidt (TATE) and Juan Pujol (GARBO). Schmidt, who was arrested after parachuting into Britain one night in 1940, was turned and used to feed misleading military intelligence via his radio to Germany. His greatest triumph came in 1944, when he radioed false intelligence about where the German V-2 rockets were landing; his "corrections" caused the Germans to redirect the rockets away from more vulnerable targets in London. Pujol, a Spaniard operating in Lisbon, was detected working for the *Abwehr* by an ULTRA decryption. Turned by MI5, he fed misleading intelligence to the *Abwehr* until 1945. Among them was a

Popov was considered the star player in the double-cross system; completely trusted by the Germans, MI5 used him carefully, primarily for high-level political intelligence. His greatest achievement was to convince the Germans, via cooked documents, that the British were militarily much stronger than the Germans assumed (although in fact Britain had no real power to halt a German invasion in 1940). The deception played no small role in Hitler's eventual decision to abandon Operation Sea Lion, the planned invasion of the British Isles.

This perceived intelligence triumph boosted Popov's stock with the *Abwehr*, which decided in 1941 to use him for a major operation: infiltrate the United States to collect intelligence on the military power of the nation the *Abwehr* believed would soon enter the war. He was given the shopping list later shown to Hoover.

The puritanical Hoover, repelled by the snappily-dressed Popov (complete with ivory cigarette holder, diamond jewelry, and pungent cologne), did not pay too much attention to the shopping list. He should have, for it contained a vital intelligence clue: at the request of Japanese intelligence, the *Abwehr* wanted Popov to find out what he could about Pearl Harbor, especially the anti-aircraft defenses and which ships normally anchored there. Hoover routinely passed the message to military intelligence without pausing to wonder why the Japanese would be so interested in Pearl Harbor. (As it turned out, neither did military intelligence, with devastating consequences.)

Given Hoover's hostility, there was no way that MI5 could get his cooperation for an elaborate intelligence sting: to have Popov feed misleading material about U.S. military preparedness to the Germans. MI5 gave up, and Popov returned to Lisbon, where he concocted an elaborate story to account for his inability to carry out his mission in the United States. The *Abwehr* apparently believed him, although there was the first faint hint of doubt: Was it possible that Popov was working for the British? Apparently as a method of settling that question, the *Abwehr* sent Popov to London, with orders to gather high-level intelligence on British war plans. Once in London, Popov fed a steady stream

---

momentous deception: he convinced the *Abwehr* that the Allied landing on the west coast of Europe would be at Pas de Calais, not Normandy. As a result, Hitler for four critical days kept his reserves near Pas de Calais, convinced that the Normandy landing was only a feint.

of cooked intelligence reports back to Lisbon, but as the ULTRA codebreakers knew from reading the subsequent Lisbon-Berlin traffic, the Germans had come to regard Popov as untrustworthy. Still, the game continued to the end of the war, and despite the German uneasiness, Berlin still believed at least some of the misleading material Popov was sending.

With the end of the war, Popov's job was over. He refused an offer of citizenship from a grateful British government, and settled in the south of France to write his highly entertaining (but inaccurate) memoirs. It was not until some years after the war, when some records were declassified, that the role of Popov as the star of the astonishing double-cross system was revealed. Still later, it was learned how he had provided a vital clue that might have prevented Pearl Harbor—if only the Americans had paid attention.

Decades of living the high life finally caught up to Popov in 1981, when he died—a happy man, so his friends said.

F. W. WINTERBOTHAM
The Spy in the Sky

1897–1990

Faced with the tedium of a German prisoner of war camp, the 20-year-old Royal Air Force pilot had plenty of time to think about a problem that had been bothering him for quite some time. How, wondered F. W. Winterbotham as he strolled the camp grounds in that summer of 1917, could he take aerial photographs from altitudes above 8,000 feet?

Admittedly, this was not a problem on the minds of his fellow prisoners—or anybody else, for that matter—but it was something that preoccupied Winterbotham. Enamored with the romance of flying, at the outbreak of war he had enlisted in the Royal Flying Corps. Early on, he became fascinated with the problem of aerial reconnaissance. Then in its infancy, aerial reconnaissance consisted largely of flying a plane low over enemy lines, sticking a camera out the cockpit, and taking a few pictures before getting shot to pieces. There had to be a better way, Winterbotham thought, a conclusion underscored when he was shot down and captured during an aerial reconnaissance over German trenches on the Western Front.

After the war, Winterbotham left the military and went back to the family farm near Sussex. But aerial reconnaissance was never far from his mind; he remained convinced that in a future war, victory would go to the nation that developed the ability to get above the battlefield and see the enemy before he moved. He also believed that aerial photography would be critical in modern

103

intelligence, for photographs would provide the objective, irrefutable proof of a nation's actual capabilities.

Winterbotham often talked about his abiding obsession around the flying clubs and with some ex-military types. What he had to say came to the attention of MI6, which had just the kind of job suited for his beliefs. In 1929, he was recruited for the agency, and a year later was assigned the job of creating MI6's first air section.

Winterbotham's instructions were simple: he was to create the world's first aerial espionage operation, capable of covering most of the world—with special emphasis on Germany. To that end, he set up a dummy aeronautical research company as cover, bought several planes, and prepared to photograph everything worth photographing all over Europe.

But he immediately encountered the same problem that balked aerial espionage in 1917: the laws of physics, which decreed that any camera lens above 8,000 feet would become fogged over by lower air temperatures. Flying any lower than 8,000 feet meant that the planes were not only easily observable, but vulnerable to ground fire from sensitive military installations. The only solution was to get those cameras to operate at higher altitudes, but how?

The answer came quite by accident. Winterbotham had convinced MI6 to invest in the very latest in airplane technology, the American Lockheed 12A, a two-engine aircraft that could operate at a ceiling of 22,000 feet. He then hired Sidney Cotton, a vagabond (and slightly crazy) Australian bush pilot to fly the plane. Cotton, assuming he would have to use subterfuge to take espionage pictures on low-level flights, devised an ingenious system: holes were cut in the fuselage, concealed by shutters operated by controls inside the plane. The idea was that the plane would overfly its target, the shutters would be opened, the pictures would be snapped via controls inside the cockpit, and then the shutters would close after the pictures were taken. Anyone looking at the plane would see only a blank fuselage, with no cameras in sight.

After installing the system, Cotton and Winterbotham took the plane for a test run above the English countryside, and made an astonishing discovery: at high altitudes, when the shutters were opened, warm air from inside the plane was drawn out over the camera lenses, preventing them from fogging. Modern high-altitude espionage was born.

Equipped with their secret, the two men set off for Europe, where they overflew even the most sensitive areas with impunity, since everyone assumed no aerial photographs were possible at altitudes higher than 8,000 feet. Winterbotham paid particular attention to Germany, and a series of flights—all of them under cover of drumming up business for Winterbotham's firm—managed to photograph nearly every important military installation in the country, at the propitious moment when Hitler was beginning his rearmament program. Winterbotham became well-known to the Luftwaffe, and in 1939 Luftwaffe General Albert Kesselring and other senior officers asked the Englishman if they could take a ride in his American plane. Winterbotham obliged, but during the flight his heart almost stopped when Kesselring wondered aloud about the series of blinking green lights at the controls. These were indicators showing continuity of the Leica automatic cameras' exposures, but Winterbotham, thinking fast, told the Germans the lights signified special controls that showed "petrol flow to the engines."

It was a close call, and Winterbotham realized that with the storm clouds gathering, it was time to end operations over Europe. He returned to Britain, where MI6 gave him a new assignment: agency liaison to GCHQ's ULTRA code-breaking operation. Winterbotham devised a system that solved the central dilemma of ULTRA. Somehow, vital information that ULTRA uncovered had to be disseminated to forces in the field without revealing that the information came from broken German codes. The slightest hint that the German codes had been compromised would destroy ULTRA, for the Germans would change all their coding systems.

Winterbotham's solution was to set up Special Liaison Units (SLU), which consisted of agents involved in the ULTRA operation who were assigned to various armies in the field to give instant intelligence about what ULTRA revealed. The system was brilliantly successful: Throughout the war, Allied generals were able to redeploy their forces immediately, reacting to information provided by the SLUs about German plans and dispositions. There was not a single breach of security about ULTRA, which remained secret until 1974.*

---

* In that year, the British decided on a limited disclosure of the great secret, part of an effort to rehabilitate the tattered image of British intelligence. Winterbotham was detailed to write a report for public consumption on the history and scope of the code-breaking operation. Published in a commercial version as *The ULTRA Secret*, it caused a worldwide sensation.

Yet, despite these great contributions to British intelligence, at war's end Winterbotham was let go by MI6—and, in the great tradition of MI6 penuriousness, without pension. Not a wealthy man, he returned to his farm, there in later years to reflect on the furious controversies surrounding the U-2 spy plane and spy satellites. He never said if he derived any satisfaction from knowing that the modern "technical means" (as the diplomats politely called overhead espionage) all stemmed from his curious obsession many decades before. Content among his cabbages and livestock, he died in 1990.

AMY THORPE PACK
The Siren Spy

Code Names: E11, CYNTHIA
Alias: Elizabeth Thomas
1910–1963

Not many people who lived anywhere near the British embassy in Santiago, Chile, were enjoying the balmy spring of 1939. The reason was Mrs. Amy Thorpe Pack, wife of a senior British diplomat assigned to the embassy. For reasons no one could understand, Mrs. Pack insisted on learning how to shoot a pistol; by the hour, under the instruction of the British naval attache, she banged away at targets on the embassy grounds.

Finally, the growing complaints of the embassy neighbors compelled her to stop. Reluctantly, she put her new pistol away and tried to settle into the stifling world of diplomatic protocol and embassy teas. Mrs. Pack did not make much of an effort to hide her boredom, a reaction that most of the embassy family ascribed to her upbringing as an American debutante, accustomed to the glitter and swirl of a much more exciting social circle.

But what no one knew was that Mrs. Pack had been an MI6 asset for the past two years, already involved in a number of true-life espionage adventures. After that experience, life in the backwater of 1939 Santiago was pretty dull stuff.

Then 29 years old, Pack was a stunningly beautiful woman, an attribute that made her a very formidable spy. Put plainly, she was an absolute man-killer, with an acute intelligence that kept her at least two jumps ahead of the many men who pursued her. The daughter of a Marine Corps captain who later became a prominent maritime lawyer in Washington, D.C., she grew up in an atmosphere of privilege and power. To the surprise of her friends, in 1930, just one year after making her debut in Washington society, she ignored the attentions of a number of highly eligible men and married a colorless minor British diplomat named Arthur Pack.

The Pack marriage proved passionless, and Amy Thorpe began a series of affairs with other men, partially as a means of stoking the fires of her restless energy. In many ways a remarkable woman, she yearned to do something useful with her life, but a dozen different things at which she tried her hand failed to satisfy that craving. Finally, in 1936, she discovered a field of endeavor that had the challenge she was looking for: espionage.

Accompanying her husband to a posting in Spain, she was approached one day by five desperate Nationalist soldiers who had been trapped behind Loyalist lines. Could she help them through the lines? She agreed, and with her charm and beauty, talked her way past Loyalist checkpoints in a car containing the five soldiers hidden in a trunk. A small incident, but she had discovered the narcotic effect of danger and conspiracy. She had found her true calling at last.

The next year, in 1937, her husband was transferred to the Warsaw embassy, where Pack simply approached the MI6 chief of station and announced her availability for intelligence work. It is a tribute to her forcefulness that the MI6 man felt he had no choice but to accept. Any reservations he might have had about enlisting this American debutante were dispelled almost immediately. Within a few weeks, Pack demonstrated a natural ability in a field for which she had never received any training. She seduced a Polish Foreign Ministry official, who provided her with top-grade intelligence on Poland's plans for dealing with Hitler and Stalin. She followed that with an astonishing intelligence coup: from another government official, she learned that a team of Polish mathematicians had begun cracking the German Enigma codes. (This intelligence was to pay dividends later for MI6; after the German invasion of Poland, the Poles turned over a complete Enigma machine and their solutions, the first step in the ULTRA operation).

A year later, following her husband to a posting in Prague, she managed to obtain the German plans for the invasion of Czechoslovakia (obviated by the Munich Agreement). That was to be Pack's last espionage for nearly two years because her husband was reassigned to Santiago, Chile. His wife followed him—and almost died of boredom. That may help explain why the Pack marriage died in Santiago. In 1941, separated from her husband, Pack went to New York to begin a new life. She had barely set foot on American soil when **William Stephenson,** MI6 chief of station, contacted her. He had heard a great deal about the beautiful American with nerves of steel; how would she like to work for his sprawling operation?

Actually, Stephenson did not want her working in New York, for he felt her amazing ability to penetrate foreign embassies was better suited for the diplomatic corps in Washington, D.C., which offered a richer field of targets. She was given only a general set of instructions to infiltrate, as best she could, some of the embassy staffs in which MI6 had the most interest—especially the Germans, the Italians, and the Vichy French. Stephenson, a shrewd judge of character, understood that with an asset like Pack, there was no necessity to weigh her down with a lot of detailed instructions. Given her talents, it was only necessary to point her in the right direction; she would take care of the rest.

Stephenson also understood that behind Pack's eagerness for intelligence work lay a complex set of psychological motives. Although she was working for MI6 in part because of her aversion to what she had seen of fascism in Europe, the real explanation, Stephenson realized, was that there was no other field of human endeavor that could satisfy her lust for danger and excitement—and that at the same time provided her with a feeling of accomplishment. Somewhat piquantly, he gave her the code name CYNTHIA, after a long-lost love.

Stephenson's faith in Pack's abilities was rewarded shortly after she arrived in Washington. She set her sights on the Italian embassy and in short order had seduced the chief of station for Italian military intelligence at the embassy. With characteristic boldness, when he asked her what she wanted in life, she replied: "The Italian navy cipher." Apparently smitten beyond common sense, he agreed to provide her with the name of an embassy code clerk, desperately in need of money, who would be willing to sell the cipher. Pack set up the deal, and the cipher came into British hands.

And just in time. The Italian navy significantly outnumbered the beleaguered Royal Navy in the Mediterranean, but equipped with the Italian cipher, the British were able to read the Italian messages, allowing them to anticipate all moves by Mussolini's navy. Even more significantly, in March 1941, knowledge of the Italian ciphers allowed the British to destroy a significant part of the Italian fleet in the battle of Cape Matapan, ending forever the Italian navy's threat to British supply lifelines in the Mediterranean.

This achievement alone would have been sufficient to put Pack in the pantheon of espionage giants, but she was to pull off still another amazing penetration of an embassy, an operation that would become one of the great espionage stories of World War II.

It began early in 1942. Pack, who with Stephenson's approval had also become an OSS asset after Pearl Harbor (under the code name E11) in addition to her work for MI6, was asked if she could penetrate the Vichy France embassy. The OSS was especially eager to get a look at the Vichy ciphers; with planning underway for the invasion of Vichy territory in North Africa, any insight into the Vichy military ciphers would be critically important. As usual, Pack's approach was direct: posing as a pro-Vichy journalist, she gradually won the confidence (and the heart) of Charles Brousse, the embassy's press attache and coincidentally an important Vichy politician. Within a month, Pack had recruited him as an OSS asset, and information began flowing out of the embassy.

The next step was the most delicate: getting a look at those ciphers, without the embassy knowing about it. The cipher books were inside a huge safe, so an elaborate operation was devised, with Pack playing the key role. The plan was for her and Brousse to enter the embassy one night for a presumed tryst. Once inside, they would unlock a window; an OSS safecracker would enter, deduce the safe combination, and remove the code books. An OSS team would be waiting outside to take the books, bring them to a nearby apartment outfitted as a photo studio, photograph all the ciphers, then return the books. The entire operation had to be completed before dawn, when the embassy security people arrived to make their first check.

One evening in June 1942, Pack and her lover Brousse entered the embassy; Brousse winked at the watchman, noting he and the beautiful lady would be in the embassy for a while to "discuss world politics." With a replying wink, the watchman bid them good night. A short while later, the OSS safecracker was about to enter through the opened window when disaster suddenly appeared: The watchman, suspicious, decided to check on the lovers. As he entered the room—and before he could spot the open window and the OSS safecracker on the top rung of a ladder—Pack took matters in hand. Hearing the watchman's approach, she stripped entirely naked; as his flashlight beam caught this vision, he murmured "*Pardonnez moi*," and quickly exited, for no gallant Frenchmen would interrupt further what was obviously a signficant moment in the couple's lovemaking.

With the watchman gone, the operation swung into motion. It took nearly six hours, but by the time the code books had been replaced just before dawn, there was no trace that anyone had even touched the safe. To make certain, Pack wiped every inch of the safe on her way out, lowering her eyes modestly as she and Brousse walked past the smiling watchman.

It would be difficult to exaggerate the importance of the Vichy embassy operation. The photographs of the cipher books were flown to London within 24 hours, and less than a few days later, the British codebreakers at GCHQ were reading all messages from Vichy military installations in North Africa. When the Allies invaded several months later, almost all Vichy opposition was neutralized.

Stephenson would say later that Pack's efforts had saved the Allies 100,000 lives. There is no way to be certain, but there is no doubt that her extraordinary efforts significantly aided the Allied war effort. But her crowning achievement, the Vichy embassy caper, would mark the end of her espionage career; a consuming affair of the heart had replaced her lust for adventure. Ironically, she had fallen in love with Brousse, the man she had originally seduced for espionage. Following a divorce from Pack, she married the Frenchman. In 1944, they went off to France to live in a castle.

In her later years, the spy known as CYNTHIA never discussed her espionage career; settled in a comfortable existence with the man who became the love of her life, she preferred to concern herself with the minutae of running a French castle. Occasionally, old acquaintances from her MI6 and OSS days would arrive for a visit, invariably urging her to write her memoirs. She eventually began working on them, and although she finished before her death of cancer in 1963, they were never published. She could not imagine that anyone would be interested in what she insisted were a few "minor adventures" in her life.

RICHARD SORGE
The Greatest of Them All

Code Names: SONTER, RAMSAY, FIX
Alias: William Johnson
1895–1944

It's always the little things, counterintelligence agents like to say, those minor frailties of the human species that will cause even the most cautious of spies to commit a fatal error. And so it was with Richard Sorge, among the greatest spies in history, who committed a very human mistake and paid for it with his life.

One night late in October of 1941, every instinct honed in a 20-year espionage career told Sorge it was time to flee Tokyo. For more than four years, he had managed a network that ferreted out nearly every important secret of the Japanese government. His superiors in the Soviet GRU agreed that his network's usefulness was at an end. As Sorge was aware, the *Kempei Tai*, the Japanese secret police, were already watching him. Two members of his network had been arrested some hours before, and under torture, it would only be a matter of time before they identified Sorge as chief of the network.

And yet, he hesitated. The reason was a beautiful Japanese dancer with whom Sorge had been intimately involved for more than a year. Sorge, deeply in love, let his heart rule his head: Despite the growing danger, he could not bear to flee without one last tryst to say goodbye. Sorge spent some time with her at the nightclub where she worked, and they then adjourned to her apartment, where he assumed he would spend his last night in Japan. The next morning, he would flee the country into China and eventually to safety in the Soviet Union. He seemed morose,

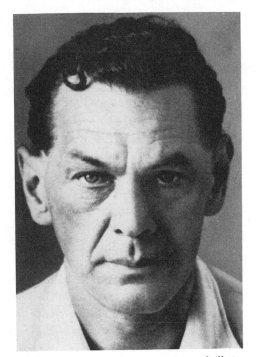

Soviet agent Richard Sorge, perhaps the greatest spy of all time, during his stay in Japan in 1940 under cover as a German journalist. (*AP/Wide World*)

and although he would not tell her why, she sensed he was under some kind of intense pressure—so intense that he violated an elementary rule of tradecraft. It was a fatal error.

Sorge had been carrying a message sent to him a short while before by a member of his network, warning that the Japanese were closing in, and that he should flee as quickly as possible. On the way to his lover's apartment, a distracted Sorge, instead of burning the note, ripped it up and threw the pieces on the ground. Not too far behind, trailing Japanese *Kempei Tai* agents retrieved the pieces. They put them together, and now Sorge's guilt was beyond question. Several hours later, Sorge was arrested as he lay in the arms of his paramour.

So the Japanese had captured the head of the network at last, but they had no idea what exactly they had ensnared. All the Japanese knew was that there had been a major espionage network operating inside Japan for quite some time. Two years of patient detective work had led them, finally, to Sorge. But for whom was Sorge working?

Since Sorge was a German citizen officially working in Japan as a correspondent for several leading German newspapers, the Japanese at first assumed he was working for either the *Abwehr* or the SD. But the Germans were adamant: despite Sorge's close relations with the German ambassador, he was not a German agent. It would take another year before the Japanese were finally able to prepare a complete picture of Sorge and his network, and the result surprised them. For one thing, Sorge was a Soviet agent. Second, and even more significantly, his espionage operation was primarily concerned not with Japan, but his native land—and it was Germany that had suffered terrible damage.

The deeper the Japanese dug, the more impressed they became with Sorge and his operation, for they encountered one of the most remarkable operations in the history of espionage. It was an operation headed by a very remarkable man.

The key to understanding Sorge lay in his deep Communist convictions, which to a certain extent could be considered genetic. His paternal grandfather had been private secretary to Karl Marx, and when Sorge was a small boy, among the first books he read was a copy of Marx's *Das Kapital* given to him by his grandfather as a gift. Born in 1895 in the Russian Caucasus to a German oil drilling engineer, Sorge enlisted in the German army at the outbreak of World War I. He was wounded twice and spent his long convalescences devouring books on Communist theory. By 1920, he was a fervent Communist, and was among the early members of the German Communist party. Meanwhile, he obtained a Ph.D. in political science at the University of Hamburg.

Sorge's rare combination of revolutionary ardor, high intellect, and eagerness to serve the cause quickly brought him to the attention of Comintern officials, who transferred him to Moscow for training at the organization's higher party schools. In 1927, he was sent to Hollywood to aid in setting up party cells in the American film industry, a task largely designed to test his abilities as a party organizer. He returned to Moscow a year later for further training, in the process demonstrating an amazing linguistic ability (in addition to his native German, he became fluent in English, French and Russian, later adding Chinese and Japanese). By 1929, the Comintern envisioned a future for Sorge as a top party organizer in Western Europe.

But GRU chief **Jan Berzin,** noted for his ability as a talentspotter, also had noticed the bright German Communist, and Sorge was recruited for a very different future. As he had done with another of his brilliant recruits, **Leiba Domb,** Berzin was planning something special for his newest recruit. After a year of training, Berzin assigned him as *rezident* in Shanghai, with instructions to revive GRU networks in China. In short order, Sorge—operating under cover as a German journalist and, on occasion, as an American journalist named William Johnson—created a series of networks that extended throughout the country and kept Moscow informed about its two main concerns: the steady rightward drift of Chiang Kai-shek, and the growing power of the Communist leader in north China, Mao Tse-tung. But his most significant intelligence discovery concerned a development that alarmed Moscow: Germany was abandoning its traditionally close relationship with China to forge an alliance with Japan. To Moscow, this shift represented the nightmare of two hostile powers facing the Soviet Union on the east and west.

This critical intelligence seems to have escaped the notice of both the GRU and KGB chiefs of station in Tokyo. Summoned home to Moscow to explain the gross failure, they confessed their errors and were promptly executed. That created an intelligence void in Tokyo, and Berzin devised a daring plan to fill it. In Berzin's conception, Japan was actually a secondary target; given the new relationship between Germany and Japan, Tokyo now offered the potential as a good listening post on German plans, for the Germans would have to consult and coordinate with their Asian allies. An intelligence operation in Tokyo would be targeted against the large German diplomatic structure, a line of attack that avoided having to set up operations in Germany itself, where the Nazi police state made espionage operations very difficult.

Berzin's idea was for Sorge to be assigned to Tokyo, with full authority to recruit whomever he wanted and operate free of direction from Moscow Center. This was an unprecedented arrangement in the tightly-controlled world of Soviet intelligence, but Sorge's performance in China had been so brilliant, it had been decided that he worked best when given total freedom of action.

Sorge laid his plans carefully. From his China network, he selected two veteran GRU agents who would work with him in Japan: Max Klausen, a longtime German Communist and brilliant radio operator, and Branko de Voukelich, an ex-Yugoslavian army officer, considered an expert on military intelligence. Sorge also selected two key GRU assets, both secret Japanese Communists whom Sorge first recruited in 1933: Ozaki

Hozumi, political correspondent of a leading Japanese newspaper with extensive contacts throughout the Japanese government and political establishment; and Miyagi Yotoku, scion of a respected Japanese family, who had extensive contacts among a group of liberal politicians opposed to the policies of the right-wing government.

Sorge's next step was to create a new legend for himself. He returned to Germany and became a fervent Nazi. Blessed with a great personal charm, Sorge soon ingratiated himself with some of the leading figures in Joseph Goebbels' Propaganda Ministry, important connections that he used to gain appointment as Japan correspondent for several leading German newspapers. It remains a mystery to this day how the Gestapo, which kept a strict watch on all forms of political dissidence, somehow missed Sorge. Given his former prominence as a Communist activist, there seems no reasonable explanation of how a man with that kind of record not only joined the Nazi party, but managed to become closely connected with the ruling hierarchy.

Whatever the explanation, Sorge, now apparently a rabidly Nazi foreign correspondent, arrived in Tokyo in April 1938. He immediately took two important steps. One, he befriended Colonel Eugene Ott, the German military attache at the German embassy. Aware that Ott, who spoke no Japanese, was supposed to gather intelligence in Japan, Sorge helped him out, passing on various little tidbits that Ott could include in his reports to Berlin. Ott, a singularly untalented intelligence officer, was very grateful, and began to pass on to Sorge a few interesting items he had heard from his superiors. (This connection would prove even more valuable when Ott later was named German ambassador to Japan.)

Sorge's second action was to expand his network. His original ring of four recruited a few more important assets, until Sorge had a network of 20 people, all in key positions, who were able to keep him informed of everything of importance occurring in a geographic area extending from Manchuria to the northern tip of Japan.

What made the Sorge network unusual, and highly effective, was the role of its chief. Instead of merely collecting intelligence and passing it to Moscow, Sorge also functioned as the network's chief analyst. He would collect all the scraps of intelligence gathered by his network, fit them together in a coherent whole, and add his own analysis and conclusions. He had trained himself as an expert on all matters Japanese, and kept a 1,000-volume library of Japanese books that reflected his deep knowledge of the country. In effect, he was a one-man intelligence agency.

Within a month of his arrival in Tokyo, Sorge was able to keep Moscow informed of the ongoing debate within the Japanese government over future policy. Basically, the Japanese had decided to go to war, but in which direction would they strike? One faction, close to the Germans, wanted to ally Japan with German war aims—which included, as Sorge found out, an eventual invasion of the Soviet Union. Another faction, however, argued that Japan's lack of raw materials mandated a strike southward, toward the oil and rubber riches of Malaya and the East Indies. This faction was beginning to gain the upper hand, although its adherents admitted their policy meant war with the United States.

Sorge's Japanese assets were able to keep him informed of the ongoing debate. Meanwhile, Sorge kept a close watch on the German end of the equation, where the ever-helpful Ott sought his advice about Hitler's latest policy decisions. In late 1940, Sorge learned an earth-shattering piece of intelligence: in a secret conference of his generals, Hitler had announced his decision to invade the Soviet Union.

In retrospect, it remains almost unbelievable that Stalin, as he did with top-grade intelligence from other sources about the imminent German invasion, discounted Sorge's report, wondering aloud why so brilliant a spy as Sorge had fallen for such a transparent "deception." Sorge was angry, but resolved to collect more intelligence sufficient to change Stalin's mind. But nothing he sent Moscow seemed to make any difference, even when in May 1941, he transmitted a warning that the German invasion of the Soviet Union would begin at dawn on June 20 (the actual invasion, planned for that date, was delayed 48 hours by bad weather). Stalin still ignored the warning.

By that point, Sorge was transmitting a huge volume of material, raising the recurring problem of his radio being on the air for too long. Aware that Japanese counterintelligence had an extensive radio-monitoring service, Sorge took elaborate steps to conceal his transmissions from listening ears. Initially, he kept the radio moving from house to house, but then hit upon the idea of using a sailboat as a radio base. The boat would transmit, then immediately move to another location. Klausen, the radio operator, used high-speed transmissions to keep on the air for as short a period as possible.

Still, the Japanese became aware that there was a clandestine radio operating somewhere in their territory. They could not pinpoint it, but the high volume of transmissions indicated the radio was probably serving an espionage network. As early as 1938, coincidental with Sorge's arrival in Tokyo, the Japanese had detected indications of some kind of network in operation, but had no idea of its size, scope, and for which intelligence service it was operating. In late 1939, the *Kempei Tai* got its first break: they had arrested Ritsu Ito, leader of the hard-line, rabidly pro-Moscow faction of the Japanese Communist party, which had been outlawed some years before. The *Kempei Tai*, notorious for its hideous tortures, extracted from Ito the interesting revelation that the party had a secret underground section whose members were involved in espionage for the Soviet Union. He did not know specifically which members were involved, but nevertheless gave his interrogators a list of all the names of party members he knew had been assigned to the underground. Among them were Ozaki Hozumi and Miyagi Yotoku, Sorge's two prime Japanese assets.

The Japanese now began the laborious process of investigating the more than 100 names wrested from Ito. It was the equivalent of looking for a needle in a haystack, but the patient sifting of all the names finally produced an interesting result: surveillance of Ozaki and Miyagi revealed a close connection with a German correspondent named Richard Sorge. Perhaps it was time to take a close look at Sorge.

Coincidentally, the SD station at the German embassy also began taking a closer look at Sorge. The SD did not suspect Sorge of being a Soviet spy, but it was struck by his close relationship with the German diplomatic staff, especially the ambassador, Eugene Ott. The SD's concern centered on the possibility that Sorge might be working for its hated rival, the *Abwehr*.

Some sixth sense warned Sorge throughout those critical months of 1941 that he and his network were in danger. Nevertheless, the Soviet Union's need for intelligence was more desperate than ever, especially anything Sorge could tell them about German intentions. In early October 1941, as German troops began closing in on Moscow, Sorge came up with a piece of intelligence that would have a dramatic effect on the course of the war, and one that would enshrine him in the Soviet Union's pantheon of intelligence demigods.

For months, the Japanese cabinet debated where the country's military machine would strike. While the Germans pressed for an invasion of the Soviet Union, the cabinet finally decided it would move south, to gain the raw materials essential for Japanese industry. That decision, passed on to the disappointed Germans, immediately became known to Sorge. In a series of three long transmissions from his moving sailboat, Klausen sent this momentous news to Moscow, including texts of the cabinet deliberations.

What happened next was unprecedented: based on Sorge's record of accuracy to that point, the Soviets decided to take an extraordinary gamble. Virtually all the front-line troops kept on alert in the east to check a possible Japanese invasion were shifted westward, where they fell upon the surprised Germans battling their way through the suburbs of Moscow. Fresh Siberian divisions, unaffected by the coldest weather in 50 years, inflicted the first defeat on the German *blitzkrieg,* a shock that caused Hitler to sack most of his East front field marshals and assume personal direction of the war—with results that would prove catastrophic.

But by this point, Miyagi and Ozaki had been arrested, and as the *Kempei Tai* began closing in, Sorge prepared to send his last transmission: the Japanese would open their southward march with a knockout blow against the American fleet at Pearl Harbor sometime during the end of the year. To their relief, the Japanese managed to arrest Klausen before he could transmit this intelligence from Sorge (who still might have gotten away had it not been for his fatal dalliance with his Japanese lover).

What Sorge underwent at the hands of the *Kempei Tai* is not known; the surviving Japanese records indicate only that he cooperated completely, telling the Japanese everything. The Japanese resisted an urgent German request for Sorge's extradition, preferring instead to keep him for possible exchange later. In 1943, the Japanese proposed an exchange deal with Moscow, offering Sorge for several Japanese spies who had been arrested by the Soviets. But Moscow never replied; apparently, Stalin was not eager to have still another witness around who knew of his blindness to the clear warnings of the German invasion.

The Japanese kept Sorge alive for three years, spending much of that time painstakingly uncovering what he had imparted to Moscow in the more than 30,000 pages of information he broadcast. Finally, in 1944, when there was nothing left to learn from Sorge, he was executed.

For years afterward, his Japanese lover regularly visited his unmarked grave and decorated it with garlands of chrysanthemums, noted for their ability to faithfully flower, despite the most adverse growing conditions.

RUTH KUCZYNSKI
The Radio in the Teddy Bear

Code Name: SONIA
Alias: Ruth Werner
1908–?

The two police constables who knocked on the door of the modest cottage near the university town of Oxford one spring morning in 1941 were already quite certain they were on a wild goose chase. They had gotten one of those calls that was typical in those jittery times, when ordinary citizens, warned to be alert for the presence of enemy spies, tended to call police with even the slightest suspicion.

The cottage hardly looked like an espionage den. It was rented by an RAF sergeant named Leon Beurton and his wife Ruth, who lived there with their two small children. Although a neighbor had told police of seeing a sophisticated shortwave radio in the cottage (ownership of shortwave radios had to be registered under wartime regulations), it did not seem likely, at first glance, that such a sophisticated piece of technology would be owned by a poorly-paid RAF sergeant.

The woman who answered the knock was a short, plump woman in an apron; a small child huddled at one knee, staring wide-eyed at the two men in uniform. Mrs. Beurton looked puzzled as the police constables explained why they were there. In a pronounced but vague European accent, she invited them inside, and showed them a child's toy radio. Could that be the "short wave radio" a neighbor had seen?

Probably, said the police constables, smiling. They expressed their apologies for bothering this charming *hausfrau*, and left.

Just another spy scare, and the two constables promptly forgot about it. Only much later would they learn they had stood in the presence of the most brilliant Soviet intelligence agent in all of Great Britain.

As usual, Ruth Kuczynski Beurton had played her role perfectly. With that frumpy look of harassed mother of small children, the constables could be forgiven for not checking further. It would not be the last time this consummate actress had fooled her enemies.

Kuczynski's appearance concealed a totally dedicated Communist who was born into a very Communist family: her father, Rene, a prominent economist, was one of the first members of the German Communist party, as was her brother Jeurgen. Daughter Ruth was enrolled in the party's youth movement in 1917 when she was only nine years old. In 1926, she joined the party as an adult. That same year, she went to New York to run a bookstore, and met Rudolph Hamburger, studying architecture in the United States. They fell in love, married, and she followed him to Shanghai in 1930, where he had taken a job as an architect.

Hamburger was not a Communist, and while he tolerated his wife's rabid political convictions, he put his foot down when she announced her intention to "work for the party" in the foreign settlement area of Shanghai. He wasn't sure what that meant, but the idea of his wife marching in demonstrations, dodging police, or manning barricades was not what he had in mind for a dutiful German wife. Ruth ignored him, and soon was busily at work within the city's foreign settlement organizing workers and carrying out a number of other duties. She soon became a striking figure in the Communist underworld, noted for her high intelligence, linguistic ability (she spoke four languages fluently), and apparent fearlessness. Precisely the kind of qualities that tend to catch the attention of intelligence agency recruiters; sometime during late 1933, **Richard Sorge,** GRU *rezident* in China, enlisted her for the GRU.

Sorge, enthusiastically recommending her as a potentially great agent, sent her to Moscow for training in cryptography and radio communications. She proved to be a brilliant pupil, and when she returned to China a year later, Sorge gave her increasing responsibilities running various networks.

In 1935, Kuczynski was ordered by the GRU to divorce her "inconvenient" husband, Rudolph Hamburger, an order she dutifully obeyed. Subsequently, she married Alfred Schultz, a GRU agent who also worked in China. (Two years later, Schultz disappeared in Stalin's purge; his wife, informed that her second husband was a traitor, calmly replied that his execution was therefore justified; she was now a widow with one child).

By that time, Kuczynski's stock was high in the GRU, which had great plans for her. Then in the midst of organizing a series of networks in Europe aimed at Nazi Germany—a sprawling octopus that came to be called the "Red Orchestra" by the Germans—the GRU intended Kuczynski to play a key role. Following a brief assignment in Danzig to perfect her skills, in 1938 she was sent to Switzerland with orders to find GRU assets among British Communist veterans of the Spanish Civil War. Her prize recruitment was Alexander Foote, who had fought in the war and demonstrated ability as a radio operator. (Foote later was assigned to a large-scale GRU network in Switzerland known to the Germans as the "Red Three.")

Kuczynski's next assignment was a real challenge: she was ordered to Britain to create a British branch of the Red Orchestra. A tall order, for as a German citizen, she could not enter Britain without a passport—something the Nazi government was not about to give a known Communist. She solved the problem with typical directness, simply approaching a number of British Communists then in Switzerland and asking them to marry her so she could obtain British citizenship by marriage. Foote turned her down, but Leon Beurton, a young Communist veteran of the war in Spain, agreed to this marriage of convenience. In 1940, with her husband called up for RAF service, she settled down in Kidlington, a small town near Oxford. The GRU ordered her to act as a sleeper—for the moment.

How Kuczynski was managing all this represents a tribute to her dedication and fortitude. She already had one child from her marriage to Schultz, and quite unexpectedly, she and Beurton had another. So now she had two small children to care for; when in May, 1941, the GRU ordered her to go into action, she somehow had to carry out that order in addition to her domestic burden.

She succeeded brilliantly. She started building a network right in her own family, which had fled to Britain after Hitler came to power. As dedicated Communists, they were ready to answer the summons of duty to the cause. Her father, now teaching economics at Oxford, had become well-connected in the British establishment, and he began to collect high-level political intelligence. Brother Jeurgen, also an economist, was working as an analyst in the British Air Ministry; he provided top-level military intelligence. (Later, after the United States entered the war, he joined the OSS and served on the staff of the Strategic Bombing Survey, giving him even greater access to high-grade intelligence). Even closer to home, her husband put her in touch with an RAF senior officer who was a secret Communist; he passed on samples of the latest British air technology, along with technical reports that Ruth arranged to ship to Moscow.

From there, Ruth went trolling among the exiled German Communist party members living in Britain. She discovered that as loyal Communists, they continued to pay their party dues and hold regular cell meetings. After the German invasion of the Soviet Union in June 1941, they were desperate to help Moscow, and Ruth Kuczynski organized them into a network of assets with varying degrees of usefulness. Most occupied low-level jobs, but they nevertheless came across bits and pieces of classified information that the GRU found useful. Her next recruit, however, had much more to offer.

In late 1941, Kuczynski met a young German emigré scientist who had fled Germany in 1933 when Hitler came to power. A rabid Communist, he continued to attend party meetings in exile, and told Kuczynski he was eager to help the Soviet Union in any way he could. He did not seem in a position to offer much; after a year in an alien internment camp at the outbreak of the war, the British recruited him to work on something called "Tube Alloys Project." When Kuczynski did not seem especially impressed, **Klaus Fuchs** told her that the project was a cover name for the greatest technical secret in the war: Great Britain and the United States were jointly developing an atomic bomb. Would the Russians be interested?

They certainly were, and Fuchs was enrolled as the star asset in Kuczynski's network. By this point, she confronted the problem of how to transmit all this intelligence to the main GRU station at the Soviet embassy in London. Much of the material she was gathering could be sent by courier, but really "hot" intelligence had to be sent via radio. She needed a transmitter, but this was no simple matter in wartime Britain; she could not simply pick one up at the store and take it home. The solution was at once ingenious and resourceful: over a period of several weeks, Kuczynski made periodic trips by train to London with her small son. They appeared ordinary enough; a mother and small son, the boy clutching a large teddy bear, on their way to London. Once there, Kuczynski met a GRU agent in a park. He handed over a package; later, she removed the radio parts from the package and put them inside the hollowed-out teddy bear. On the way back home, she and her son were just another ordinary mother and son travelling on the train.

Once on the air, Kuczynski began transmitting, careful to keep her transmissions short as British counterintelligence was on the alert for any signs of clandestine radios. She even had a neighbor help string her aerial, telling him it was a clothesline. This was all part of a facade she maintained of domestic ordinariness. It was a facade that served her well, for despite the heavy volume of material she sent to Moscow during the war, she was never detected. She even managed to survive a development that should have meant her end: in 1945, Fuchs was arrested in Britain on charges of espionage, and gave a confession. But he avoided mentioning Kuczynski, so she was still safe.

It was not until two years later, in 1947, that she finally was unmasked. Alexander Foote, the British Communist she had recruited a decade before, defected to the British. He revealed all the GRU agents with whom he had ever had any contact, including Kuczynski—although he claimed that she had stopped working for the GRU in 1940. For reasons he never made clear, Foote apparently meant this semi-revelation to protect her in some way. It did: MI5 agents appeared at her door and began asking questions about her connection to Soviet intelligence. She put on another of her *hausfrau* acts, and by the time the MI5 agents left, they were wondering if Foote was mistaken, somehow. It did not seem possible that this plump lady whose wide-eyed innocence protested any knowledge of such nasty things as espionage could be the spy Foote claimed her to be—even before 1940, when the GRU and KGB were known to have enlisted *anybody* who agreed to help them.

Before MI5 could decide what to do next, Kuczynski realized her time was up. She, her husband and the two children left on what she told her neighbors was a trip to see relatives in Germany. But they never saw Kuczynski again; Mr. and Mrs. Beurton and the children disappeared into East Germany, followed shortly by the rest of the Kuczynski family.

MI5 was not especially upset by her disappearance, assuming that at worst, she had been a very low-level asset for Moscow years before, and in any event probably had not injured British security, since she had not arrived in the country until 1939. It was not until 1959, when more of the VENONA decryptions came to light, that MI5 realized its error. The decryptions, of traffic from the GRU station at the London embassy to Moscow during the war, revealed a small ocean of material from a source—obviously head of a network—code-named SONIA. From several clues sprinkled in the transmissions, it did not take long for MI5 to deduce that SONIA was in fact Ruth Kuczynski, the little house-wife who had hoodwinked them years before.

Kuczynski, meanwhile, settled in East Germany, where she became a loyal follower of the regime and worked in a government job that apparently had nothing to do with intelligence. (It is unclear whether she is still alive). In 1982, now retired, she published her memoirs and basked in the glow of a tribute from Soviet intelligence, which said of her, "If we had five Sonias, the war would have ended sooner."

HERBERT YARDLEY
The American Black Chamber

1890–1958

T he restless 22-year-old former railroad telegrapher who arrived at the huge Victorian mausoleum on Pennsylvania Avenue in Washington, D.C., in 1912 to report for his new job as code clerk in the State Department realized at once that his presumption that the job entailed excitement was quite wrong. The place was a tomb; in the torpor of pre-World War I Washington, the State Department, and the War and Navy departments located in the same building, had all the drama and excitement of a birdwatchers' convention.

Herbert Yardley had arrived from Indiana assuming that the very center of American power would be teeming with intrigue and activity. Instead, the State Department reflected the country's overall mood of isolationism; it had very little idea of what was really happening in the rest of the world, and did not seem to care, particularly.

Yardley settled into the dull routine of his job, and passed the idle hours, of which there were many, pursuing his hobby of cryptography. He haunted the Library of Congress in every spare moment, reading everything he could find on the subject, and by the beginning of 1914, the $900-a-year code clerk was the leading American expert on cryptanalysis. Not an especially difficult feat, since American cryptography at that point was some 30 years behind Europe.

The more Yardley studied the creaky American codes then

Herbert Yardley, the legendary American codebreaker whose Black Chamber was to dramatically affect the course of World War II in the Pacific. (*AP/Wide World*)

in use, the more he was convinced that they were so simple as to make them useless for modern coded communications. Rebuffed by his superiors when he complained about the codes, Yardley decided on direct action to make his point: over a period of several months, he solved every single American code then in existence, and wrote up a report entitled *Exposition on the Solution of American Diplomatic Codes.* He concluded that European nations, known to have a first-class cryptographic ability, undoubtedly were reading the simple American codes with ease. He impolitically presented this report to his superior, who just happened to be the man who devised the codes in the first place. To further make his point, Yardley coolly walked into the man's office and opened his safe—whose combination, Yardley figured out, was based on the telephone number of President Woodrow Wilson's fiancée.

Word of Yardley's feat got around the small American military establishment, and in 1917, as America entered the war, he was recruited by Colonel Ralph H. Van Deman, then head of the

Army's Military Intelligence Division. Following only a 15-minute conversation with Yardley, Van Deman concluded that he was just the man to bring the United States into the forefront of cryptography. An entirely new Army intelligence unit, called MI-8, was created for Yardley, who was given an Army commission, told to recruit and train a staff of the best minds he could find, and sent off to France.

Yardley then began one of the most amazing careers in the history of American intelligence—and one of the most tragic.

A highly energetic man, Yardley in short order had a cadre of trained cryptanalysts in an organization that he modelled on the famous wartime French *Chambre Noir* (Black Chamber), one of the most brilliant cryptographic organizations in the world. By 1918, Yardley added to a glittering record by organizing an effort that cracked the German ciphers used to keep in touch with spies in France; as a result, every single German spy dispatched to France was caught.

At the end of World War I, MI-8 was scheduled to be eliminated in the wave of postwar cutbacks, but Yardley and his staff's feats were so well known at the upper levels of the government that an unprecedented arrangement was worked out: MI-8 would continue to operate under cover of a civilian commercial code-making company, secretly funded by the State Department. Setting up headquarters in a New York City brownstone, Yardley unofficially called his group the "Black Chamber," in tribute to the French organization that had taught the Americans so much.

Yardley began churning out a river of yellow flimsies that began "We learn from a source considered reliable in the past . . ." and continued with the text of the actual message as decrypted by the Black Chamber. The codes of a dozen nations fell before Yardley's efforts, but in late 1919, on orders of the State Department, the Black Chamber concentrated its efforts on the codes of Japan, already considered to be a potential enemy of the United States. Given the intricacies of the Japanese language and the complexity of the codes, it took the Black Chamber nearly two years to crack them; according to Yardley's later account, the solution came to him one night in a dream.

At any rate, the solution came just in time to play a role in one of the more amazing diplomatic episodes of the pre-World War II era, an episode that would make Yardley a hero and a pariah at the same time.

In 1921, the Washington Naval Limitations Conference opened, with the objective of reducing the world's naval fleets by means of a ratio system: each nation would be permitted a certain number of capital ships in a proportion to the size of other naval fleets. The presumption was that large maritime nations such as the United States would need larger fleets to protect their interests than smaller nations. Japan was a participant in the conference, but was determined to get as close a ratio as it could in relation to the American fleet.

The Japanese negotiators had been instructed to hold out for a 10:7 ratio (700,000 tons of Japanese warship tonnage for every 1,000,000 tons of American), but given further instructions to compromise at 10:6 if the Americans proved intransigent. Which is precisely what the American negotiators held out for; given the transcripts that Yardley provided of the coded messages exchanged between the Japanese negotiators and their superiors in Tokyo, the Americans held fast. The Japanese finally gave in, and the consequences would prove enormous. Some 15 years later, the Japanese renounced the treaty, but by then it was too late; in the brief period before Pearl Harbor, Japan was unable to make up for lost time and build a navy sufficiently strong to challenge American superiority.

For Yardley, the feat cemented his vaunting reputation as a cryptographic magician. But that did not save the Black Chamber: In 1929, the new Secretary of State, conservative Henry L. Stimson, learned the source of those yellow flimsies that so accurately revealed what the diplomats of other nations were thinking. Shocked, Stimson ordered the Black Chamber closed down with the immortal words that would haunt him the rest of his life, "Gentlemen do not read each other's mail."

Out of work, Yardley suffered a further blow when the money he had invested in the stock market was lost in the crash. To support his family, he wrote an immensely popular book called *The American Black Chamber*. The book infuriated the American government, and when Yardley tried to write another, called *Japanese Diplomatic Secrets*, government prosecutors went to court and won a landmark ruling that upheld the government's right to prepublication review of the writings of its intelligence agents. The government was aggravated by *The American Black Chamber*, and no wonder: it revealed American intelligence's greatest secret, a revelation certain to cause all the nations whose communications had been read by Yardley to tighten up their cipher systems.*

Yardley professed to be unconcerned about all the controversy, preferring to invest his energies in a business career. But however talented a cryptanalyst, Yardley was no businessman; every scheme he tried failed, including one spectacular failure involving his invention of a nearly undetectable secret ink, the market for which proved to be obscure.

In 1938, by then desperate for money, Yardley returned to the field in which he had won his fame, accepting a job with Chinese leader Chiang Kai-Shek to work on solving Japanese army ciphers. The appointment displeased the Japanese, who began to regard Yardley as a nemesis. After Pearl Harbor, Yardley volunteered his services to Washington as a codebreaker, but the American government, still furious about his book, would not take him up on the offer. The Canadians, interested in upgrading their codebreaking efforts, hired Yardley, but soon dispensed with his services under strong U.S. government pressure.

Embittered, Yardley served during the war as a lowly official in the Office of Price Administration. After the war, he faded into obscurity. He wrote one book about his work in China, and another, this one a treatise on poker that still ranks as the greatest work ever written on the subject. A heavy drinker, the habit began to exact its toll on Yardley's health, and he died in 1958. The general public had forgotten him, but the government had not, although its long animosity had finally mellowed. Accordingly, former Lieutenant Herbert Yardley, ex-chief of the MI-8 section of the United States Army Military Intelligence Division, the man who singlehandedly revolutionized American cryptography and created the groundwork for the great American code-breaking triumphs of World War II, was buried in Arlington National Cemetery with full military honors.

---

* Among them was Japan, where Yardley's book was a best-seller. Appalled at learning how easily their codes were compromised, the Japanese government overhauled its cipher sytems, ultimately producing a complex cipher machine code-named PURPLE by the Americans. It required a herculean effort by U.S. Army cryptographers to crack the machine, and as a result, the Americans were able to read all high-level Japanese diplomatic traffic before and during World War II.

ERIC ERICKSON
The Counterfeit Traitor

1891–1983

On a crisp fall day in 1944, the weapon Nazi Germany was convinced would turn the tide of war slowly rolled to a takeoff position at an airfield in southern Germany. The Messerschmitt 262, the world's first operational jet fighter plane, was ready for one of its final test flights.

Once deployed, the Germans were convinced, the ME-262 would dramatically alter the air war then pounding Germany to pieces. The new jet, much faster than the fighter escorts protecting the fleets of Allied bombers, would quickly decimate the slow-moving bombers. Free of bombing attacks, German industry would then turn out the "wonder weapons" to finally win the war.

But the very circumstances of the ME-262's appearance on the airfield underscored why Germany had no hope of winning anything, much less the air war. This triumph of German technological genius was pulled onto the airfield by a team of cows. Once airborne, it could only fly a few minutes because of Germany's acute shortage of aviation fuel. Some miles away, the factory producing the ME-262 was having trouble getting parts and raw materials, because the trucks needed to carry them had very little fuel. And even if maximum production was achieved, there simply was not sufficient fuel to keep enough of the planes airborne.

All these problems devolved upon Nazi Germany's Achilles heel in 1944: lack of oil. It was a critical deficiency that finally wrecked the German war machine. And one man was responsible for that fact, the man who had ensured that Nazi Germany's oil supply dwindled to a mere trickle, a man that the Germans never would have suspected. His name was Eric Erickson.

At the outbreak of World War II, Erickson was a 48-year-old oilman who travelled frequently around the world working out various deals. Like most men in the business, Erickson loved the rough and tumble world of oil. Born in Brooklyn, he had emigrated to Sweden in 1924 to start his own oil production company. Nicknamed "Red" for his shock of red hair, Erickson was known as a burly, easygoing man who liked nothing better than hoisting a few with his oil industry cronies, exchanging stories about the latest big find in the Persian Gulf.

But the mild exterior concealed an extremely shrewd man who had strong moral convictions. Which is why his friends found it all the more puzzling when in 1939, shortly after the outbreak of the war, Erickson suddenly became something of a pro-Nazi. To their further puzzlement, Erickson, never known for any prejudice, began to become openly anti-Semitic. He stopped talking to his Jewish friends, and loudly insulted one prominent Jewish businessman in a restaurant. Coupled with his open admiration for Hitler, the transformation struck everybody who knew Erickson as very strange. They learned to avoid the Erickson home in Stockholm, lest they be subjected to a tirade about the "dirty Jews" and the genius of Adolf Hitler.

There was one group of men in Stockholm who did not find such behavior so strange; in fact, they delightedly watched Erickson's growing infatuation with Nazi ideology. The men of the SD station at the Stockholm embassy had taken notice of Erickson as he veered suddenly rightward. This offered possibilities: Germany had an acute need for oil, and Erickson, one of the world's leading experts on that subject, could prove valuable. A careful, tentative approach was made: would *Herr* Erickson be interested in helping the Nazi regime? Erickson replied enthusiastically.

And so the bait had been taken. In fact, Erickson loathed the Nazis, but had been instructed to cultivate an image of pro-Nazi to lure an SD recruitment. Some months before, Erickson had been approached by an acquaintance, an American diplomat named Laurence Steinhardt, who was on his way to Moscow to serve as ambassador. Steinhardt, himself an expert on the oil business, concluded that the war between great industrial powers would be decided in large measure on the issue of oil; the nation that had sufficient oil to fuel its planes and tanks and keep its industrial machinery going would be the nation that won the war. Steinhardt proposed a daring plan to Erickson: posing as a pro-Nazi, he would allow himself to be recruited by the Germans as a helpful expert willing to advise the Nazi regime on oil production. Naturally, that meant Erickson at some point would have to take a look at the German oil production facilities.

And that is what American intelligence wanted to see. Since World War I, the Germans had led the world in the technology of synthetic oil, which involved an industrial process that converted coal into oil. It removed a dependency on imported oil—easily cut off in the event of war—although the process was quite expensive. The Americans wanted to know how advanced the German synthetic oil industry was, and, even more importantly, where the plants were located. (The plants were under heavy security, and neither the British nor American intelligence had much information about them.)

Toward the end of 1939, Erickson began to make regular trips to Nazi Germany to consult with oil experts. Blessed with a photographic memory, Erickson remembered every detail he either saw or heard about; following each return to Stockholm, he sat with several State Department aides and repeated it all to them.

Actually, as Erickson discovered, there was not much he could help the Germans with; their synthetic oil industry was very far advanced, to the point where Hitler believed he could fill almost all the petroleum needs of his war machine from the output of synthetic oil plants. To keep the game going, Erickson proposed an idea that delighted SS leader Heinrich Himmler himself: the Swede would construct a huge synthetic oil plant in Sweden, using German capital. Thus, in the event the German plants were damaged or destroyed, the Germans would have a guaranteed source of oil.

As Erickson anticipated, that led the Germans to approve an extensive series of inspection trips to their oil plants, all in the name of Erickson becoming familiar with the German technology that he was to build in Sweden. By 1943, Erickson had a virtually complete picture of the German plants. Concidentally, they began to be struck by persistent American bombing attacks. The bombers not only seemed to know the precise location of the plants, they were uncannily punctual in return bombings when a damaged plant was restored to production.

The Germans did not make the connection between the accurate American attacks and the presence of Erickson at the very same plants. Erickson artfully stalled while the Germans pressed him to finish arrangements for the new plant in Sweden; their anxiety was understandable, considering that synthetic oil production was dropping precipitously.

By mid-1944, German synthetic oil production was drying up, and the German war machine was tapping into precious reserves in order to keep going. Nevertheless, that machine was clanking to a halt: most of the Luftwaffe was grounded for lack of fuel, and there was not enough gas for those Panzer formations that once swept across Europe. By the end of that year, the synthetic oil industry in Germany collapsed altogether.

Erickson's mission was over. There was no point for him to make any more trips to Germany, for there was nothing left to bomb. While the Germans hitched up a team of cows to pull their technological wonder, the ME-262, onto an airfield, Erickson was at a large dinner in Stockholm that had been arranged by his American friends. At the dinner, it was announced that Eric Erickson was not a pro-Nazi after all; it was only a facade to aid his "great work" on behalf of the Allies. The "great work" remained unspecified, but the important fact was that Erickson now became reconciled with the friends whom he once spurned in the name of perfecting his cover.

With the end of the war, Erickson returned to his oil business. Praised by Dwight D. Eisenhower as the man who "shortened the war by at least two years," he shunned publicity. He endured a best-selling book about his role in the war, and later a movie, *The Counterfeit Traitor*, that starred William Holden in a somewhat exaggerated account of Erickson's work as a spy.

The book and the movie appeared to say everything there was worth saying about Erickson, but there was one secret he took to the grave with him when he died in 1983: a list, given to him by the Germans, of Swedes who secretly had agreed to serve in a Nazi government should Germany invade Sweden. At Eisenhower's request, Erickson burned that document to forestall a witch-hunt.

ELSBETH SCHRAGMUELLER
Fraulein Doktor

Aliases: Henrichsen, Christiansen, Rennmueller
1894–1939

The man in the clutches of two burly military policemen appeared miserable, a not unreasonable emotion considering he was about to be shot as a spy. Facing a grim-looking British officer seated behind a desk as a heavy rain in that wet summer of 1915 pelted the tent, the man tried not to look at the evidence of his espionage spread before him: the innocent-appearing letter whose invisible writing between the lines had been developed, the Belgian identity card proven to be a forgery, the small pieces of rice paper with coded writing found in the sole of his shoe.

The British officer made an offer: if the spy would tell all he knew, then he would be treated as a prisoner of war, and put into a prison camp. If not, he would be shot within the next 20 minutes. The spy, a native Belgian recruited by the Germans, didn't hestiate a second, and began telling his story.

To the British army intelligence officer, his story had a very familiar ring, because he had heard it at least a dozen times before. It was always the same: an offer to spy for the Germans, a mysterious summons in the dead of night, a ride in a car with shades over the side windows, arrival at a building somewhere in German-occupied Antwerp, and then a greeting by a woman who announced she would be his spy trainer. She was a tall, blonde woman with a pair of the most penetrating ice-blue eyes he had ever seen. Like a drill sergeant, she barked out the orders that would govern his every waking moment for the next three

136

months: he would be known only by a code name, he would speak to no other person at the school, he would spend 12 hours each day training in the espionage arts, he would spend the remaining part of each day locked in his room, and if he was a successful graduate of this regimen, he would be sent behind British lines to work as a spy. Any violation of these strictures would result in his immediate execution.

Like almost every other spy trained at the spy school, he was terrified of this blonde woman, who screamed and ranted at the recruits. He did not know her name, but there was a rumor she had been an academic with a Ph.D. in economics. As was the German custom, which dictated that male holders of the degree be addressed respectfully as *Herr Doktor*, the lady spymaster, reputedly unmarried, was known among the trainees as *Fraulein Doktor*.

And it was as *Fraulein Doktor* that she became an espionage immortal. Not until after the war did the British discover that her real name was Elsbeth Schragmueller, and that despite her reputation as a stern taskmaster (hinting of a possible military background), her actual history was much more prosaic.

In 1914, Schragmueller, then 20 years old, was just finishing her graduate studies in economics at the University of Freiburg (her dissertation was on the medieval stonecutter guilds), and when the war broke out, she volunteered her services. A fanatic German patriot, Schragmueller actually suggested to military recruiters that she be trained in the infantry and sent to fight as an ordinary front-line soldier. That was considered out of the question, but since she spoke four languages fluently, she was shuttled off to the army's Postal Censorship Bureau in German-occupied Brussels, a sleepy backwater where battalions of men and women censored mail.

The energetic Schragmueller converted her dull job into a flourishing intelligence operation. To the surprise of her superiors, she showed how the mails were being used by clever spies who managed to convey a great deal of intelligence in even the most innocuous messages. A man writing to his cousin about the family farm, she lectured, was probably a spy; just look at this detailed accounting of how many pigs, chickens, and horses he was recounting for his cousin. Obviously, these referred to the types and numbers of German units he had observed. And this letter, ostensibly by a woman recounting how many sailboats she had seen on a trip to the seashore; obviously, she was in fact reporting on the number of German warships she had spotted in the area. Schragmueller, in a presentation that dazzled her listeners, demonstrated how she had developed a system of textual analysis that would betray letter-writers who were conveying military information, rather than idle family gossip.

Word of this feat soon reached the higher levels of German military intelligence, which concluded that Schragmueller's talents were better suited for a job of greater responsibility. Schragmueller had just the job in mind: she wanted to run training at the military intelligence's training school in Antwerp. It was not a very good school, Schragmueller complained: army officers with minimal intelligence experience trained recruits in a quick once-over in espionage techniques, then sent them on their way. Most never were heard of again.

Impressed with her determination and boldness, military intelligence gave her the job. Within a month, the old mansion at 10 Rue de Pepiniere (an address Belgians learned to fear because they would be arrested if they showed any curiosity about the place) was humming with activity. Schragmueller introduced an entirely new curriculum, ranging from lessons on how to recognize the latest in enemy military technology to cryptography. None of the several hundred recruits who went through the exacting training schedule ever forgot the woman they sometimes called "Tiger Eyes," the single-minded blonde in German army uniform, complete with pistol and riding crop—which she didn't hesitate to use on doltish students. Above all, they learned that Schragmueller was not to be trifled with. She would fix an errant student with a malevolent glare, and when especially infuriated, tended to brandish her pistol.

British counterintelligence on the Western Front soon became aware that a new vigor had entered German intelligence operations. They began to turn up indications that German spies had managed to infiltrate some of the channel ports, and what made things more difficult, they apparently were a lot better trained. Gradually, the British also heard about the "Fraulein Doktor," and mounted a series of operations to infiltrate her operation and identify her. They never succeeded; Schragmueller was adept at shifting identities, and lived at various addresses under multiple disguises, including that of an old washerwoman.

Meanwhile, she kept churning out highly trained spies, and it is for her curriculum that she is best known in the history of modern intelligence, for virtually all modern spy agencies copied her training regimen. She is also known for a particularly cynical technique she contributed to the field: the "discard," an agent deliberately sacrificed as part of an effort to conceal another, more important, agent. One of her "discards" became much more famous than her teacher.

In 1915, she was sent a new recruit to train for eventual operations at the highest levels of French society, a plumpish Dutch woman who had already won some fame as an exotic dancer named Mata Hari. Margareta Zelle did not impress Schragmueller, and seemed to have difficulty in mastering even the simplest techniques. "A dud shell," Schragmueller pronounced her, despairing that Mata Hari would ever amount to anything. (She turned out to be right, and it was Schragmueller who arranged to have her dull student betrayed to French counterintelligence.)

In 1918, following the liberation of Belgium, Schragmueller went back to Germany, and there disappeared into total obscurity. By this time, fueled by a series of revelations from wartime British intelligence operatives, "Fraulein Doktor," along with Mata Hari, had become one of the most glamorous spies in history. Schragmueller refused all offers in Germany to write her memoirs, preferring a quiet life taking care of her aged mother (she never married), and working as a lecturer in economics at the University of Munich. She briefly emerged into the limelight in 1932, when a woman admitted to a Swiss sanatorium for drug addiction claimed to be the legendary *Fraulein Doktor*. There was a furious burst of publicity, in which the stories about Schragmueller got wilder and wilder. Some newspapers ran a picture purported to be of Fraulein Doktor, showing a stunning blonde in an army cap and brandishing a cigar.

It was too much. Schragmueller broke her long silence to deny she was a drug addict in Switzerland, to cite just one of the wild stories. She faded back into obscurity, and died in 1939. One can imagine what her reaction would have been, 29 years later, to see the now-cult movie *Fraulein Doktor*, which featured the Schragmueller character as a lesbian dope addict.

MARGARETA ZELLE
Mata Hari, The Eye of Dawn

Code Name: H21
Alias: Mata Hari
1876–1917

A nd how did the accused propose to explain the 30,000 marks she received from an official of German intelligence? The prosecuting officer, with a flourish meant to impress the military court, brandished the records of several money transfers from German banks to Swiss accounts of the accused.

Margareta Zelle shrugged. "He was my lover," she said. "That was the price of my favors."

"This amount seems rather large for a simple gift," the prosecutor said, allowing a pause before the word "gift."

"Not to me," Zelle snapped. At that moment, she was doomed; the worldwise senior officers who constituted the French court martial were not prepared to believe that even the famed Mata Hari—to use Zelle's stage name—was worth the then-astonishing sum of 30,000 marks for a night of pleasure. They unanimously voted that Maragareta Zelle was a spy in the pay of the Germans.

A few months later, on October 15, 1917, she was taken to the rifle range at Vincennes and, declining a blindfold, stood before a firing squad at dawn and was executed. Instantly, she became a legend. In the more than 75 years since that morning, Mata Hari has become shrouded in myth as the greatest, the most beautiful, and the most mysterious spy of all time. She has been the subject of more books, articles, and movies than any other

Margareta Zelle, in costume as the "Eye of Dawn" (Mata Hari). (*AP/Wide World*)

spy; she remains the one instantly recognizable name in the public's mind when the subject turns to spies.

And yet, ironically enough, the fact is that Mata Hari was not very mysterious, she was not a great spy, and, if truth be known, she was not very beautiful. Her legend was created for reasons of statecraft, for it suited certain political objectives having little to do with espionage.

For a long time, much of the legend centered on her origins, which were reputed to be in Java, where a union of a Dutch adventurer and a Javanese temple dancer produced a beautiful daughter. As a young girl, so the story went, she learned sensuous temple dances, and adopted the stage name Mata Hari ("eye of dawn" in Javanese) to bring those dances to the world.

In fact, her origins were much more ordinary. Margareta Zelle was born in 1876 to a middle-class Dutch family. She attended convent school, and at age 18, was swept off her feet by a Scottish sea captain named Macleod. She followed him to the East Indies, where it turned out that Macleod was a mean drunk and a man of violence. In 1901, the marriage collapsing, they returned to the Netherlands, and were divorced.

Subsequently, Margareta Zelle became Mata Hari. In special private concerts all over Europe, she gave demonstrations of the "secret Javanese erotic temple dances" that actually may have had more to do with burlesque than East Indian art. Whatever the case, she became a sensation; at a time when public nudity was quite rare, Zelle presented dances in which she slowly divested herself of seven veils to reveal a nude body that apparently a fair number of aristocrats, political leaders, and senior military officers found alluring. In a short period of time, she became not only a highly sought performer, she also was a highly paid courtesan for the ruling circles of Europe.

This access made her a natural recruit for intelligence, and the Germans, with the deepest pockets, enlisted her after World War I broke out. She proved inept, so she was sent to the famous German spy school in Antwerp, run by *Fraulein Doktor*, **Elsbeth Schragmueller**, and dispatched into France to seduce French officials and gather intelligence.

But French counterintelligence was already aware of her links to the Germans. They moved to deport her, but Zelle surprised them by admitting she was close with some German officials, although denying she had ever spied for Germany. She then offered to become a double agent for the French. The French did not trust her, but as a test, sent her to Belgium with a list of six agents she was to contact. Within a fortnight, one of those six agents she contacted was arrested and executed by the Germans.

At this point, though she had given up the name of a French asset, the Germans didn't trust her, either. Schragmueller became convinced that Zelle's betrayal of the French agent was simply a discard operation to bolster her bona fides, part of a larger French operation to infiltrate German intelligence. Schragmueller recommended that Zelle be betrayed to the French. Accordingly, German intelligence assigned her to return to France, and announced the move via a coded radio message to other assets in France—in a code the Germans knew the French had broken. When Zelle returned to France, she was arrested for espionage, the decoded message having noted the imminent arrival of H21 (Zelle's German intelligence code name), along with enough details to allow any counterintelligence officer to deduce that the code name referred to Zelle.

She could not have picked a worse time to be arrested. The French, at that time wracked with army mutinies, needed a convenient scapegoat to explain military disasters at the front. Mata Hari was perfect; she was now described by the French as the greatest spy of all time, the woman who had managed to obtain all the secrets of the French High Command from officers fatally lured to her beauty. In the French version, virtually all the military setbacks on the Western Front could now be attributed to the female spy. The French public, notoriously susceptible to the idea of romantic entanglement as the cause of most world events, lapped it up. In the process, the dimwitted French generals who had sent their men to slaughter now had their alibi. The legend of Mata Hari was born.

The verdict in Zelle's trial was thus a foregone conclusion, but she didn't help her case by her idiotic explanation of why some German official was paying her all that money. Nor did she aid her defense when she claimed to have served French intelligence by revealing where in Morocco German U-boats were refueled. Too late, she realized she had entrapped herself, for the prosecutor then asked the natural question: considering the fact that she had never been to Morocco in her life, how could she have known of such vital information unless the Germans had told her?

She had no effective reply, except to insist repeatedly during her trial, "Harlot, yes. But traitress, never!"

That statement may have been closer to the actual truth than anyone in France realized, but no one was in a mood for subtleties. It was enough for everyone to believe in the myth of Mata Hari the super-spy.

It took some years for the record to be set straight, finally, but by then, it hardly mattered. Margareta Zelle, the Dutch convent girl who danced naked and made the mistake of dabbling in the dangerous world of espionage, had already passed into immortality. And there she remains, for no single individual has ever done so much to glamorize the world of espionage.

WOLFGANG LOTZ

Aliases: Rusty Bey, Ze'ev Gur-Ayeh
1921–1993

ELIYAHU COHEN

Code Names: ALEX,
OPERATIVE 88, MENASHE
Alias: Karmal Amin Taabet
1928–1965

The Eyes of Israel

At dawn on June 5, 1967, Israeli warplanes streaked in at low level to attack, with pinpoint accuracy, a half-dozen large military airfields in Egypt and Syria. The most devastating first strike in military history destroyed the air forces of Israel's two most dangerous enemies on the ground. Within 24 hours, an Israeli military *blitzkrieg* recaptured Sinai and shattered six Syrian divisions guarding the Golan Heights.

At the end of six days, when a truce stopped the fighting, the Israelis had won a stunning victory, a triumph that clearly owed a great deal to their superior intelligence services. Arab planes, armor, and fortifications were hit by Israeli pilots and tank gunners who often operated with maps and diagrams showing the precise location of their targets.

The triumph indeed owed much to Israeli intelligence, and the lion's share of that credit should go to two extraordinary men. Together, they were able to provide the intelligence that underwrote the victory, and their exploits demonstrated the effectiveness of human intelligence sources when properly trained and motivated. It also helped that both men were perfectly placed by an intelligence agency that knew how to make the best use of human spies.

Of the two men, Wolfgang Lotz was the more interesting. Born in Germany, he was 12 years old when Hitler came to power in 1933. The son of a Jewish mother and a Christian father, he grew up in a non-observant home; his mother was so agnostic, she didn't bother to have her only child circumcised. This omission, as it turned out, would save her son's life many years later.

Lotz's father died in 1932, and a year later, sensing what Hitler would do to the Jews of Europe, his mother decided to emigrate with her son to Palestine. When he was 16, Lotz joined the underground Haganah, working as a guard at the Ben-Shemen Forest near Jerusalem, a job which to his delight allowed him to patrol on horseback. A passionate horseman, Lotz was nicknamed "sus" (horse in Hebrew) by his friends, who also marvelled at his complicated personal life. Married and divorced three times by the time he was 20, Lotz pursued women avidly, and clearly enjoyed the high life.

Even a stint in the British army during World War II failed to dampen his *joie de vivre*, nor did a stint in the Israeli army during the 1948 war. Immensely popular, the garrulous, fun-loving Lotz was well-liked by both native Israelis and the Eastern European immigrants because in their view he was not *yekke*, a contemptuous Israeli term for the snobbish and fanatically neat German Jews whom most Israelis despised.

Lotz assumed he would spend the rest of his life in Israel pursuing his chief passion and avocation, horse ranching. But in 1956, Aman, Israeli military intelligence, asked him to volunteer for a mission that was to change his life.

At the time, the Israelis were most worried about Egyptian President Gamal Nasser's recruitment of former German rocket scientists and other military specialists to build a modern miitary capable of waging a first-strike war against Israel. Aman needed an agent to infiltrate this tightly guarded entity and identify all those involved (for whom the Israelis planned assassinations). The problem, of course, was that the agent had to play the part of a German, with a legend that would withstand detailed checking.

Lotz seemed ideal for the part. Blonde and blue-eyed, he did not look Jewish, and spoke German fluently without a trace of accent. Given his open friendliness and his ability to get people to like him, it was assumed he would be able to infiltrate the German community—many of them ex-Nazis—in Egypt and find out what the Israelis wanted to know. It would take a consummate actor to pull off this dangerous infiltration, but as things turned out, Lotz was not only a great actor, he was a nerveless one, as well.

To prepare Lotz for the mission, Aman went through a curious exercise in reverse legend-creation. When his mother emigrated to Palestine, Lotz Hebraicized his name to Ze'ev Gur-Ayeh. But now he would revert to his German identity of Lotz—with some important differences. Lotz, instead of a Jewish boy who fled Hitler, was now an ex-German soldier who had fought with Rommel in North Africa during the war. He was not a Nazi, but clearly had sympathized with Nazi aims and ideology. After the war, he became a wealthy horse rancher and was now looking to expand his business in the Middle East, especially Egypt.

With the help of the West German BND, the Israelis meticulously created the Lotz legend in Germany. Old documents attesting to Lotz's Jewish birth were destroyed, replaced by new documents making him the offspring of impeccably German parents, along with military records noting his devoted service in the *Wehrmacht.* Other false documents created a paper trail of his successful horse business.

By 1959, the Israelis were ready. Wolfgang Lotz the German horse rancher appeared in Cairo. Buttressed by extensive capital, he opened a stud farm and riding stable just outside Cairo. He immediately set to work.

Lotz was patient; as he anticipated, word of his riding school soon spread among the Egyptian officer corps. Gradually, some of them began enrolling for horsemanship lessons and were charmed by the friendly German, who occasionally reminisced about his wartime service with Rommel, a figure of immense respect to Egyptians. Lotz further cemented his relationships by sprinkling anti-Semitic and anti-Israeli comments into his conversations. In all, his cover was very solid, further strengthened by the presence of his blonde German "wife," who happened to be a BND asset lent to Lotz for purpose of constructing his legend. (This move was accomplished with the reluctant acceptance of Lotz's real wife, a very Israeli woman.)

The Egyptians were as cautious as Lotz, but after apparently having him checked out in West Germany, they relaxed. Lotz furthered the process by hosting a series of lavish parties to which he invited top Egyptian officials, as well as military men. His image as wealthy German playboy fixed, Lotz then moved to the next phase, infiltration of the enclave of German scientists and military advisers.

That task proved easier than he thought; some of the senior Egyptian military officers with whom he became close also happened to be involved with the German rocket scientists, and their willingness to vouch for one of Rommel's officers gained him quick entree. Delighted to meet a fellow German, and one who apparently shared their pro-Nazi sympathies, they welcomed Lotz as a long-lost brother. In the process, they had the habit of discussing the progress of their work in Egypt, all of which Lotz radioed back to Tel Aviv.

Over a period of time, Lotz was to develop a complete picture of the structure, size, and personalities of the German presence in Egypt. Aman did the rest: a campaign of letter bombs, pressure against relatives, and sheer terror finally persuaded the scientists and military experts that it was time to go home. Lotz's mission had been brilliantly successful, but *Mossad* now saw further benefit in Lotz's presence in Egypt. In 1963, Lotz was formally transferred to *Mossad* to carry out a different mission, which was nothing less than developing a detailed picture on the entire Egyptian military structure.

The operation sought to make use of Lotz's already-established advantages: He was bosom buddies with senior Egyptian military officers and government officials, he had an established cover business in the country, and thus far, he was completely above suspicion. A new round of lavish entertaining began, and the escalating expenses (Lotz never stinted) moved *Mossad* auditors to call Lotz the "champagne spy," the nickname by which he became part of espionage lore.

However much the Egyptians regarded Lotz as an amusing, boisterous playboy with more money than sense, he in fact didn't miss anything. Lengthy conversations with senior Egyptian military officers—sometimes in drunken revels when Lotz only pretended to be drunk—uncovered the plans, dispositions, and strength of the Egyptian armed forces. The Egyptians could not be more helpful to their German friend: they often invited him to visit them at military bases, where they freely talked about the state of their forces, the quality of their fortifications, the capabilities of their aircraft, and a virtual laundry list of everything the Israelis would want to know. Assuming him to be an ex-Afrika Korps officer, some Egyptians asked his advice on their planned tactics for a desert war against the Israelis.

The sheer volume of all this intelligence created the problem that had confronted spies for a long time: radio. Even with modern spy radios and their high-speed "burst" transmissions that could send a large volume of material in a very short time, Lotz was still vulnerable to an attack by radio direction-finders. The moment Lotz had been dreading came early in 1965, when the authorities began receiving complaints about heavy static that interfered with ordinary radio reception. Suspecting that the heavy static might be caused by an illegal transmitter, the Egyptians consulted with their largest arms supplier, the Russians. An expert crew of GRU direction-finders was sent to Cairo from Moscow, and in short order they tracked an illegal transmitter to a horse farm just outside Cairo. A raid found that transmitter; Lotz and his "wife" were arrested.

The first task of Egyptian counterintelligence was to find out for whom Lotz was working. Their initial suspicion of Lotz as an Israeli agent was discounted immediately, for an inspection of their prisoner revealed he was uncircumcised. So, the Egyptians concluded, he was probably working for the West German BND. But the BND played it deliberately coy, refusing to admit that Lotz was its man, but not exactly denying it, either.

In an attempt to confirm that suspicion, the Egyptians subjected Lotz to extensive torture, including sensory deprivation that drove him nearly mad. But he held on, insisting he was German. Finally, Lotz was put on trial on charges of espionage for Israel, and in the hope of an eventual exchange, he was sentenced to life in prison, along with his "wife," who had also been actively engaged in collecting intelligence.

The Egyptians did not learn positively that Lotz was an Israeli until just after the 1967 war, when Israel offered to exchange the incredible total of 500 Egyptian prisoners for Lotz and his presumed wife. The Egyptians, reluctant to let an Israeli spy go free, but also determined to get back its soldiers, assented to the deal.

By that time, of course, the Egyptians knew how truly damaging a spy Lotz had been. Thanks to his intelligence, the Israelis had been able to construct a complete order of battle for the entire Egyptian military, even which pilots flew which planes. When the Israelis struck in June of 1967, their intelligence on the Egyptians was thorough, right down to the platoon level.

While Lotz was performing this feat, possibly an even greater espionage coup was being carried out several hundred miles to the east, in the heartland of Israel's other great enemy, Syria.

The Israeli spy in that case was Eliyahu Cohen, a very different man than Lotz. Quiet and introspective, Cohen had been born in Egypt in 1928. As a young man, he was active in the Jewish underground's illegal immigration operations, which consisted of smuggling Egyptian Jews (who had been denied exit visas to go to Palestine) out of the country. This dangerous work was good training for a clandestine operator, and in 1952, he was recruited by *Mossad* for operations in Egypt. Following a one-year course of espionage training in Israel, which Cohen covered by claiming to have studied abroad, he returned to Egypt. It was a bad operational mistake: the Egyptians already knew him as a Jewish activist. Luckily for Cohen, he had not yet become too deeply involved in espionage, so in 1958, the Egyptians merely kicked him out of the country.

Two years later, *Mossad* devised a much more ambitious operation for Cohen. Under the plan, Cohen would work in Syria, where his real identity was presumably unknown. It amounted to a complex infiltration operation: Cohen would assume the identity of a wealthy, playboy-type Syrian named Karmal Amin Taabet and initiate contacts with the Syrian military and governmental elite. With that infiltration complete, he would then learn top-flight intelligence on Syrian military and political plans. Essentially, Cohen would be on his own, authorized to make operational decisions as he saw fit.

After a year of intense training in his new legend, Cohen flew to Zurich, Switzerland. He entered the airport terminal as Eliyahu Cohen; at the exit, he was met by a stranger who wordlessly handed over a packet of documents and took from him his passport and papers in the Cohen name. With that exchange, Cohen became Karmal Amin Taabet.

Cohen next flew to Buenos Aires, where he established himself in the large Syrian community in the Argentine capital. With some flamboyant spending as a wealthy businessman (but not, the *Mossad* auditors discovered with a sigh of relief, the dimension of Lotz's expenditures) Cohen soon established himself as a playboy who hosted lively parties that featured plenty of luscious women. He made it a point to become close friends with the Syrian military attache at the Syrian embassy, a connection that led to the next step: introduction to the attache's well-connected friends in the Syrian hierarchy.

In January 1962, Cohen went to Damascus, where his reputation preceded him. Quickly, the playboy businessman had a wide circle of friends from the Syrian military and government. Their guard weakened by those lavish parties, the availability of beautiful women, and magnificent gifts proffered by their friendly host, Syrian military officers took Cohen to their bases, showing off their latest weapons. Cohen's most productive contact was the Syrian colonel in charge of defenses on the Golan Heights; proud of the "invincible" defense lines he was constructing to forestall an Israeli invasion, he showed everything to Cohen. (Transmitted back to *Mossad*, Cohen's intelligence, amazingly specific in its detail, allowed the Israelis to construct a 3-D model of the Golan Heights, in which every single Syrian position, down to individual foxholes, was pinpointed.)

By 1964, there was almost nothing about the Syrian military that Cohen did not know. At one point, he learned the names of all the pilots in the Syrian air force—intelligence which the Israelis later used to fake radio transmissions that lured the pilots to their deaths. Yet, despite these intelligence bonanzas, Cohen was getting worried. On the excuse of a business trip, he returned to Israel for a rest from his nerve-wracking double life. During a *Mossad* debriefing, he indicated his worries, which convinced him he probably should not return to Syria.

First of all, Cohen noted, the volume of the intelligence required him to be on the air too long with his radio. That radio was concealed in his apartment in an area where a number of foreign embassies were located; the risk was that he might cause interference with an embassy radio, and a complaint would lead to his unauthorized transmitter. Second, and more ominously, he had managed to charm virtually the entire Syrian hierarchy, with one ominous exception: Colonel Ahmed Sue'edeni, head of Syrian military intelligence. Everybody was afraid of Sue'edeni, a secret police chief noted for his brutality and horrible tortures. Apparently jealous of Cohen's access to high-level officials, Sue'edeni had been openly suspicious of Cohen, and seemed to be working actively to check his bona fides. It would only be a matter of time, Cohen warned, before Sue'edeni discovered that "Karmal Amin Taabet" was a fiction totally created by the *Mossad*, since no such person actually existed (a simple check of birth records would uncover that fact in nothing flat).

But *Mossad* was desperate for the kind of intelligence that Cohen was providing. While Israel was locked in a life-or-death struggle with Syria's radical regime, war could break out at any moment. Against his better instincts, Cohen agreed to return to Syria.

It turned out to be Cohen's death warrant. As he feared, Sue'edeni had focused on Kamal Amin Taabet, suspecting that there was something not quite right about the playboy. As he also feared, his lengthy radio transmissions caused problems. The nearby Indian embassy complained of interference, and another GRU radio-finder team was dispatched. It found Cohen's radio with little trouble, and as Cohen was in the middle of a transmission, a squad of secret policemen burst into his apartment.

Cohen's terrible torment now began. An infuriated Sue'edeni subjected him to the full range of his tortures, designed to force Cohen to operate his radio under Syrian control. Cohen refused, and the Syrians finally gave up. Sue'edeni sent a message to Tel Aviv via Cohen's radio:

> KAMAL AMIN TAABET AND HIS FRIENDS ARE OUR
> GUESTS IN DAMASCUS. ASSUME YOU WILL SEND
> ALL HIS COLLEAGUES. WILL GIVE YOU NEWS OF
> HIS FATE SHORTLY.

The Israelis did not have long to wait: on May 18, 1965, Eliyahu Cohen was hung in a public square in Damascus. Nearly 200 Syrians who had enjoyed Mr. Taabet's hospitality and counted him among their friends—and were now regarded as traitors—paid the price a police state exacts for such folly: they were rounded up and taken to Sue'edeni's torture cellars for their own torments. Many were later executed.

But it was too late. What Cohen had passed to the Israelis was a virtual template for conquest. In June 1967, Israeli soldiers and airmen exacted a terrible toll on the Syrian military, avenging Cohen's death a thousand times over.

Shortly after the war, Israel's other great spy of the 1967 triumph, Wolfgang Lotz, returned in triumph to Israel, where the "champagne spy" was hailed as one of the great agents in its history. However, the bubbles suddenly went flat when it was learned that Lotz had fallen in love with his German "wife," who had converted to Judaism. He divorced the real Mrs. Lotz, and headed off to California and, later, Germany, to become a wealthy businessman. He died in 1993. As the Israelis learned the hard way, even a great hero is human, after all.

THE TRAITORS

LARRY WU-TAI CHIN
The Spy in the Casino

1923–1986

The Las Vegas casino managers could not have been more pleased when the shy, quiet, Asian man began to show up periodically. He seemed of a type the casinos were happy to have as patrons: rich Asian businessmen, mostly from Hong Kong, with money to burn. They were also notoriously bad gamblers.

Larry Wu-Tai Chin was among the most consistent losers whenever he dropped in. For that reason, he had a line of credit at a number of casinos that were aware Mr. Chin had never heard of the mathematical law of probability. No one was quite certain what Chin did for a living, but no matter: he was a heavy gambler seemingly unbothered by big losses. Win or lose, that inscrutable face behind thick eyeglasses remained impassive.

But Chin was not a wealthy Hong Kong merchant, or any other kind of businessman, for that matter. In fact, he was an ordinary GS-9 federal bureaucrat. So where did he get the money that allowed him to bet $100,000 or more during a night of gambling? The money came from the People's Republic of China's intelligence service, the Central External Liaison Department (CELD). Chin was worth every cent of the largesse, for he was the greatest asset Chinese intelligence had ever recruited in the United States. Indeed, the Chinese were pleased that Chin had a gambling habit, because as long as he needed a lot of money to feed that habit, he would have to keep betraying his adopted country.

How Chin arrived at that point represents a curious progression from political idealist to mercenary. Born in Peking in 1923 of a moderately wealthy family, Chin was a university student in 1943 when he was hired by a U.S. Army detachment as an interpreter. A gifted linguist, Chin already had mastered three Chinese dialects, and was fluent in English. Chin had postwar ambitions to become a professional translator, and enrolled at Yenching University in 1945 to perfect his skills. One day, he was approached by a fellow student, Ou Quiming, who began to talk to him about Chinese-American relations. Chin had gotten to like Americans as a result of his wartime job as an interpreter, and told Quiming of the sadness he felt over the growing estrangement between the Chinese Communists and the United States. Only through Chinese-American understanding could world peace be assured, Chin said, and he regarded such a rapprochement as his "personal mission" in life.

Quiming agreed enthusiastically. Tragic, he told Chin, how the Chinese and Americans did not understand one another, and how few Chinese were in a position to do anything about it. The problem, Quiming said, was lack of information; the Chinese simply had no insight into the way Americans thought. Too bad there were no Chinese in a position close to the Americans who would be able to properly "interpret" American attitudes for the Chinese and thus foster greater understanding.

It was a subtle recruitment, for Quiming was actually a young operative for the CELD, assigned the mission of recruiting among Chinese university students for assets who had any contacts with Americans—or who were about to. Quiming was careful not to reveal his hand too openly; he simply told Chin that he had "important friends" who were in a position to influence Chinese policy toward the United States. These people, Quiming claimed, wanted close friendship with the Americans; if Chin would be willing to help, then his own personal mission could be achieved.

Chin swallowed the bait. Following graduation in 1946, he approached the Americans, offering his services as a translator and interpreter. By 1948, he was the leading translator for the U.S. consulate in Shanghai, at that time the key American listening post in China. It was the chief conduit for nearly all American intelligence reports on China, which Chin began to pass to Quiming. To Chin, he was not committing espionage, merely passing on intelligence reports by means of demonstrating to Quiming and his friends how ill-informed the Americans were about the civil war then raging in China.

In 1952, the CELD's recruitment paid off when Chin hit an intelligence gold mine: He was assigned the task of translating all the American interrogations of Chinese military POWs during the Korean War. Passed on to Quiming, it revealed to the Chinese not only how much sensitive military information the POWs had given the Americans, but also which prisoners had been especially cooperative. As a result, thousands later found themselves thrown into prison camps for "thought reeducation," and an unknown number of others were executed outright.

By this point, Chin had developed a reputation as a linguistic wonder-worker, the man who could handle almost any Chinese dialect flawlessly and a linguistic scholar who could spot the most subtle shift of emphasis in the spoken or written Chinese word. He not only worked for the State Department, he also was lent out to various other government agencies—among them, to Quiming's delight, the CIA.

Whether Chin realized at this juncture he was working for Chinese intelligence is not known. However, it is known that at some point, Quiming gave Chin a large payment of money "for expenses." As Quiming perhaps had foreseen, Chin, living on a meager U.S. government salary, was bedazzled by that sudden infusion of cash. It opened a new world to him: expensive restaurants, vacation trips, women, and gambling, a vice Chin suddenly discovered was irresistible.

From then on, Chin was a mercenary spy. As he passed more and more intelligence to the Chinese, the larger the payments became. Chin was living a double life: by day, a self-effacing government bureaucrat, by night a bon vivant who also began dabbling in real estate and other investments. He bought some property (he eventually wound up with a portfolio worth over $700,000), and deposited more than $200,000 in Hong Kong banks, drawing high interest for his retirement. Most of the money, however, went to his gambling habit. He was a consistent loser, sufficient to have casinos routinely "comp" him, meaning the practice of providing free hotel rooms and other services for high-rollers.

In 1970, Chin's recruitment finally reached full flower: he was hired by the CIA, which put him in charge of handling the bulk of its translation chores for material from China. In that position, Chin saw all the reports from CIA assets in China, reports of CIA agents based in Taiwan (mostly from Nationalist Chinese-recruited assets), and, for good measure, most of the more sensitive diplomatic reports on China. In other words, Chin was now perfectly placed. The Chinese had a window into everything the Americans knew about China, an advantage that allowed them to learn in advance of the CIA's most sensitive program, U-2 spy flights over China that used Nationalist pilots. (As a result, most of the planes were shot down).

Chin's greatest coup came in 1972, when he was able to provide complete details of the dramatic change in American policy, the Nixon-Kissinger "opening" toward China. As an extra benefit, Chin had access to Kissinger's reports on his impressions of Chinese leaders.

Completely unaware of this leak, the American government rewarded its star Chinese language expert with American citizenship, and in 1981, when Chin officially retired from the CIA, he was awarded an intelligence medal. Chin did not bother telling his employers that Chinese intelligence had awarded him one of its own medals at about the same time, thus making him one of espionage's great rarities: awarded a medal by the nation he was betraying, while receiving a medal from the nation for whom he was committing the treason.

Even after his retirement, Chin was retained by the CIA as a consultant, giving him continued access to sensitive intelligence. Since there was still not the slightest hint of suspicion attached to him, Chin might have continued indefinitely except for an event he could not have anticipated. In 1983, his control, Ou Quiming, disillusioned with the Communist regime, defected to the CIA. Among his first revelations was a grave shock: Chin was a Chinese intelligence asset.

Interrogated by the FBI, Chin glumly listened as the agents recited a detailed catalog of his treason. "You have details that only Ou knew," he said finally, realizing that he had been blown by what must have been a defection by Quiming. Arrested on espionage charges, Chin never went to trial. On February 21, 1986, he tied a plastic bag over his head and committed suicide.

KLAUS FUCHS
The Man Who Stole the Atomic Bomb

1913–1988

To William Skardon, the man seated before him seemed almost a comic book caricature of what a nuclear physicist was supposed to look like: a tall, thin man with rimless eyeglasses, a pronounced German accent, and a high-domed forehead. But however much Klaus Fuchs looked like a cliche, Skardon knew something very important that was not so evident: Fuchs was a Soviet spy.

Skardon, considered MI5's most brilliant interrogator, was facing a major challenge that January of 1950. Somehow, he had to get Fuchs to admit what both British and American counterintelligence already knew. The super-secret atomic bomb program had been penetrated by Soviet intelligence, mainly through the efforts of Klaus Fuchs. But although they were certain, they dared not use the source of their information in a court case involving espionage, because prosecuting Fuchs on the basis of that source would reveal the greatest secret of Western intelligence.

Code-named VENONA, it was the patient decryption of the mountain of Soviet intelligence radio traffic during World War II. By 1949, the cryptanalysts had found the trail of a huge Soviet effort to obtain the secrets of the atomic bomb. One of its key sources, spelled out via a series of personal references in the coded traffic, was Fuchs. So a decision was made to confront Fuchs, and hope that Skardon's abilities would compel an admis-

Klaus Fuchs, the German emigré nuclear physicist who betrayed the secrets of the atomic bomb to the Russians. (*AP/Wide World*)

sion from him. Without it, as Skardon was aware, there would be no legal case against Fuchs.

Skardon, renowned for his ability to "read" suspects, decided to play a game of bluff with Fuchs. In his quiet way, occasionally puffing on his pipe, he hinted that MI5 had a stack of evidence that made Fuchs' guilt a foregone conclusion, so his "cooperation" would merely confirm what MI5 already knew as established fact. Fuchs listened quietly, but Skardon sensed that he was wavering, mentally considering his options. Skardon then played his high card, expressing understanding why a man in Fuchs' position would see betrayal of secrets as a tactic to advance the cause of world peace. Certainly, Skardon said, almost in a fatherly tone, one could understand how a man like Fuchs would come to believe that this very worthwhile cause would be best served by ensuring that the Soviet Union shared in the great secret of the atomic bomb.

Skardon had scored; the mushy idealism that coexisted in Fuchs' mind with his Communist convictions now came to the forefront. With a sympathetic listener, Fuchs began to pour out his heart to Skardon. When he was finished, he had admitted to an achievement for which he felt great pride: almost singlehand-edly, he had given the Soviet Union the atomic bomb.

A year later, Fuchs' admission would earn him a 14-year prison term for espionage, but by that time, the great VENONA spy hunt had already passed him by, deep into a pool of even greater mysteries for which Fuchs was only the proverbial tip of the iceberg.

Among those mysteries was Fuchs himself. Born into a family of German Quakers, most of whom were committed leftists, Fuchs joined the German Communist party in 1932, when he was only 19 years old. Then studying at the University of Kiel, he was con-sidered a brilliant physics student with a bright future in research or university teaching. That career was cut short in 1933 when the coming to power of Hitler threatened to make life impossible for German Communists. Fuchs fled to Great Britain, where he worked in some humdrum scientific jobs and joined the party's exile group in Bristol. By then a hardened Communist slavishly devoted to the Soviet Union, Fuchs actively searched for ways to aid Moscow. He had no access to anything of importance, but in 1941 was recruited to work in something called the Tube Alloys Project. Fuchs was told only that he was joining a very hush-hush wartime scientific project, but on the first day he started working at the project's laboratory, he realized Tube Alloys Project was an innocent-sounding cover name for what was in fact work on an atomic bomb. Apparently, Fuchs deduced, the British and Amer-icans had made great strides toward overcoming the considerable scientific and engineering obstacles in making a nuclear bomb. Fuchs also learned that the British and Americans were keeping this great secret from their ally, the Soviet Union. Now, at last, he had something he could contribute to the cause. Already a re-cruit of **Ruth Kuczynski**, the GRU master spy in Great Britain, Fuchs told her the news. Within days, he began stealing docu-ments from the project for Kuczynski to photograph onto micro-film, adding his own scientific evaluations.

It was at this point that the first mystery about Fuchs arose. Given the fact that he was an avowed Communist who partici-pated openly in the activities of the exile faction of the German Communist party, how was it possible that he received a security clearance to work on so security-obsessed project as the atomic bomb? A special section of MI5 in those days kept close tabs on Communist activities in Britain; how had it missed Fuchs? Years later, mole-hunters from MI5 would examine this sequence of events and conclude that a KGB mole inside MI5 had arranged for Fuch's Communist leanings to be overlooked. The same mole (never identified) may also have been responsible for another, subsidiary, mystery about Fuchs.

In 1945, British intelligence managed to capture almost intact all the Gestapo files from the agency's field office in Kiel. The cache included detailed records on all known Communists in Kiel, records that had been collected since well before Hitler came to power. Among them was an extensive dossier on Klaus Fuchs. MI5 examined those records in an attempt to find any Communists who might have emigrated to Britain during the 1930s and gone to work for Soviet intelligence. Curiously, there was no record that MI5 had ever investigated Fuchs, an unbelievable lapse never explained.

These sort of lapses later stood in stark relief in light of the damage that Fuchs caused. In 1943, he was assigned to the Manhattan Project at Los Alamos, New Mexico, where an elaborate security screen was supposed to keep out any enemy agents attempting to infiltrate the project. But it was no help against a man like Fuchs, equipped with a lofty security clearance from MI5 that permitted him access to any aspect of the project. By 1944, he had provided the Soviets with the key secrets of the bomb, most importantly the unique implosion design that created the weapon's tremendous destructive power. But at this moment of triumph, Soviet intelligence committed a grave mistake, a lapse that ultimately would prove very costly.

Desperate for the intelligence Fuchs was providing, the GRU decided to assign one of its important American assets, Harry Gold, the job of picking up some material from Fuchs during a brush contact near Los Alamos. But six years later, when Fuchs was giving his confession, he revealed the contact with Gold. That revelation was of acute interest to the FBI, which already suspected Gold.

Again, the VENONA decryptions had played a key role. They hinted at the existence of three major espionage rings operating in the United States during the war that had been assigned the job of obtaining secrets of the atomic bomb project. One ring operated at the University of Chicago, where Enrico Fermi had conducted the world's first controlled nuclear reaction. The second operated at the Radiation Laboratory at the University of California, Berkeley. The third, and most extensive, was a ring of 22 American Communists who had been recruited years before to steal American industrial and technological secrets. It operated out of New York and in 1943 had been diverted into atomic espionage.

It was this ring for which Gold worked, primarily as a courier. The FBI had some indications of the ring's existence, primarily through its investigation of the theft of radar technology early in the war. Later, in 1945, Elizabeth Bentley, a disillusioned Communist, approached the FBI and told them she was an aide to the chief GRU controller for a number of rings, including a large technology theft network. She did not know its members, but remembered that her boss had contacted one of its members, a man he called "Julius."

VENONA provided further clues, among them the revelation that there was a man and wife team of assets involved in the atomic espionage operation who had a relative working in the Manhattan Project. Those circumstances, it turned out, fit Julius and Ethel Rosenberg, whose brother, David Greenglass, worked as a technician at Los Alamos.

Fuchs provided the final link. Shown an array of photographs of suspected American GRU assets, Fuchs picked out the one of Gold as the man to whom he turned over information in Los Alamos. The FBI pounced on Gold, who confessed, leading the FBI to the other members of the ring. The GRU's operational error in using Gold to service two different sets of assets had now borne bitter fruit.*

If Fuchs was bothered by the wreckage his confession had caused, he didn't show it. He served his prison time quietly, teaching an elementary science course to fellow inmates. Released in 1959, he emigrated to East Germany and went to work at a nuclear physics institute, where he labored in obscurity until his retirement in 1979 (he died nine years later). In 1993, in a belated tribute, Soviet nuclear scientists admitted that they had built the Soviet Union's first atomic bomb largely on the basis of material provided them by Klaus Fuchs.

---

* In a tragic irony, the two most minor members of the ring, the Rosenbergs, were convicted of espionage and executed in 1953. The more important assets were evacuated eastward by the GRU: Alfred Sarant and Joel Barr, who went to work in a Soviet high-technology institute; and Morris and Lena Cohen, who resurfaced in 1962 as Peter and Helen Kroger, working for an important Soviet spy ring in Great Britain.

ALFRED REDL
Feasting with Panthers

1864–1913

It is possible that if Hans Wagner had shown up to play for the Storm I. soccer team on May 25, 1913, no one would have ever known of the greatest traitor in history—and one of the biggest attempted cover-ups of all time.

Wagner was the star player on the amateur Storm team, one of the strongest in Prague. Scheduled to play another strong team, Union V., that spring Sunday, Storm was counting on a stellar performance from Wagner, its talented fullback. But Wagner, a locksmith, was called away on an urgent job just before game time; to the fury of his teammates, Storm lost, 7–5.

Wagner was preparing for the Sunday afternoon game when a captain and a general of the Austro-Hungarian army, in full dress uniform, appeared at his home and told him that he was urgently needed for a job that had to be done immediately: opening the doors of a locked house. When Wagner protested he was about to play in an important soccer game, he was told the job was "of the highest national urgency." He accompanied the officers to a house in the fancy section of town. He picked the lock of the front door; once inside, he was instructed to open a number of locked cabinets and closets. Wagner performed the job easily enough, but wondered why virtually every space in the house was crammed with maps, documents, and thick bundles of cash. Apparently anticipating Wagner's curiosity, the two officers warned him he was never to mention to anyone what he had seen

163

in the house; in fact, he was never to mention even being there. As a means of assuring future discretion, the officers pressed a lavish payment into Wagner's hands.

Wagner might have remained mute had it not been for an angry encounter that night with his infuriated teammates. They demanded to know why he didn't show up. Wagner replied simply that he had to go out on a job. When that failed to appease them, Wagner then told them of his mysterious encounter with the army officers, the house, and the trove of papers and money. He re-counted the warning never to say anything, although he did de-duce that the house apparently was owned by a fellow officer of the two men who hired him for the job. One of the teammates came fully alert: Two days earlier, he heard of the mysterious suicide of Colonel Alfred Redl of the Austro-Hungarian Army General Staff. The army had taken great efforts to keep news of that suicide from the public. Was there a connection between the suicide and the search of the document-laden house?

This was no ordinary weekend soccer player asking the ques-tion; he was an editor on the staff of Prague's most important newspaper, the *Prager Tageblatt.* He went right to work, and by the next day had enough for a cautiously-worded story that neverthe-less created a public sensation, for it reported that Redl was a Russian spy. The modern equivalent would be a revelation that General Colin Powell was working for the KGB. The possibility that Redl, one of the stars of the Austro-Hungarian military es-tablishment, a man whose brilliant career was an inspiration to an entire generation of young officers, had committed treason was unthinkable.

The very circumstances of Redl's career made the charge hard to grasp. One of 14 children of a poor Austrian railroad official, Redl went to military school as a boy of 14 in 1878 and later joined the army, determined to become an officer, despite the fact that the officer ranks amounted to a caste system based on aristocratic birth and wealth. But Redl was one of the most brilliant minds the army had ever encountered: Fluent in six lan-guages and an organizational genius, by 1900 he was considered a candidate for future chief of staff.

In that year, Redl was named head of the *Kundschaftsstelle,* (KS) the army's counterespionage organization, with orders to reorganize and reinvigorate it. The KS, as it was known, soon responded to Redl's direction, and began to roll up a number of networks run by the Okhrana, the intelligence service of Austro-

Hungary's hated enemy, Russia. KS officers were armed with a series of innovations invented by Redl, all of which later passed into standard counterintelligence practice: fingerprint and photo files on all suspected assets, monitoring of political dissidents, and bugging of meeting rooms (in Redl's day by use of phonograph wax cylinders).

The Russians, unhappy about this course of events, took a close look at Redl's operation, determined to find some kind of weak link they could exploit. They found it in Redl himself: to the immense satisfaction of the Okhrana, it was learned that the Austro-Hungarian colonel was a pedophile. Armed with that priceless piece of information, the Okhrana set him up with a boy, took some compromising photographs, and the colonel was hooked.

Initially, this had all the trappings of a classic blackmail operation. But it turned out that Colonel Redl was money-hungry, too, so the Russians happily began paying him huge sums, eventually reaching a total of over $1 million in 1913 dollars. The Russians got a good bargain, for Redl gave them everything except the crown jewels. He handed over the names of all Austro-Hungarian agents operating in Russia, details of KS operations, complete military plans for use of the Austrian railway system in the event of war, Austro-Hungarian military cipher systems, schematics for all Austrian forts and military installations, and, most damaging of all, the complete Plan 3, the detailed Austro-Hungarian mobilization and deployment plan to be used in event of war with Russia.

Redl had access to just about everything, because in 1905 he had been promoted to chief of staff for the Eighth Corps, the most important unit in the Austro-Hungarian army. In that position, he was involved with the full scope of the country's military mobilization plans and other important intelligence, all of which found its way to Russia. In 1908, he was able to warn Russia of the Austro-Hungarian annexation of Bosnia-Herzogovina, an action that led to an alliance between Russia and an infuriated Serbia, with consequences that resonate to this day.

All the while, Austro-Hungary had no idea that its secrets were open books to the Russians. They did not learn of the disaster until March 1913, when several KS agents who had been assigned to keep watch on mail from and to border areas noticed something interesting. They had come across two letters, both addressed to a post office box in Vienna, from Eydtkuhnen in

East Prussia near the Russian border, notorious as the site of numerous Okhrana letterboxes. The KS agents carefully steamed open the envelopes, and found 6,000 kronen in one, and 8,000 kronen in the other (about $2,700, an average workingman's annual salary in those days). No letter, no note, just money. They resealed the letters and sent them on with a surveillance operation set up to see who picked up the cash-laden envelopes.

The KS agents trailed the man in civilian clothes who eventually arrived to pick up the envelopes. They tracked him to a hotel; a check of the register revealed that the guest's name was Alfred Redl. The agents called headquarters, which went into shock. Colonel Redl? There must be some mistake.

But there wasn't. When word reached the General Staff level of Redl's treachery, a plan of action was worked out, which amounted to a coverup. Redl would be offered a pistol to be used in the traditional officer's honorable way out: suicide. It would then be explained to the public that Redl had committed suicide from the "stress of overwork." Only 10 senior military officers would know of the real circumstances of Redl's death; sworn among themselves to secrecy, no word of the colonel's treason would leak out. Not even the Emperor Franz Joseph would be told the truth of the highly-regarded colonel's death.

A few nights later, four grim-looking officers in full uniform appeared at the hotel room in which he was staying. "I know why you have come," Redl said. He asked for a pistol, which one officer handed him. With a slight bow of thanks, Redl asked to be alone. The officers waited outside the front door. In a short while, they heard a shot. Reentering the room, they found Redl sprawled in front of a dressing mirror; he had stood in front of the mirror and watched himself as he blew his brains out.

The next stage of the coverup began with the entry into Redl's home to retrieve evidence; when the two officers assigned the job couldn't find Redl's keys, they hired a locksmith. It might have worked except for Hans Wagner, the locksmith who had to explain his absence to angry soccer teammates. The first newspaper story only whetted the public's appetite for more, and within a few days, the Austro-Hungarian government had a full-fledged scandal on its hands. Like a military force retreating before a huge enemy host, the army high command handed out one cover story after another, each one looking more frayed with still further revelations. Gradually, the whole truth emerged, but it was rendered somewhat academic by the onset of World War I.

And it was then that the full impact of Colonel Redl's treason became apparent. Although the Austro-Hungarian high command knew the Russians possessed Plan 3, such plans—involving mobilization schedules, troop movements, and logistics—were extremely intricate and often ran to many volumes. The plans were not easy to change, so the Austro-Hungarians went to war against an enemy who knew their main operational plan. As a consequence, the Austro-Hungarians suffered a military disaster in Galicia, with 500,000 casualties, a defeat from which it never recovered. Less than four years later, the empire of Austro-Hungary collapsed into the dustbin of history.

Redl's suicide prevented any full exploration of the mental process that had led him to treason. He left only a brief suicide note that explained very little: "Levity and passion have destroyed me. Pray for me. I pay with my life for my sins."

THE SPYMASTERS

K'ANG SHENG

Alias: Zhang Shuping
1898–1975

TAI LI

1895–1946

Terror in China

Shanghai in 1927 was not a city for the faint of heart. With its large international settlement, headquarters for almost all major businesses operating in China, and competing Chinese political factions, the city was in ferment. It was also an important crossroads of international espionage and the main battleground in a no-quarters struggle between the Communists and non-Communists seeking to take control of the country.

This seething cauldron produced two remarkable spymasters who were to spend the next 20 years in a deadly battle that would ultimately cost millions of lives. One would triumph, although the word must be used advisedly in a nation where the price in blood for that victory was very high. In truth, the Chinese people faced something of a choice of two evils with these two men, since one was known as "the **Beria** of China," and the other as "the Himmler of China."

The eventual victor was K'ang Sheng, the Communist spy chief who ranks as the most remarkable man in the long history of Chinese espionage. Unlike most of his Communist revolutionary contemporaries—particularly his close friend Mao Tse-tung—Sheng came from a wealthy background. He was born in 1898 as Zhao Jung, the son of a wealthy landlord, but as a teenager, turned away from his family and adopted the name K'ang Sheng as a protest against his father's exploitation of the peasants. By 1922, he was a revolutionary; two years later, a university student, he was among the early members of the Chinese Communist party. Soon,

170

K'ang Sheng, Communist China's spymaster. (*Eastfoto*)

he came to the attention of party leaders by demonstrating a flair for espionage. He organized an informal spying operation to ferret out police spies from the party, an operation he extended to include spying on "dissidents" in the party who failed to demonstrate sufficient zeal in toeing the latest party line.

In 1927, Sheng was to cross paths with the man who would become his hated rival. Tai Li, born in 1895 in the same village that had produced Chiang Kai-Shek, was the son of a poor peasant. Like Sheng, Li also became a revolutionary, but his zeal took a very different turn. At the age of 14, he joined a warlord army, and later enrolled in Chiang Kai-Shek's organization. Fanatically loyal to Chiang, Li turned his energies toward espionage, creating a network that kept tabs on Chiang's supporters for any sign of deviation.

The 1927 clash between Sheng and Li took place in Shanghai, where a Communist uprising convulsed the city. Sheng, one of the leaders in the city's Communist underground, was simultaneously running spying operations against the Shanghai police to detect its next moves and unleashing a rule of terror against defectors from the Communist cause. Many of them were murdered by a platoon of killers Sheng had recruited from among the city's underworld.

Li, meanwhile, was in charge of operations to put down the uprising. Demonstrating the kind of ruthlessness that would make his name as infamous as Sheng's, Li subjected the city to his own reign of terror. He played a key role in the suppression of the revolt, which featured the special fate he meted out to captured Communist revolutionaries: they were thrown into the red-hot boilers of steam locomotives.

And so the battle lines were now drawn between Sheng and Li. Both men rose rapidly in the hierarchies of their respective political movements. In 1931, Chiang named Li head of the innocuously-named Bureau of Information and Statistics, the Nationalist movement's intelligence agency. Li recruited over 300,000 agents and blanketed China with a network of informants and agents directed to concentrate all their energies on Li's consuming obsession, the Communists. Li sought to create the impression that his agency had eyes and ears everywhere. His reach even extended to prostitution: he created a network of brothels staffed with women trained to wheedle out secrets from their customers. The brothels were highly specialized, ranging across every possible sexual taste. His most famous, called "The House of One Thousand Assholes," catered to a homosexual clientele, with the aim of obtaining information from homosexuals on what they might know about Communists—or any other subject of interest.

Sheng, meanwhile, had been named head of a special party section known as *Shehuibu* (Department of Special Tasks), which was the Chinese Communist intelligence service. The energetic Sheng organized his own networks of informers and mounted elaborate operations to infiltrate his agents into the ranks of Li's intelligence agency. The result was a clandestine war in which bodies from both sides routinely littered the streets. In an espionage war of no quarter, both sides played by the same rule: a man or woman even suspected of working for the other side was tortured to death, the body left for all to see as a warning. Li rarely took part personally in these atrocities, but Sheng did. A sadist, he enjoyed participating in the most horrible torture sessions, and became known even among his closest aides as "the king of hell" for his love of inflicting agony on other human beings.

There were other character defects that made some of the senior party leaders nervous about Sheng. He was a heavy user of opium, an opportunist, power-mad, and totally ruthless. But given his close friendship with Mao, nobody was about to criticize the man Mao thought essential for the security of the beleaguered Communist movement. (Sheng further cemented his relationship with Mao by providing the party's leader with a steady supply of nubile young women to slake Mao's apparently limitless appetite for female flesh).

By 1938, Sheng's influence within the party leadership was very high. He had been elected to the party's Central Executive Committee, and in that role was sent to the Soviet Union at Stalin's invitation to receive KGB training. His stay in the Soviet Union would prove significant, for Sheng, a shrewd judge of men, concluded that the Russians were not really the fervid supporters of Chinese Communism they claimed to be. Sheng's misgivings, conveyed to Mao, mark the real beginning of the Sino-Soviet split. For evidence, his agents had collected a considerable amount of intelligence on how the KGB was actively recruiting within the Chinese Communist party to develop its own assets who spied on Mao and other party leaders.

Sheng hurried back to China to help combat the Japanese invasion, but it never crossed his mind to join forces with his enemy Li in the name of fighting a common enemy. Throughout the war, Sheng and Li both spent most of their time trying to infiltrate and neutralize their respective competing intelligence services. Both men were looking ahead to the day when the Japanese would be defeated—an eventuality considered inevitable— and the final battle in their own private war would take place.

Li sought to improve his chances by an alliance with the Americans by means of an extensive propaganda campaign that sought to portray the Nationalist movement as the "true" representative of the Chinese people. He extended his Bureau's operations worldwide, recruiting a number of prominent Chinese-Americans who formed the nucleus of what would become the influential "China Lobby." The result was a growing Nationalist-American bond that was to create serious problems later when the United States decided to give full backing to the Nationalists in the Chinese Civil War. During World War II, Li forged close links with the American military and intelligence establishments, climaxed in 1943 when he was named director of the Sino-American Cooperation Organization (SACO), a joint operation to run anti-Japanese guerrilla units.

But Li's abiding concern remained the Communists, and throughout the war, he and Sheng remained at each other's throats. Both sides routinely murdered each other's agents as they jockeyed for the dominant position after the war. Sheng, the better organizer and planner, gradually began to get the upper hand, an advantage he demonstrated in 1944 by obtaining a piece of intelligence that later would have significant consequences.

Both Li and Sheng worked actively to infiltrate the groups of assets recruited by American intelligence in China, especially the OSS. Sheng developed one source—never identified—who passed on the astonishing news, obtained from a talkative senior OSS officer, that the United States was working on an atomic bomb that would soon bring the war in the Pacific to an end. Sheng pointedly did not pass on this intelligence gem to the Russians, and prepared his own plans. He began an immediate operation to recruit Chinese-born scientists working in the United States, especially those involved in nuclear physics. He succeeded in luring two of them back to China, where they went to work to develop a Chinese atomic bomb. Some years later, when the Chinese government decided on a crash program to develop nuclear weapons, Sheng already had a scientific nucleus that had been at work on the problem for some time.

Li had no equivalent intelligence triumph, but he did have an advantage Sheng lacked: the United States. As the relationship between the Americans and the Nationalist government deepened, the American supply line began to hum with weapons and supplies to help defeat Mao's forces. Li, who handled many of the arrangments, further cemented his relationship with American intelligence. The Americans, in the name of political pragmatism, tended to overlook some of Li's less attractive qualities, including the network of concentration camps he set up to imprison "enemies of the state," defined as any Chinese citizen who ever uttered even a mild criticism of Chiang.

By early 1946, as the civil war raged across China, Sheng decided that Li would have to go. Not a simple task, for Li was always surrounded by tight security, kept his movements secret, and avoided sleeping in the same bed for more than two nights in a row. Some of Sheng's agents finally managed to infiltrate Li's inner circle and made an interesting discovery: Li was totally smitten by a beautiful actress named Butterfly Wu. She happened to be married, an inconvenience Li removed by offering the husband a huge bribe to disappear. That problem out of the way, Li began a regular series of trysts with Wu, secretly flying to her home in Shanghai (where she acted in Chinese movies) from his base of operations in Chungking.

Armed with this intelligence, Sheng then approached the pilot of Li's personal plane with an extraordinary offer: In exchange for a suicide mission, in which he would dive his plane into the ground the next time Li was aboard, the pilot's entire extended family would be lavishly compensated for the rest of their lives. The pilot accepted, and one night in May 1946, he dove the plane into the ground a few minutes after takeoff. He and Li were instantly killed. The pilot's family never did collect their reward, however. Li's agents, suspecting some kind of murder plot in the crash, ultimately found out out what happened, and kidnapped all the members of the pilot's family, then tortured them to death.

With Li the spymaster gone, his Bureau of Investigations and Statistics gradually withered on the vine. Bereft of his energetic leadership, the agency fell apart before repeated assaults by Sheng and his agents. In 1949, when Mao's forces triumphed, Sheng became the intelligence master of all China. Anyone who thought the replacement of Li by Sheng in that role would lead to less oppression was soon disabused. Sheng organized the vast purges that swept China, and opened his own concentration camps, which he called "reeducation centers," where "improper thought" was corrected in conditions that rivalled Auschwitz. As a result, party leaders began calling Sheng the "Beria of China" behind his back.

There was much worse to come. In 1958, Sheng, at Mao's behest, organized the "great leap forward," an industrialization campaign that turned China into an anthill, with all individuality suppressed in the name of "Mao's thought." Later, he organized the "great cultural revolution" that further suppressed the last flicker of individual freedom in China. The total number of victims in all these violent spasms may never be known for certain, but the estimates run into the tens of millions.

In the process, Sheng became a fanatical ideologue who had drawn even closer to Mao; it was Sheng's well-known Russophobia that played an important influence in Mao's decision to split with the Soviet bloc. Sheng became indispensable to Mao, but his service ended in 1970, when he became incapacitated by cancer. He died five years later, but by that time, things had started to change in China. In 1980, the new Chinese leadership posthumously expelled Sheng from the Communist party, calling him "an enemy of the Chinese people."

MARKUS WOLF
The Hour of Karla

1923–

On a warm spring day in 1979, an East German HVA agent named Werner Stiller walked through Checkpoint Charlie in East Berlin and announced his intention to defect. In that crossroads of Cold War espionage, defections were not especially rare, but this one was quite different. Stiller was greeted as though he had arrived with the Holy Grail.

The avid interest shown in Stiller by the West German, American, British, and French counterintelligence services was only partly related to the fact that he knew the identity of HVA and KGB moles operating in West Germany. (Stiller blew 17 of them, and another five fled eastward the moment they became aware of his defection). The real focus of interest in Stiller was because for the first time the West could gain insight into the man they called "Karla," the mysterious East German spymaster who had been making fools of them for years.

"Karla" was not the spymaster's code name; it was used in the novels of John Le Carre to represent the fictional superspy based on a real character, Markus Wolf of the HVA. Stiller, a close personal friend and protégé of Wolf, could now shed some light on the man who was ranked as the most brilliant spymaster in Cold War espionage.

Like the fuzzy outlines of a photo print becoming sharper in a developing tray, Stiller's debriefings fleshed out the details of Markus Wolf, both as a man and as a spy chief. In terms of

East German spymaster Markus Wolf, the model for John Le Carre's fictional "Karla," in 1989 as his country's regime was collapsing. (*AP/Wide World*)

background, Wolf's antecedents revealed a certain familiar pattern for German Communists. Born in 1923, Wolf was the son of the Communist playwright Friedrich Wolf, who as a Jew and a Communist, realized he had no future under a Hitler regime. Two months after Hitler took power, Wolf and his family fled to the Soviet Union.

Initially, Wolf's son had ambitions of becoming a diplomat. He studied at the Comintern schools in Moscow, then took university degrees in diplomacy. In 1945, he was first consul of the new East German mission in Moscow. In contrast to the colorless *apparatchiks* who dominated the first East German government, Wolf was independent-minded, youthful, energetic, had an amazing grasp of technical detail, and was highly intelligent. These qualities attracted the attention of a number of younger Soviet officials who were chafing under the deadening hand of Stalin; in Wolf, they saw a kindred soul who represented the future of communism. Chief among them were Alexandr S. Panyushkin, an important *eminence grise* in the Soviet diplomatic and intelligence establishments, and his own protege, Yuri Andropov, then a diplomat with a finger in KGB operations. (Some 30 years later, Andropov became head of the KGB). Both men decided that Wolf's considerable talents were better suited for intelligence work in the newly-created East Germany. It was in Germany, Panyushkin argued, that the great battles between east and west intelligence would be fought. As he was aware, the first East German intelligence structure was dominated by "old fighters" from pre-Hitler days, the kind of men who spent two decades in underground work against the Nazis. Commendable, but not very good preparation for the very different world of postwar espionage.

To a certain extent, the Soviet calculation took note of an interesting figure on the other side. Reinhard Gehlen, the wartime head of *Fremde Heeres Ost* (Foreign Armies East), the German military's front-line intelligence unit on the eastern front, had won a reputation for honest and amazingly accurate evaluations of Soviet military strength while demonstrating ability in running a huge structure. Fired in 1945 by Hitler—who demanded that he be locked up in a lunatic asylum—Gehlen deserted to the Americans. Later, they set him up in West Germany with lavish CIA funds to run something called The Org, a sprawling intelligence apparatus designed to infiltrate East Germany and the rest of the Eastern Bloc.

Faced with this sort of challenge, the KGB reached out to Wolf and recruited him for a revised East German intelligence structure. The key component of that structure was an arm called Main Department IX, which ran foreign intelligence operations, with emphasis on West Germany. When Wolf was named its head in 1954 at the young age of 31, it was a clear signal of the regard in which he was held by the KGB. He repaid that confidence almost immediately, organizing a vast infiltration operation against West Germany that eventually was to honeycomb the country's governmental structure with interlocking rings of assets who kept the HVA (and, by extension, the KGB) informed of just about everything worth knowing.

Two years later, in recognition of his brilliance, Wolf became head of the HVA. Known as the KGB's fair-haired boy, it turned out that he had a few tricks to teach his masters. His most striking innovation was the concept of "seamless penetration," a technique involving obtaining the passports and other papers of West Germans who had moved to other countries. Wolf would then recruit East German assets who matched the personal details in those papers as closely as possible. Subsequently, they would be infiltrated into West Germany with "clean" backgrounds very difficult for counterintelligence to spot.

Another innovation was his "secretaries offensive," which involved the recruitment of handsome young East Germans assigned the specific task of infiltrating West Germany under the guise of refugees and striking up relationships with government secretaries. Not just any secretary; the idea was for the men to woo the plain-looking, lonely spinster types who seemed to make up a large portion of the government secretarial force. Wolf's young men prowled the bars, resorts, and vacation spas to find lonely, middle-aged secretaries who would be swept off their feet by the amorous attentions of handsome men. Once the seductions had been completed, the men would get the secretaries to bring home government documents to be photographed and dispatched eastward via microfilm.

At the same time, Wolf was busily combatting Reinhard Gehlen's Org, which became the West German foreign intelligence agency BND in 1955. In a covert war later immortalized in John Le Carre's *The Spy Who Came in From the Cold*, Gehlen and Wolf conducted the battle of moles, infiltration, counter-infiltration, double agent, and triple agent. The battle was even until Wolf went to work on Gehlen's chief vulnerability, his tendency to hire ex-SS, SD and Gestapo agents without detailed background checks on the assumption that such men obviously had no pro-Communist sympathies.

The assumption proved wrong in the case of Heinz Felfe, an ex-SD official who during the war worked in counterespionage operations against the KGB. Felfe had been a rabid Nazi, but was also virulently anti-American and anti-British for the terrible destruction of his beloved birthplace, the city of Dresden, during Allied fire-bombing raids in 1945. Aware of this interesting schizophrenia, Wolf and the KGB went to work on Felfe, who was recruited as an asset. The next step was to have Felfe infiltrate the BND, accomplished by providing Felfe with a lot of low-level (but nevertheless impressive-looking) material on the KGB and the HVA. Gehlen enlisted the ex-SD man, and Felfe was off and running. In a brilliantly-managed operation, Felfe was fed a steady diet of material from the east that enhanced his credentials as a brilliant counterintelligence officer. In some cases, the KGB and the HVA deliberately sacrificed some of their lesser agents in West Germany to further bolster Felfe's credentials. The Felfe operation reached its pinnacle in 1958, when he was named head of the Soviet counterintelligence section of the BND and the agency's liaison with the CIA and other Western intelligence agencies.

The later exposure of Felfe* as a KGB/HVA asset destroyed Gehlen, who was forced to resign in the ensuing scandal. Wolf then moved to his next operation, which would become the crowning achievement of his career.

The idea, basically, was to infiltrate the office of German chancellor Willy Brandt. Not by means of a seduced secretary or other low-ranking asset, but a full-scale mole who could get close to Brandt and obtain access to all the material that came across the Chancellor's desk. Wolf studied the problem for some time, emerging with a plan that illustrated the kind of patience necessary for long-term mole operations.

Wolf learned that in his pre-World War II days in the anti-Nazi underground, Brandt had been treated by a Communist doctor, Max Guillaume, who later fled Germany, eventually settling in East Germany after the war. He remained a committed Communist and his son Guenther, Wolf learned, had also become a devoted Communist. Wolf approached both men and recruited them for what he described as a "long-term operation" in West Germany. The first move was for Guenther Guillaume to become a refugee; he "fled" across the border and wound up in a refugee camp. The next step: in 1956, Max Guillaume wrote a letter to his old friend, asking him to give the younger Guillaume a job. The father regretted the son's decision to flee westward, but understood and respected the decision. Could Brandt help the son of an old friend?

Brandt arranged for the younger Guillaume to be plucked out of the refugee camp and hired as an administrative assistant in Brandt's political organization. Not much of a job, but as Wolf had calculated, officials in the organization were aware that Guillaume had been given the job through connections with Brandt himself, a circumstance that tended to enhance Guillaume's career prospects. Guillaume helped things along by demonstrating a talent for organization and administration. In 1969, he was appointed private secretary to Brandt, and was switched on. A 13-year-long operation had now finally paid off; Guillaume was in a

---

* Felfe was blown by Mikhail Goleniewski, a Polish UB agent and KGB asset, in 1961. Arrested on espionage charges, he was sentenced to 14 years in prison. In 1969, he was exchanged in a spy swap, went to East Germany, and disappeared.

position to see every secret that crossed Brandt's desk (including the rather interesting information that the Chancellor had been on the CIA payroll since 1947).

The Guillaume operation ended in 1973, when it was detected by a British GCHQ decryption (Guillaume was sentenced to 13 years in prison), but the damage had been extensive: All of West Germany's diplomatic and military secrets flowed to the HVA for four years. Wolf, the man behind the operation, by this time had become something of a legend in the espionage world, with a record unmatched by any other intelligence agency. He had emasculated his chief opposition, the BND; infiltrated more than 3,000 assets into West Germany, with another several thousand sleepers; balked a number of attempts to infiltrate his own organization; and topped off all that by planting a mole inside the West German Chancellor's office.

Western counterintelligence was aware of Wolf, but since he had never served as an agent outside his own country, it was difficult to get a handle on him. Not until 1979, when his protege (and presumed successor) Werner Stiller walked into West Berlin did any of Wolf's opponents begin to get a real sense of the man. The Stiller defection was to severely dampen Wolf's operations, and he retired in 1987. But he was not ready for the rocking chair yet. Still close with the KGB, he became involved in an operation to replace East Germany's ailing leader, Erich Honecker, with a faceless "moderate" whom Moscow assumed would be able to rescue the faltering East German regime. One of Wolf's few operational failures, it was to be his last operation.

In 1990, following the collapse of East Germany, Wolf fled to Moscow under KGB protection. That shield was removed when the Soviet Union itself collapsed, and Wolf went back to Germany, proclaiming that despite the shattering events of the previous two years, he was still an unrepentant Communist. But the new German government had a long memory, and arrested him for espionage. Out on $150,000 bail, he filed a series of motions challenging Germany's right to try him, setting off complicated legal arguments that continue to this day. In 1993, he finally went to trial.

Whatever his espionage talents, Wolf seems to have no appreciation for irony. In his autobiography, written in 1992, he complained bitterly about the inequities of the German legal system that put him on trial for espionage, apparently unaware that he was undergoing due process that none of his East German countrymen ever enjoyed.

WILLIAM STEPHENSON
The Saga of Intrepid

Code Name: INTREPID
1896–1989

The most frustrated official in the entire United States government during the spring of 1941 was Assistant Secretary of State Adolph A. Berle. Assigned the major responsibility for ensuring that the United States adhered to the Neutrality Act and stayed out of the war raging in Europe, Berle found almost daily evidence that there was a British intelligence agent who had recruited many Americans to flagrantly violate the law. And no one in the American government wanted to do anything about it.

That man's name was William Stephenson. To Berle, he was a prototypical example of the British upper crust, complete with Saville Row suit, what seemed to be a permanent ironic expression, and a snobbish arch of his eyebrows. Officially, Stephenson was MI6 station chief in New York, but as Berle knew, Stephenson's mandate reached very wide: His mission was nothing less than getting the United States into the war on the side of Great Britain.

The source of Berle's frustration was the White House; every time he brought evidence of Stephenson's lastest transgressions there, he heard promises to get the problem straightened out at a high diplomatic level with the British. But nothing was ever done, and Berle began to get the impression that the White House was in collusion with Stephenson. Berle was absolutely right.

Stephenson occupied a unique niche in British intelligence, one that has not been duplicated since. In espionage terms, he

One of the few existing photographs of William Stephenson. (*AP/Wide World*)

had been assigned a dual mission: first, a traditional intelligence function, to keep an eye on German intelligence operations in the United States; second, he was to work as a covert action specialist with the objective of getting the United States into the war by any means, fair or foul. It was to this second mission that Stephenson was to devote most of his time and energy.

That mission came direct from Winston Churchill, who had ordered Stephenson's posting to New York. Churchill knew Stephenson very well, enough to know if there was one man who could carry it out, it was the man nicknamed "Little Bill" (for his bantamweight physique.) Churchill ignored the restiveness in MI6 over the appointment; Stephenson was not an MI6 officer, and had virtually no intelligence experience. But as Churchill argued, his conception of the mission in New York was very special, requiring a special man. Stephenson certainly was that.

Interestingly, despite Berle's perception of Stephenson as typical English upper class snob, in fact Stephenson was a Canadian, having been born in Winnipeg in 1896. A restless youth determined to make something of his life, Stephenson dropped out of high school to join the Royal Flying Corps and fight in

World War I. Shot down in 1917, he escaped from a German prison camp, making his way back to Allied lines by walking the entire length of Germany. On his return, Stephenson immediately sat down and wrote out a lengthy report on everything he had seen in Germany, an incredibly detailed catalog drawn from his photographic memory.

He had demonstrated the qualities necessary for a good spy, but Stephenson had higher aspirations than espionage. Fascinated with radio, he went into the radio business and invented a process of transmitting photographs via radio signals. The invention made him a multimillionaire by the age of 30, but Stephenson, a workaholic, was determined to push further. He went into the plastics and steel industries, and a few more inventions by the high school dropout brought him even further millions.

By this point, having obtained British citizenship, Stephenson had become a very patriotic Englishman. Like many of his generation, he was concerned about the rise of Hitler. To his frustration, the British government did not seem to grasp the threat that Hitler represented. But one British politician, then out of power, did: Winston Churchill. And around Churchill gathered a group of like-minded men, among them a number of industrialists and businessmen. This latter group, including Stephenson, began to function as Churchill's private intelligence service; with strong connections in German industry, they were the first to warn Churchill that Hitler was reorganizing German heavy industry for war production. Stephenson, an expert on steel mills, had visited German production facilities, and told Churchill that entire production lines were being set aside for large-scale manufacture of tanks and artillery, sufficient to equip a very impressive military force.

Churchill was impressed with Stephenson. In the spring of 1940, having decided on a bold plan for a special MI6 operation in the United States aimed at getting America into the war, he selected Stephenson for the task. Stephenson set up headquarters in New York on the 35th and 36th floors of Rockefeller Center that officially were the offices of the British Passport Control Office. But the office conducted very little official business; with only three regular MI6 officers as aides, Stephenson went right to work. He set up his radio link to London and tapped out his chosen code name, INTREPID, the first step in what would become the most successful covert action operation in history.

Stephenson had arrived in New York with two high cards. First, his appointment came from Churchill, and it was to Churchill that he reported directly, bypassing the MI6 bureaucracy— and a number of MI6 officials who were convinced that this energetic amateur would cause a disaster. Second, Churchill and President Roosevelt had reached a "private understanding" that everything would be done to evade the U.S. Neutrality Act and aid Great Britain. In effect, that made the President of the United States a co-conspirator.

Stephenson was in very murky waters, but emboldened by his top-level sponsorship, he created an empire. He took charge of all British intelligence operations in the United States, ranging from counterintelligence to port control. Given their sheer scope, it would be difficult to summarize all of Stephenson's operations. A pure buccaneer, he was in favor of any plan that worked, the bolder the better: a platoon of beautiful prostitutes hired to seduce German diplomats and pro-German American politicians; a squad of thugs retained to carry out kidnapping operations; a group of experts detailed to open and reseal diplomatic mail without a trace; several professional safecrackers assigned break-ins at embassies and consulates to steal code books.

Stephenson's firm principle was that dedicated amateurs under the proper guidance will handle intelligence operations better than the professionals. For one thing, Stephenson liked to argue, amateurs had no records as intelligence operatives and were thus unknown to counterintelligence agencies. For another, the amateurs were inexpensive to maintain, since they were working for patriotism, not money.

Stephenson recruited nearly 300 such amateurs, ranging from the unknown to such famous movie stars as Greta Garbo, Marlene Dietrich, and Erroll Flynn. Anyone who had even the slightest value would be the subject of a recruitment by the tireless Stephenson. Most were recruited for his extensive propaganda and infiltration operations against his two key targets: the intelligence and propaganda operations of Germany and its allies in the United States, and the powerful America First organization, a significant political movement that lobbied actively to keep the United States out of the war. Stephenson mounted an extensive dirty tricks campaign against the isolationists with derogatory items planted in the newspapers and on radio by means of assets he recruited among the upper levels of American journalism. He also enlisted the top newspaper columnists of the day—Walter

Lippman, Walter Winchell, and Drew Pearson—to plant items alleging indiscretions by isolationist senators.

By early 1941, Stephenson had an army of 2,000 men and women who worked on his disinformation, propaganda, and dirty tricks campaigns. Among his key assets were the mystery writer Rex Stout, who wrote propaganda pamphlets, and the famous advertising genius David Oglivy, who churned out newspaper ads for an apparently inexhaustible series of front groups Stephenson created to urge U.S intervention in the war. Americans were also bombarded with a series of lurid newspaper stories about assorted Nazi plots allegedly boring away from throughout the hemisphere. None of them were true, but they sounded good: a Nazi plan to sponsor a military coup in Bolivia and thereby seize Bolivia's deposits of wolfram, essential in the manufacture of military planes; an army of Spanish fascists being trained at secret camps in Mexico by the Nazis for an eventual invasion of the United States; a plan by Hitler to outlaw Christianity in Europe and replace crosses on churches with swastikas; and Stephenson's disinformation masterpiece, a map, said to be obtained from "secret sources" in Germany, showing a plan by the Germans to take over several weak Latin American governments and gradually extend influence northward, into the United States. The map was used by Roosevelt in a speech to underscore his plea for Congress to repeal the Neutrality Act.

Aware that Stephenson was behind all this—and a lot more, besides—Berle's complaints grew sharper. Stephenson decided to deal with the Berle problem by instituting a massive surveillance operation against him, hoping to find some dirt he could use to discredit the irksome State Department official. Stephenson's agents didn't find much, except the amusing intelligence that Berle had two adjoining bathtubs installed in his home so that he and his wife could bathe at the same time—when she would have to undergo the ordeal of listening to her husband's apparently endless political lectures.

The attack on Pearl Harbor, and the declaration of war against the United States by Germany two days later, effectively brought Stephenson's operation to a close. He spent the rest of the war running a much-reduced MI6 station and urging the Americans to set up a centralized civilian intelligence agency. His influence on that score was considerable. A close friend of William Donovan, intelligence adviser to Roosevelt and later head of the OSS, Stephenson was the guiding spirit behind Donovan's

proposal for an American centralized intelligence agency. The
plan was rejected by Roosevelt, but most of it was later adopted
in creating the CIA.

In 1945, he was knighted by a grateful sovereign; Churchill
scrawled across the nomination letter, "This one is dear to my
heart." The knighthood made no mention of Stephenson's specific services to the crown, and most people assumed he was being
rewarded because he was a prominent industrialist. Very few knew
that he was the spy chief who had organized the vast covert operation that turned around American public opinion in the two
years before Pearl Harbor. No one will ever know whether Stephenson, in the absence of the Japanese attack and Germany's
declaration of war, would have succeeded in getting the United
States directly involved in the war. But it is a fact that Stephenson
created the proper conditions for Lend Lease and the vast American supply effort that kept Great Britain alive. For that alone, his
knighthood was well deserved.

Stephenson himself was content to remain in the shadows
(rarely photographed, only one picture of him during the years
1933 to 1945 is known to exist). With the end of the war, he
decided to retire from government service, from which he never
drew a penny in salary. He had one, but very significant, last
contact with the espionage world that year when he rescued **Igor
Gouzenko**, the defecting Soviet code clerk in Canada, an action
that initiated the era of Cold War espionage.

Stephenson retired to his palatial home in Bermuda. He
emerged into the public spotlight in 1964, when one of his former MI6 aides, H. Montgomery Hyde, wrote a book that revealed
for the first time the bare-bones outline of the story of INTREPID
and the New York operation. Some years later, Stephenson cooperated in the writing of another book, *A Man Called Intrepid,* a
much fuller account that put him in the espionage pantheon.

Stephenson became a public figure again in the burst of
publicity that followed publication of the book, and settled back
into retirement when all the attention ebbed. He died in 1989,
surrounded, as he had been for many years, by newswire tickers
and telex machines that spewed out the one commodity that the
multimillionaire could never get enough of: information.

CLAUDE DANSEY
The King of Z

Alias: Haywood
Code Name: Z
1876–1947

"An utter shit," an MI6 colleague once summed up the man who was known by the deliberately sardonic nickname of "Uncle Claude" around MI6 headquarters. Apparently, it was an accurate evaluation, for there is no record that Claude Dansey was ever regarded by his colleagues except as a thoroughly miserable human being. But no one seemed to doubt that this nasty man was one of the greatest spymasters who ever lived.

Dansey's prickly personality stemmed in large measure from what modern psychiatry would call a "dysfunctional" family. Born in 1876 to an army officer, Dansey was one of nine children who grew up in an atmosphere of strict military discipline that included regular beatings for even the slightest infractions. All the siblings came to hate each other, as well as their father. At age 20, he joined the army, intending a military career (his father would not have tolerated any other choice), and in 1910, ill from the effects of service in North Borneo, he joined a new military intelligence unit known as MO5. The forerunner of MI6, the agency was almost exclusively concerned with the Irish nationalist movement. Dansey received on-the-job training in the intricacies of modern intelligence during the relentless underground struggle between the British and the Irish revolutionaries: double agents, triple agents, moles, penetrations, wiretapping. Above all, Dansey learned the value of intelligence in anticipating the kind of disasters a revolutionary movement was capable of carrying out; on at least two occasions, assets he developed within the revolutionaries were able to warn British intelligence about plans to dynamite Buckingham Palace.

In 1911, Dansey was sent to Washington, D.C., to organize operations against Irish revolutionary supporters in the United States, an assignment that brought him into contact with America's miniscule intelligence organizations. More importantly, he also made other significant contacts with American industrialists, from whom he obtained intelligence on organizing efforts by the Irish revolutionaries among their Irish workers. By then a talented administrator, Dansey was lured away from the army by an offer to run the Sleepy Hollow Club in upstate New York, an exclusive playground for American and British corporation executives, developing a network of contacts that also would prove significant.

At the outbreak of World War I, Dansey returned to MO5. Because of his extensive American contacts, he was assigned to Washington, there to work with the Americans in combating German intelligence operations in the United States. At the end of the war, he was recruited by a number of corporations to work as a general troubleshooter. But like many men who have come into contact with intelligence work, corporate life paled beside the excitement and intrigue he had known in the intelligence world. Bored, Dansey in 1929 returned to MO5, by this time renamed MI6. He was assigned as chief of station in Rome, with instructions to keep a watch on Mussolini's Fascist movement, which threatened British interests in the Mediterranean.

Dansey was not impressed by what he saw of MI6. Like every other MI6 station chief, he was given diplomatic cover in the British embassy as Passport Control Officer. MI6 had been using this cover for years, and as Dansey discovered, even the lowliest taxi driver knew that the head of MI6 operations in any given city was always the Passport Control Officer. That was just part of the problem. Its budget drastically cut back in the postwar austerity, MI6 was a mere shadow of its reputation. With little operating funds, for the most part it hired retired military officers who were expected to draw little or no salary and live on their pensions. Most were incompetent. The agency itself was under the direction of retired Admiral Hugh Sinclair, a half-mad paranoid who preferred to communicate with his people exclusively via messages left in a locked box—to which only his equally half-mad sister had the combination.

As a result, Dansey realized, MI6 didn't have a clue as to

what was going on in Europe, a continent in ferment. For his own intelligence-gathering, Dansey preferred to rely on the network of corporation contacts he had developed; businessmen, he discovered, knew much more about the true state of the world than MI6 intelligence officers. Accustomed to cold-blooded assessments that focused on the bottom line, they were unencumbered by some of the prejudices that tended to afflict intelligence officers. Moreover, they traveled widely, had intimate contacts with foreign businessmen, and were their own experts. A steel company executive, for example, could walk into a foreign steel manufacturer and in a glance estimate the state of the plant's technology, its capacity, and the quality of its workers. An airplane manufacturer, with just one look, could accurately estimate the state of manufacturing technology in a foreign airplane.

As a result, Dansey began to formulate a plan. The more he saw of the MI6 networks then operating in Europe, the more he was convinced he was looking at a disaster waiting to happen. In the event of a war, Dansey concluded, those MI6 stations and the halfwits who ran them would be rolled up in a moment. There would have to be a parallel MI6 structure, in effect a second, hidden, MI6 that could take over when the inevitable happened.

Dansey slowly began to build that shadow network. From his business world contacts, he put together a network of businessmen happy to help out, and by 1936 he had a structure of some 200 executives providing him with intelligence from all over Europe. Some of them were delighted to participate for the sheer thrill of working in espionage. Their involvement, as per Dansey's firm instructions, tended to be low risk: they were never to write anything down, or attempt to take photographs, or to carry any spy paraphernalia. They were simply to keep their eyes and ears open, and later recount what they had witnessed. (Others were somewhat more ambitious, especially the film producer Alexander Korda, a born conspiratorialist, who used his film company as cover for an excuse to visit sensitive areas in Europe under the guise of scouting film locations).

Dansey called his private network the "Z Organization" after his code name, Z. Dansey got them ready for the war he was certain to begin soon. Meanwhile, he was promoted to head MI6's covert intelligence operations from its London headquarters. He had no sooner arrived in London when war broke out—as did the intelligence disaster he had long predicted.

The blow fell in the Hague, which served as the major transshipment point for all MI6 operations in Europe; the station collected material from other stations around the continent and transmitted them to London. But the Hague station, run by two retired military officers with little intelligence experience, Payne Best and Richard Stevens, had already been penetrated by one of its assets, a Dutchman who was actually working for the German SD. The SD gradually uncovered the identities of all the station's agents and assets.

But instead of simply attempting to neutralize the station, the SD decided on a radical plan to cripple British intelligence and at the same time discredit the anti-Hitler underground movement in Germany. The plan, a brainchild of a young SD officer named Walter Schellenberg (who years later would become SD chief) called for him to pose as a German military officer involved in the underground. Via his Dutch asset, he would approach the two MI6 men who were running the station and offer to provide information, in exchange for MI6 aid to the underground.

The incautious Best and Stevens snapped at the bait and agreed to a dangerous arrangment: they would meet this German officer in the town of Venlo, on the Dutch-German border. On November 9, 1939, they arrived at the meeting in a restaurant. Within minutes of their arrival, an SD squad roared across the border, kidnapped the two MI6 agents and sped back to Germany in a fusillade of gunfire with Dutch border guards.

Once in Germany, a few days at the hands of the Gestapo's tender mercies compelled Payne and Best to reveal everything they knew. It was the greatest disaster ever to befall British intelligence. Because Payne and Best occupied the critical Hague post, they knew the identities of every important MI6 agent in Europe, along with the more important assets. Within days, the entire MI6 structure in Europe was destroyed.

Having anticipated this disaster, Dansey immediately switched on his Z Organization. It is no exaggeration to say that at this moment, Dansey saved MI6. But however great his contribution, it won only grudging respect within MI6, even though he was promoted as deputy to the new head of the agency, Stewart Menzies. The problem was Dansey's personality: spiteful and vindictive with a foul temper, he hated anyone who had a university degree as a worthless dilletante; only his businessmen friends, he insisted, had the kind of down-to-earth appreciation of the real world to serve effectively. In a word, Dansey was impossible; half-blind from the effects of diseases contracted during his military service, he seemed to spend much of his time raging at the world.

Menzies grew to hate him, as did just about all other MI6 officials who came in contact with him.

But there was no question of his brilliance as an intelligence officer. Within weeks of the Venlo disaster, his Z Organization, overseen by several MI6 officers personally selected by Dansey, was up and running, providing more and better intelligence than did the old MI6 structure. Its strength was in the vital area of economic and technological intelligence; thanks to the businessmen with firsthand experience in visiting German industrial plants, Dansey had a comprehensive overview of the size, scale, and capabilities of the German industrial machine (an insight which convinced him that machine was not up to the demands of total war).

In 1941, Dansey was handed an assignment that looked impossible to fulfill. It represented an especially knotty problem: thanks to its ULTRA decryptions, the British concluded that Germany was about to invade the Soviet Union. With the actual source concealed, the intelligence was passed on to Stalin, along with information pinpointing the exact day of attack and a list of all the German units participating. Stalin, who had rejected all intelligence from his own spy services that told him the same thing, rejected the British intelligence as a "provocation."

The invasion, when it took place, created a dilemma for the British. Thanks to ULTRA, they had a precious insight into German military plans on the Eastern Front, but they were not about to let Stalin know that this intelligence came from the greatest code-breaking operation of all time. The concern was only partly related to fears that if given to the Russians, the ULTRA would leak out somehow to the Germans; actually, the British had plans to use ULTRA for reading Soviet traffic at some point—plans that would be obviated by any premature disclosure. On the other hand there was a lot at stake, for the bulk of German military power after June 1941, was occupied on the Eastern Front. At all costs, the Soviet Union had to be kept in the war, for in Churchill's cynical but accurate phrase, the two scorpions were bleeding each other to death. The idea that all that military might now directed against the Soviet Union would be turned against Great Britain in the event of a Soviet defeat was unthinkable.

So the question was how to convey ULTRA intelligence while concealing the great secret and at the same time convince Stalin that it did not emanate from the British, whom the Russian dictator intensely disliked and distrusted. Dansey's solution was at once intricate and elegant.

One of Dansey's operatives in Switzerland was aware of the existence of a large-scale Soviet espionage network in that country known to the Germans as *Rote Drei* (Red Three) because it used three separate radios to transmit to Moscow. One of the network's intelligence sources was a German expatriate named **Rudolf Roessler**, who had some contacts in his homeland providing low-scale information. Working with friends in Swiss intelligence, Dansey arranged for Roessler to be fed a diet of intelligence from ULTRA, all dealing with German plans and dispositions on the Eastern Front. At first distrustful, Moscow Center came to appreciate Roessler's intelligence, which was unfailingly accurate.

The operation ended in 1943, when the Russians, having gained the upper hand militarily, no longer needed the concealed ULTRA intelligence. Although they did not know it, Dansey's operation often provided the difference between victory and defeat on the Eastern Front.

It was to be Dansey's last achievement for MI6. Increasingly estranged from colleagues repelled by his abrasive personality, Dansey's career went into decline. As it became clearer that a German defeat was inevitable, there was less reason to overlook Dansey's character flaws for the sake of keeping him around for his brilliance in intelligence work. Put plainly, Dansey had outlived his usefulness. In 1944, he was assigned a meaningless post without much to do, and a year later, was pressured to resign from MI6 on the grounds of ill health. He left without a word of thanks (or any pension) from the organization he had done so much to save.

Ailing, he took a job as a director of Korda's Lion Films movie studio. In 1947, he died in a nursing home of heart disease. No one from MI6 came to see him in his last days, nor did any member of his family. His funeral was attended by a few old friends from the Z Organization, including Noel Coward.

Toward the end of his life, Dansey had been bothered by a strange incident. One morning he woke up to discover a large "Z" had been painted on his front door. Since only a handful of people knew his MI6 code name, Dansey tried to figure out who among them had taken this puzzling action. He never did find out, and until the end of his life he wondered aloud about it, the old intelligencer frustrated by one of the few mysteries he could not solve.

FELIKS DZERZHINSKY

1877–1926

JAN BERZIN

1889–1937

Midnight in Lubyanka

There were not many men who could make demands to Vladimir Lenin and get away with it, and Feliks Edmundovich Dzerzhinsky was one of those few. And so Lenin sat meekly nodding his head in assent one night in the fall of 1917 as Dzerzhinsky laid down his demands for the job the Bolshevik leader wanted him to do.

These demands were pretty stiff: Dzerzhinsky told Lenin he would head up a new entity called the "security subcommittee" only on condition that he be given full, unquestioned authority and not be subject to any supervision whatsoever. Lenin's acquiesence had everything to do with his respect for Dzerzhinsky, one of his oldest comrades in arms. It also bespoke a supreme confidence in Dzerzhinsky's abilities, for the task clearly was impossible.

In Lenin's conception, the security subcommittee would handle the considerable security tasks for the upcoming Bolshevik coup. As Lenin was the first to admit, the putsch was a bold gamble, fraught with danger. It could be snuffed out in a moment by either the forces of the Kerensky government then in power, or its more numerous Menshevik opponents, or its Social Revolutionary opponents, or the large remnants of Czarist forces still roaming the country, or the remaining forces of the Czarist Okhrana intelligence service—or a combination of all five. Lenin would later say that "power was laying around in the streets, waiting to be picked up," but in truth it was Feliks Dzerzhinsky who made the Bolshevik coup possible.

Feliks Dzerzhinsky (center) strategizing over a map during the October Revolution. (*Ullstein Bilderdienst*)

He moved with decisive swiftness. He had all the Okhrana officers he could find rounded up and offered a role with the Bolsheviks, under pain of death or imprisonment. From the Bolshevik power base in St. Petersburg, he seized all communications, including the post, telegraph, telephone, and even messengers. All "non-Bolsheviks" were banned from using any of these communications, so when Lenin carried out his coup, many members of the Kerensky administration did not know what was happening until it was too late. The communications blackout also served to paralyze Lenin's other opponents; by the time they tried to mobilize a countercoup, the Bolsheviks already had seized the reins of power.

However, it was one thing to seize power, quite another to keep it. In December 1917, only a month after the Bolsheviks took over—and at a time when their hold on Russia was very tenuous—Lenin asked Dzerzhinsky to set up a security force to protect the infant revolution and expand its power to the vast country. Again, the insistent Dzerzhinsky demanded, and got, total authority to do whatever he wanted without any direction whatsoever. With that authority, Dzerzhinsky proceeded to create the CHEKA, an entity that would become the largest, most extensive, and most successful intelligence organization in history. And it would make Dzerzhinsky a legend, the man commonly acknowledged to be the greatest spymaster of all time.

In the dark days of December 1917, the possibility that Dzerzhinsky and his organization would ever rise to such heights seemed remote. At the moment of its creation, the CHEKA consisted of exactly two dozen men, no headquarters, no cars or other vehicles, no budget, and no experience of any kind in either internal security or intelligence operations. But it had the mind and heart of Dzerzhinsky, the man whom Russians came to believe had been born a secret policeman.

Actually, despite his revolutionary background, Dzerzhinsky had been born in 1877 to a wealthy family of the Polish aristocracy. But he turned away from a life of privilege in 1897 when, as a university student, he joined the Social Revolutionary Party. He never explained his political transformation, but it would prove costly. Working as a courier between Social Revolutionary cells in Russia and exiles abroad, he was arrested twice by the Okhrana, and served a two-year prison sentence in a Siberian labor camp, where he worked as a coal miner. In 1903, when the Bolsheviks and Mensheviks split, Dzerzhinsky made a fateful decision: He threw in his lot with the Bolsheviks. He met Lenin, and the two men immediately hit it off, becoming lifelong friends. What attracted Lenin to this thin Pole with a wispy beard were the qualities he most admired in certain men: ruthlessness, cold-blooded dedication to the revolutionary cause, acute clear-headedness, and organizational talent. As Lenin understood, there were two obsessions that dominated Dzerzhinsky's life: serving as the "sword and shield" of the Bolshevik revolution; and, even more importantly, creating a Communist government in his homeland of Poland.

But before such dreams could be achieved, Dzerzhinsky faced the considerable challenge of keeping the infant Bolshevik regime alive. There were plenty of threats to that regime. For one thing, Russia technically was still at war with Germany, and German forces were decimating a demoralized Russian army. Second, there were large forces of anti-Bolsheviks (known as "Whites") who had seized entire chunks of Russian territory and were proclaiming a holy crusade to destroy the Bolsheviks. Third, Western nations, concerned over Lenin's vow to sign a separate peace

treaty with Germany and take Russia out of the war, were openly
threatening intervention.

Within weeks of creating the CHEKA, Dzerzhinsky began to
demonstrate the talents that led fellow Bolsheviks to nickname
him "Iron Feliks." He recruited thousands of agents, most of
them brutal and semi-educated, who were subject to their boss'
simple rule of discipline: do what you're told, otherwise face immediate execution or life imprisonment. "We stand for organized
terror," Dzerzhinsky announced, as he unleashed his flying
squads all over Russia, with orders to wipe out any dissent to the
Bolshevik regime. Almost overnight, he created a sprawling
CHEKA bureaucracy, moving its headquarters from St. Petersburg (renamed Leningrad) to a Moscow building that had once
been the headquarters of an insurance company. Dzerzhinsky
converted it into offices and jail cells. The CHEKA's new location,
on Lubyanka Street, soon became the most infamous address in
all Russia; Muscovites actually would walk blocks out of their way
rather than use the sidewalk in front of the building. Their fear
was understandable; thousands of their fellow citizens were dis-
appearing behind those walls, the only clue to their fates arriving
some weeks later in the form of a short, curt notice to their families that they had been found guilty of unspecified "counterrevolutionary activities" and executed.

In Lubyanka, as the CHEKA headquarters became known,
Dzerzhinsky worked up to 20 hours a day. Like an ascetic monk,
he spent days and nights closed off in a small room poring over
records and files. Constantly wracked by coughs, the result of the
tuberculosis he contracted during his Siberian imprisonment, he
sat for hours under the glare of a single, powerful electric light,
absorbing details and slowly hatching his plans. Occasionally,
brought a stack of death warrants, he scribbled his name across
the bottom.

By the early months of 1918, Dzerzhinsky had established
tight CHEKA control of the country, an astonishing feat considering the outbreak of civil war, pressure from outside powers (the
United States, Britain, Japan, and France had dispatched troops
to seize territory), and the general breakdown of communications. CHEKA strength neared 100,000, supplemented by a huge
network of informers Dzerzhinsky created.

With tight domestic control established, Dzerzhinsky now
turned his attention to some of the foreign intelligence threats
confronting the new regime. He recruited a staff of some of the

brighter CHEKA agents* and formed a counterespionage section, which targeted several Western embassies as the probable sources for a large-scale covert operation to overthrow Lenin's regime. They turned out to be right: The Americans, British and French were jointly organizing anti-Bolshevik elements to overthrow the Bolsheviks in a Western-supported coup that called for the arrest of all Bolshevik leaders, who would be paraded down the main street of Moscow in their underwear—to be followed by their execution.

Dzerzhinsky devised a typical solution to the problem. He created a whole new organization of alleged dissidents, a group of Latvian soldiers who served as Lenin's praetorian guard. The commander of the unit approached Western diplomats and offered to put his men at their service. Subsequent meetings with the incautious diplomats revealed most of the details of the coup plot. Aided by still another asset he had developed—a Communist French diplomat—Dzerzhinsky soon had a complete picture of the coup plan, along with details of a series of networks that had been recruited by MI6 and U.S. State Department Intelligence.

In the fall of 1918, Dzerzhinsky struck. In a series of sweeps, he arrested all the agents and assets, including the chief American spy in Russia, Xenophon Kalamatiano, a Greek-American businessman. (One MI6 agent was killed in a shootout). Dzerzhinsky's victory was total: Virtually all Western intelligence assets in Russia, more than 200 people, disappeared behind the walls of Lubyanka, a blow from which the West never recovered.

This was but a mild prelude to the next spasm of terror, which erupted after a Social Revolutionary tried to assassinate Lenin. Infuriated by the attempt on the life of the man he almost worshipped, Dzerzhinsky unleashed what he called the "Red Terror." For starters, he rounded up 500 ex-officials of the Czarist regime, none of whom had any connection with the assassination attempt that resulted in the severe wounding of Lenin, and

---

* Among them was Jakov Peters, a Latvian revolutionary who had fled to London in 1903 after imprisonment by the Okhrana for revolutionary activism. Working as a pants-presser, Peters joined a group of Anarchists who carried out a jewel robbery in which four policemen were killed during a shootout. Peters was acquitted of murder in a trial that featured his alibi, one that became the most famous in British legal history: He claimed he was home fixing a mousetrap at the time of the robbery. Later, he went to Russia to join Lenin, and was recruited for the CHEKA by Dzerzhinsky. He was executed in 1937 during Stalin's purge.

had them shot on the spot. Then, thousands of Russians were rounded up and shipped off to Lubyanka; almost all of them never returned.

Such terror had Lenin's full-hearted approval, and he began to use Dzerzhinsky as a general trouble-shooter for various intractable problems. For example, concerned that foul-ups in the railway system were preventing food from reaching Russian cities, Lenin named Dzerzhinsky Commissar of Railroads. The first day on the job, Dzerzhinsky traveled to one station where delays of food shipments were reported. He called a meeting of all railway officials in the area, announced that two of them were primarily responsible for the delays, and had them shot on the spot. No further delays were reported.

But there was one problem Dzerzhinsky could not solve: Poland. Determined to bring that nation back into the Russian fold, the Russians had invaded in 1920, and early successes led Lenin to appoint Dzerzhinsky as head of a Polish Soviet, with instructions to prepare for a Communist government following the inevitable Russian victory. But Polish resistance stiffened, then rallied to inflict a defeat on the Russians.

Dzerzhinsky returned to Russia to face a new threat, but this one came from within the Bolshevik government. Not all the Bolsheviks had been enamored of his methods, most prominently Leon Trotsky, head of the Red Army. In Trotsky's view, Dzerzhinsky had too much power; having one man in charge of both internal security and foreign intelligence was a dangerous precedent. To clip Dzerzhinsky's wings, Trotsky decided to form his own intelligence organization, first known as the Fourth Department of the Red Army, later the GRU. To staff it, Trotsky recruited a number of promising army officers, along with some CHEKA agents. Among this latter group was a Latvian who had already demonstrated a flair for espionage. His name was Jan Berzin.

At the time, Trotsky had no idea of the significant role Berzin's recruitment would play in the history of Soviet intelligence. Berzin, whose real name was Peter Kyuzis, had been a revolutionary most of his youth, and by 1919, considered among the brightest of the revolutionaries, at the age of 30 was one of the leaders of the Latvian Soviet. Their attempt to impose a Bolshevik-style revolution in Latvia failed, and Berzin fled to the Soviet Union. There, he was recruited by Dzerzhinsky for the CHEKA. His abilities were recognized early, and by 1920, he was an official in the agency's Registry Section, which handled foreign intelligence operations. A year later, to Dzerzhinsky's annoyance, he transferred to the new GRU.

Berzin had been critical of the way the CHEKA ran its first foreign intelligence operations. He was unhappy with its reliance on foreign Communists for espionage assets—Communists tended to be known by police and counterintelligence agencies, he argued—and was further displeased by the CHEKA's tendency to use some of its heavy-handed killers as foreign intelligence agents without much in the way of training. In Berzin's view, modern intelligence, especially in Western Europe, required sophisticated, cosmopolitan agents capable of working under business or other such cover.

Berzin had a chance to demonstrate his theories in 1924, when he became head of the GRU. Known by the nickname *starik* (old man) because of his completely bald head and prematurely aged features, Berzin was very popular among his agents. He instituted a rigorous training program whose every detail he supervised personally. He was close friends with many of his agents, who regarded him as brilliant and innovative. In time, some of his recruits would enter espionage immortality, among them **Leiba Domb,** Walter Krivitsky, **Ruth Kuczynski,** and **Richard Sorge.**

Dzerzhinsky was not pleased by the rise of the competing GRU, beginning a rivalry that was to continue for the next several decades—and one that finally would consume Berzin himself. Meanwhile, Dzerzhinsky was preoccupied by his own political troubles. The terror of his CHEKA had begun to cause restiveness among the Soviet public, and Lenin decided to rein in the agency's chief. First, he was ordered to carry out no further summary executions, and told that suspected "enemies of the state" would face the death sentence only if convicted in a trial. Then a government decree eliminated the CHEKA altogether, replacing it with a new entity called State Political Administration (GPU), which among other powers would have the job of screening future intelligence recruits.

Even with his powers reduced, Dzerzhinsky remained a formidable figure who still had exclusive power in running internal security and counterintelligence operations. In that capacity, Dzerzhinsky's chief worry was the nearly one million anti-Bolshevik Russians who had fled the country in the wake of the Bolshevik coup. They represented a multifaceted threat: a fertile source of recruitment for foreign intelligence agencies, a potential military force, and a possible source of infiltrators who could enter Russia across still-porous borders. Dzerzhinsky began to formulate a plan to neutralize this threat. His solution would become the most famous counterintelligence operation of all time.

The CHEKA had managed to wipe out all opposition groups during the terror, with one exception: a group of former Czarist officials who had gone to work for the Bolshevik government, but had gathered themselves into a secret opposition group that plotted ways to bring down the government. These men, known to the CHEKA as "radishes" (red on the outside, white on the inside), pontifically called their group the Monarchist Union of Central Russia, or, more commonly, The Trust. Dzerzhinsky was perfectly aware of the group, having infiltrated it with his own men. But instead of simply arresting all its members, he stayed his hand for a bigger game he had in mind.

His first move was to secretly arrest Alexander Yakushev, one of the highest-ranking leaders of the group. Dzerzhinsky's choice was deliberate: Yakushev hated the Bolsheviks, but he was not a fanatic and did not share the group's passion for violence and sabotage operations. Dzerzhinsky went to work on him, and in a series of protracted interrogations, convinced Yakushev that the anti-Bolsheviks were just as bad as the Bolsheviks. A middle ground was needed, Dzerzhinsky argued to the egostisical Yakushev, and Alexander Yakushev would be that man. Of course, there remained the problem of those fanatical anti-Bolsheviks in Europe; would Yakushev be willing to make contact with those people and tell them that The Trust, operating right inside Russia, should now be the sole representative of the anti-Bolshevik movement?

Yakushev bought it. He was let go, and began visiting various emigré groups in Europe. He told the emigrés about The Trust, as proof presenting his listeners with a ream of interesting intelligence (all of which had been carefully prepared by the CHEKA). Next, Yakushev proposed that since The Trust controlled all the safest "windows" (border entry points), the emigrés should infiltrate their saboteurs and agents only via those points.

Dzerzhinsky trumped this achievement with an even better twist: to prove that The Trust was real, he had Yakushev arrange special "tours" inside Russia. Emigré leaders were smuggled into Russia, where they were introduced to Trust leaders (all of them CHEKA agents), and shown a wide range of Trust activities.

Among them was a large underground religious service, complete with Orthodox priest (another CHEKA agent). Impressed, the emigrés returned to Europe with tales about how the Trust was running an actual underground government. As Dzerzhinsky anticipated, such wondrous tales soon attracted the attention of various intelligence agencies, who began funnelling money to The Trust, in return for apparently genuine intelligence that in fact had been cooked up by the CHEKA.* It was a perfect closed circle: Dzerzhinsky was not only in the process of infiltrating the emigré movement's operations against Russia, he was also feeding doctored information to Western intelligence—which was actually financing this grand deception.

All deceptions eventually come to an end, and so did The Trust. Increasingly suspicious about the emigrés who infiltrated Russia and never came back, the intelligence that never seemed to be quite accurate, and the odd lassitude of the CHEKA in confronting this presumably greatest of all internal security threats, the operation's targets finally concluded that they had been hoodwinked. Having achieved its purpose (and more), The Trust was closed down in late 1925.

It was Dzerzhinsky's greatest triumph—and his last. Increasingly plagued by his tuberculosis, he finally died of the disease in 1926. Without his leadership, his organization, now the KGB, entered a period of decline. Into that vacuum moved a resurgent GRU under Jan Berzin.

By 1936, when Berzin was assigned to Spain to direct Soviet intelligence operations in the civil war, the GRU reigned supreme. As a result, relations with the KGB were very tense. Berzin had made enemies in the KGB, most importantly its rising star, **Laventri Beria**, who was close to Stalin. In 1937, Berzin was summoned to Moscow "for consultations." Urged by GRU colleagues to flee, Berzin told them resignedly, "They can shoot me here or shoot me there." He went to Moscow; within an hour of his arrival, he was shot in the cellars of the infamous building on Lubyanka Street. His fate there was ultimately shared by almost everyone involved in the Trust operation, including poor Alexander Yakushev.

---

* One MI6 agent was so impressed he decided to see The Trust for himself. Dzerzhinsky was delighted, for the agent, the legendary Sidney Reilly, had escaped a CHEKA dragnet in 1918, when he worked in Moscow as part of the coup plot against Lenin. In early 1925, Reilly infiltrated Russia, and was executed.

History was to render curious verdicts on Dzerzhinsky and Berzin, the two greatest spymasters the Soviet Union ever produced. Following his execution, Berzin became a non-person; not until Stalin's death in 1953 could his name even be mentioned. He was rehabilitated, and memorialized as a great spymaster. Dzerzhinsky, on the other hand, became a near-cult figure in the Soviet Union. The area around Lubyanka Street was renamed Dzerzhinsky Square in his honor, and a huge statue of him was erected. Inside KGB headqarters, a smaller statute was built; each day, fresh flowers were placed around it. KGB officers, in a tribute to their founding father, preferred to call themselves *Chekisti* (Chekhists).

But in late 1991, the Russian people rendered their own final verdict on Feliks Dzerzhinsky: they pulled down the statue on Dzerzhinsky Square and dragged it away to a junkyard.

KENJI DOIHARA
The Snake in the Basket

1883–1948

For a man consumed with ambition, Japanese army Major Kenji Doihara did not look the part, which was precisely his problem. Despite his mastery of 11 languages (including three Chinese dialects), a brilliant mind, and membership in the Japanese Black Dragon Society, an elite club of officers dedicated to an expansionist Japan, Doihara's career in 1926 was completely stuck.

At 43 years of age, he was a little old to be a major; in a few more years, he probably would be forcibly retired, having missed his chance. Doihara was determined to do something great in a military career which to that point had featured only brief service in the Russo-Japanese War. Many of his contemporaries were moving up, to bigger and better things. Behind his back, they snickered about how the "ugly duckling" had been left behind. "Ugly duckling" was quite accurate, for Major Doihara did not give the air of a leader of men: Short and fattish, he had a plump face with a Charlie Chaplin mustache and an odd, duck-like walk that made him a comical figure.

Aware that other officers found him a laughable figure, Doihara was determined more than ever to succeed—in what, he had no real idea yet. It took some doing, but in the end the officers who laughed at him would stand in awe of Lieutenant General Kenji Doihara, the greatest spymaster in Japanese history.

How Doihara broke out of the dead-end career rut in which he found himself at middle age reveals much about the man. He approached a beautiful 15-year-old first cousin, convinced her to pose in the nude for him, then sent a batch of the more pleasing photographs to one of the princes in the imperial family. Impressed, the prince summoned the beauty to his presence, and although a relationship developed, he could not marry a commoner. But they were devoted lovers, a circumstance Doihara patiently waited to see reach full flowering. At that point, his cousin was instructed to mention to the prince about her incredibly clever and brilliant army relative who was at that moment wasting his talents in some boring staff job in Tokyo. Within a week, Doihara received orders to take a post as assistant military attache in Peking.

As far as Doihara was concerned, it could not have been more perfect: Japan had designs on China, so for a career-minded officer, that was the right place to be. Even better, Doihara discovered, upon arriving in Peking, that the Japanese embassy was busily engaged in espionage and covert political operations against the Chinese. Like a duck discovering water for the first time, Doihara had found his real milieu.

Within weeks, to the delight of his superiors, Major Doihara demonstrated a real flair for plots, sabotage, assassinations, subterfuge, bribery, corruption, and espionage. The object was to weaken the Chinese republican government, using any means, in the hope that it would gradually collapse and pave the way for Japanese conquest. His greatest stroke was his infiltration of a powerful Chinese business organization called Anfu that had high-level connections in the Chinese government. He recruited several of its members who kept him informed on what was happening inside government councils.

Doihara was also involved in much less benign actions, including his recruitment among the city's underworld for "mobs" who "spontaneously" demonstrated against the government. In one case, he fomented a riot, then gallantly dashed inside a government building to rescue several trapped government officials. In gratitude for saving their lives, they agreed to become assets for Doihara. He followed that up with a few more similarly successful operations, and by 1928, he had been promoted to colonel and hailed by his immediate superiors in reports to Tokyo as a brilliant spymaster who should now be promoted to a post of more responsibility.

Tokyo had just the assignment for him: Manchuria. China's mineral-rich easternmost province was coveted by the Japanese, who planned to seize it as soon as conditions permitted. Kenji Doihara was to create those conditions. Given carte blanche to act as he saw fit in Manchuria, Colonel Doihara was named head of Japanese military intelligence in the province.

His first step was to create a vast espionage network to cover the entire province. Actually, it amounted to three separate networks: One was composed of 5,000 Russian criminals who had fled to Manchuria after the Bolshevik revolution; the second enlisted White Russians eager to curry favor with Tokyo; and the third represented an army of 80,000 spies formed from a Chinese sect whom Doihara promised independence from the Peking government. Once he had all these men working, he then moved to the next phase of his destabilization plan, which consisted of taking control of the province's opium trade. Doihara took over the opium dens and put the traffickers on the payroll to make opium a monopoly for Japanese intelligence. He sought to enlarge the number of addicts by setting up booths at county fairs where "free medicine" was offered to tuberculosis sufferers. Actually, it was an opium derivative. He also convinced the Japanese government to manufacture a new brand of cigarette called Golden Bat, which was available for export only. No wonder: it contained small doses of opium and heroin. Sold at rock-bottom prices to Chinese, it created a whole new generation of addicts who had to buy the drug from what Doihara had made into a Japanese monopoly. In other words, the Manchurians were financing their own destruction.

Doihara's final preliminary move was to arrange the assassination of the warlord who then controlled Manchuria by means of a bomb planted on the train he was riding. While provincial authorities tried to figure out what to do next, Doihara struck: he deliberately instigated a shootout between Japanese and Manchurian troops. The Japanese, called upon by some front groups Doihara had created for just this purpose, graciously sent in large military forces to seize the province and "protect" its citizens from "rampages" by Manchurian troops. The central government in Peking, weakened by its own divisions and the years of strife engineered by Doihara and other Japanese, was in no position to argue. Japan seized all of Manchuria.

To forestall international problems, Doihara had to maintain the fiction that all the turmoil in Manchuria was strictly indigenous. To that end, he hit upon a curious stratagem: He went to Peking and tried to enlist Henry Pu-Yi, the last emperor of

China (at that point a strictly ceremonial post) into becoming emperor of Manchuria. Pu-Yi hesitated, and while he was trying to make up his mind, received a basket of fruit at his front door—which contained a poisonous snake at the bottom. Doihara hurried to his side, and convinced the naive aristocrat that he was now the subject of plots by unspecified enemies and needed Japanese protection. Doihara, not bothering to mention that it was he who had sent the fruit basket, whisked Pu-Yi to Manchuria to become emperor. Too late, Pu-Yi realized he was nothing more than a puppet (an incident later reprised in the movie *The Last Emperor*).

With Manchuria firmly in Japanese hands, Doihara next turned his attention to the rest of China. Following his standard pattern, he created a full range of destabilization efforts in China's southern provinces, including riots, murders, and a tenfold leap in the opium trade. Doihara's reach seemed to be everywhere; Chiang Kai-Shek executed eight of his divisional commanders after he discovered they were on Doihara's payroll. By 1938, when the Japanese invaded southern China, Doihara had created the proper conditions, defined by one Japanese authority as a "moral desert" in which the Japanese army could move unimpeded.

But Doihara could only do so much. The Japanese simply did not have sufficient strength to simultaneously carry out a major land war in China and an invasion of the South Pacific. After Pearl Harbor, war with the United States preoccupied Japan, and China became a military backwater. Doihara continued to work in China until 1944, when he was reassigned to Malaya. In 1945, he was ordered back to Japan, where he was to organize the last-ditch defense against the anticipated American invasion. From his Tokyo headquarters, he heard the reports of Japan's disaster in Manchuria, where Soviet forces in four days destroyed Japanese forces. At home, whatever plans he might have made to fight the Americans were obviated by Japan's surrender.

Doihara was captured by the Americans, who put him on trial as a war criminal. There was much he had to answer for, none of which was even remotely defensible—notably, the chief count in the indictment against him, his role in the opium trade. Convicted, he languished in prison while his appeals were underway. In November 1948, he was executed, representing one last achievement of Japan's ugly duckling: He was the only spymaster on record ever convicted for crimes committed in the name of espionage.

THE INFAMIES

LAVENTRI BERIA
"Give Me a Man"

Alias: Yenon Lidze
1888–1953

" Give me a man and I'll give you a case," Laventri Beria was fond of saying with his tight, reptilian smile. Uncounted millions of Russians learned the hard way that this was no joke; in the more than 15 years that Beria headed the KGB, no human being who had fallen into his clutches ever failed to do exactly what Beria wanted him to do.

There was no mystery about how Beria managed to achieve this. He created the largest and most efficient secret police organization in history, a vast empire that included hundreds of thousands of agents, millions of part-time informers, a network of prisons, hundreds of slave labor camps, and an internal security control system that regulated the movements of more than 200 million Soviet citizens. At the same time, he directed a foreign intelligence service that was the world's largest.

The man who presided over this empire was a truly terrifying human being, one of the real villains of history. Despite his reputation, he did not cut an impressive figure: balding and plump, he regarded the world with a pair of cold, lifeless eyes from behind a pince-nez. He had a small, delicate set of hands that were perpetually chilly and moist, and spoke in a flat monotone that never betrayed the slightest emotion. An unfeeling, lifeless killer, he was reputed to have no friends—except Joseph Stalin. In terms of Beria's job, Stalin was the only friend he needed.

Beria first met Stalin in 1915, when, as a 27-year-old revolutionary, Beria was a fugitive in the hills of his native Georgia.

He had just escaped from a Czarist prison after being sentenced to death for "revolutionary activity," defined as agitating for communism among university students. In the hills, he contacted the leader of the Georgian Communist underground, Stalin, from whom Beria obtained arms and an order to foment an armed revolution among the oilfield workers at Baku. The uprising failed, and Beria had to flee for his life, escaping through Czarist police checkpoints disguised as a woman.

When the Bolshevik revolution broke out, Beria was head of a group of 500 Austrian prisoners of war who had converted to communism and were now willing to become shock troops. Under Beria's command, they successfully fought in the civil war, a success that brought Beria's talents to the attention of **Feliks Dzerzhinsky**, who recruited him for the CHEKA. By 1920, he was considered among Dzerzhinsky's best agents, and was assigned to Prague to keep an eye on anti-Bolshevik exiles. In 1929, now working for the new KGB, he appeared in Paris with a new identity: Col. Yenonlidze, a former Czarist army officer who claimed that his estate and fortune had been seized by the Bolsheviks and was now eager to wreak revenge. With that legend, he was able to lure several ex-Czarist officers with him on a "mission" to Russia from which they never returned.

A year later, Beria was named head of the KGB's Foreign Office, the section that oversaw all foreign intelligence operations. The appointment represented a meteoric rise in the organization, and it had everything to do with the Beria-Stalin friendship. As Stalin consolidated his power, Beria rose with him, and in 1938, Beria was named head of the KGB. In tandem, they would become a frightening combination; it was Beria who came to represent Stalin's right arm. While Stalin maneuvered to overcome his political opponents, Beria was the man who collected the files of derogatory information, who arranged for certain anti-Stalin politicians to disappear, and who, when necessary, would fabricate evidence to discredit opponents. It was said that as their relationship deepened, Beria could actually read Stalin's mind, often anticipating where his friend's next move would come. When that move came, Beria already was prepared with the dossiers of the targets, along with tidbits of derogatory information about their sexual peccadillos and other weaknesses.

Although Beria was in charge of the KGB's foreign operations, he left that task largely to deputies and concentrated on the job of consolidating Stalin's power. In that function, Beria was to demonstrate a frightening talent for efficiency, systematizing repression of the people to a degree Dzerzhinsky could never have dreamed of.

As Stalin tightened his grip on the Soviet Union in a bloodbath of purge and liquidation, Beria developed the machinery that made the very mention of his name strike cold fear into the hearts of Russians. Among his innovations was the "conveyer" system, which amounted to a multi-step process by which those arrested would be processed, like so many sausages, along a stepped series of beatings, round-the-clock interrogations, and tortures to emerge at the final stop as totally compliant prisoners willing to confess to anything. A sadist, Beria liked to personally participate in this process; he kept a set of truncheons in his desk drawer that he used to beat certain "politicals" (men and women arrested for presumed opposition to Stalin), often to death. He ordered his top aides to participate in the beatings as a means of insuring that they shared in the dirty work and could never claim later that they knew nothing of such abuses.

For certain special cases, Beria created a "sincerity laboratory," where doctors and scientists developed new techniques of torture, along with mind-altering drugs. For those victims who were supposed to disappear without a trace, he built a special "death house" in a fancy Moscow apartment, where they were lured by experts on poisons and dispatched with an "accidental" scratch from a cane whose tip had been dipped in a deadly toxin. For defectors who had fled overseas, Beria founded a chilling organization called SMERSH (from the initials of the Russian phrase "death to spies"), a squad of expert killers dispatched around the world to murder anyone whom Stalin felt might represent a threat to his regime. (Later, during World War II, SMERSH was expanded to a small army that shot deserters, collaborators with the Germans—and all Soviet prisoners of war on the grounds that they had "betrayed" the motherland by getting captured).

As head of the KGB, Beria had the important threads of power in his hands. He carried out an extensive purge of KGB ranks, first eliminating all Jews (he shared his friend Stalin's virulent anti-Semitism), and later the Old Guard from the CHEKA days. At the same time, his repressive machinery grew inside the Soviet Union. Millions of Russians disappeared into Siberian labor camps; countless others were simply done away with. Those unfortunate enough to be put on the "conveyer" could expect to encounter a repressive machinery that had become so specialized, specific blocks of time had been allotted to convert a suspect from innocent citizen to a bloody pulp, complete with signed confession as a CIA spy, or MI6 saboteur, or anything the KGB wanted that confession to say. Beria introduced many efficiencies into the system, including a special room where suspects were brought to have mug shots taken. The camera release mechanism would be pressed twice: once to snap the picture, the second to fire a bullet into the back of the subject's head after the picture was taken.

Beria spent the war tightening the screws of his repressive machinery even further. His reach extended to careful reading of soldiers' mail; even the slightest hint of doubt about Stalin's direction of the war or the certitude of a Soviet victory would land the writer in a Siberian labor camp for 10 years. (One such victim was a young artillery officer named Alexander Solzhenitsyn, whose mild criticism of Stalin in a letter to his mother landed him in a Siberian camp. He used the experience to compile a history of the camps, *The Gulag Archipelago*).

In 1945, Stalin enhanced Beria's powers still further by naming him head of the Ministry of Internal Affairs, making him head of all Soviet intelligence, border control, and internal security forces. With that power, never achieved before or since by any intelligence chief, Beria was given two very difficult, but essential tasks: run the Soviet Union's crash program to develop an atomic bomb, and develop a strategic rocket capability. Beria accomplished both tasks in characteristic fashion, mobilizing a million slave laborers, the entire Soviet scientific establishment, and his intelligence service to produce an atomic bomb in only four years, less than a quarter of the time Western intelligence assumed it would take. Beria had mobilized Soviet intelligence to steal the bomb's secrets, then harnessed that information to a huge undertaking which constructed the test facilities, uranium mines, processing plants, and other vast enterprises necessary to build nuclear weapons. His approach to the problem of developing rockets was even more direct: he ordered a group of German rocket scientists kidnapped from Germany and brought to the Soviet Union, where they were offered lavish salaries to build a Russian version of the V-2 rocket. Beria did not need to mention the alternative; the Germans could see the vast armies of slave laborers working around the clock on the rocket testing facilities and bases the Russians were constructing. It did not require much imagination to conclude that if the Germans refused to cooperate, a man like Beria was perfectly capable of making them slave laborers, too. The Germans had no doubt of Beria's ruthlessness: they watched one day as an early rocket experiment exploded on the pad, killing over 100 Soviet technicians and army personnel. "Clean the mess up and get back to work," Beria snapped.

The success of these two projects drew Beria even closer to a grateful Stalin, who was willing to overlook some extremely odious aspects of his spymaster's private life. With a supreme power second only to Stalin's, Beria could indulge his vices, the chief one of which was little girls. Beria had little girls kidnapped all over Moscow; they were taken to his luxurious *dacha*, where he raped them. Parents of these unfortunate girls did not dare to complain. Often, Beria, on his way to work in his chauffeured limousine, would spot a pretty little girl on the street. He would order his chauffeur to pull over. Two of his accompanying bodyguards would seize the girl and throw her in the back of Beria's limousine, there to be raped and brutalized. Afterwards, more often than not, Beria would have the victim killed.

With his power at an apex, this terrifying character began to make plans for a post-Stalin Soviet Union. Aware that Stalin was ailing, Beria assumed he would succeed the dictator, a possibility that alarmed the Soviet military. Aside from their personal revulsion and fear of Beria, they also had long memories, having never forgiven Beria for slaughtering so many of their soldiers during and after the war. Curiously, despite his acute political sense, Beria was unaware of the military's hostility toward him, an oversight that was to cost him his life.

In 1953, when Stalin died, Beria made his move, in effect declaring himself the new Stalin. But Georgi Malenkov, a Politburo member who was Beria's most implacable enemy, had been busy lining up military support. One fall morning that year, when Beria arrived for a Politburo meeting on the question of succession to Stalin, he was surprised to be met by a delegation of senior military officers, who informed him he was to be put immediately on trial for "crimes against the Soviet people." Shocked, Beria heard himself pronounced guilty, whereupon one officer pulled a pistol and shot him dead on the spot.

REINHARD HEYDRICH
A Terrible Secret

1904–1942

On the morning of June 14, 1931, a recently-cashiered German naval officer traveled to a chicken farm near Munich to meet its owner, Heinrich Himmler. Named a year earlier to head Adolph Hitler's *Schutzstaffel* (SS), the Nazi leader's personal bodyguard, Himmler had summoned Reinhard Heydrich to offer him a job.

Himmler had no idea if Heydrich had any qualifications for the post, chief of a new Nazi intelligence service. But he was impressed with the 27-year-old Nazi, who had demonstrated the requisite qualities of ambitiousness and ruthlessness Himmler so admired. In 1920, Heydrich had joined the *Freikorps*, the roving paramilitary bands that plagued Germany after World War I, and two years later enlisted in the German navy. While still a naval officer, Heydrich had joined the Nazi party, where he found his true calling. By 1931, when he was dismissed from the navy by an officers' honor court for refusing to marry a prominent man's daughter whom he had impregnated, Heydrich had become a full-time Nazi functionary in the SS.

Upon his arrival at Himmler's house, Heydrich was confronted with an assignment: sit down and write out a plan for a new Nazi intelligence organization. Himmler gave him 20 minutes to complete the job.

The assignment put Heydrich in something of a quandary. He did not have the vaguest idea of how an intelligence service

The sinister Reinhard Heydrich, called by Hitler "the man with an iron heart." (*AP Wide World*)

was organized—or, for that matter, did he know anything about intelligence. Nevertheless, drawing on his memories of spy movies and novels, he quickly sketched out how he thought a modern intelligence service ought to be organized. Himmler, who didn't know anything about intelligence either, was impressed; on the spot, he appointed Heydrich head of the new service, which he called the *Sicherheitsdienst* (SD).

Although Himmler intended the SD to function as a collector of foreign intelligence, Heydrich discovered his new organization for the moment had more pressing domestic concerns, namely consolidating Hitler's grip on Germany. Heydrich first demonstrated his skills in this area in 1933, when Himmler named him to head a new "political section" of the Munich police, genesis of an organization that later became the *Geheime Staatspolizei* (Gestapo). His performance in rooting out anti-Nazis and stifling all dissent prepared him for Himmler's next big assignment, a bloodbath that became known as "the night of the long knives."

The impetus for the bloodbath was a cynical deal between Hitler and the German military. In 1934, the military agreed to support Hitler, with the proviso he eliminate his own private army, the Brownshirts, led by Ernst Roehm. The Brownshirts, known officially as the *Sturmabteilung* (storm troopers) were a collection of thugs and misfits who had achieved worldwide infamy by attacking Jews in the streets and vandalizing Jewish-owned businesses. Although Hitler had consented to the removal of Roehm and the disbanding of the Brownshirts, he hestitated; Roehm, a World War I comrade, was his oldest and closest friend.

Himmler, a rival of Roehm, called on Heydrich for assistance in inciting Hitler to action. Heydrich responded by preparing a thick set of documents that proved Roehm was planning a coup against the *Fuehrer* (all the documents were forgeries). For good measure, he also collected (true) dossiers full of graphic details about Roehm's homosexual escapades among his staff. Presented with evidence that he assumed proved Roehm was planning to overthrow him, the homophobic Hitler's resolve was further strengthened by evidence of his old comrade's "depravity."

In June 1934, armed with lists prepared by Heydrich, SS squads rounded up the entire *Sturmabteilung* leadership, including Roehm, who was thrown into a prison cell and murdered. But the SS men had other targets as well, for the lists also contained the names of Hitler's opponents across the entire political spectrum. By the time the SS men were finished, some 4,000 of Hitler's enemies had either been murdered or taken to a new institution in Germany, the concentration camp. With his enemies dead or behind the barbed wire of such places as Dachau, Hitler had become the unchallenged master of Germany.

Heydrich, the man who had collected the files and prepared the lists, basked in his share of the credit for the massacre. "The man with an iron heart," Hitler said of him admiringly, while Himmler proclaimed him the "true Nazi" and miracle worker whose ruthlessness and organizational genius would ensure the triumph of Nazism everywhere. But what neither Hitler nor Himmler knew was that at the very moment they were proclaiming the young SD chief as the very embodient of the Nazi cause, he was busy concealing his greatest secret.

The secret was something unthinkable: Heydrich was in fact part-Jewish. His maternal grandmother was Jewish, a circumstance Heydrich now moved to erase. He had all her marriage and birth records destroyed, and even arranged to have her cemetery headstone with its Star of David rooted up and replaced with a Christian headstone.

However thorough Heydrich was in erasing this secret from his past, one man in Germany knew all about it, a critical piece of information he hoped to use as insurance in a deadly bureaucratic struggle. Wilhelm Canaris, head of the *Abwehr* since 1929, was aware that Heydrich had been assigned the task of creating a Nazi intelligence service that obviously was intended at some point to subsume Canaris' non-Nazi *Abwehr.* Canaris intended to keep a close eye on his rival, and to that end, his agents had been collecting secrets about Heydrich, notably his Jewish background. (This fact of Heydrich's life later would assume a terrible irony.)

The *Abwehr* made a number of other interesting discoveries about Heydrich. Among them was the fact that Heydrich had secretly set up an expensive brothel in Berlin to service foreign diplomats stationed in the city. Called Salon Kitty, it was honeycombed with microphones and cameras to record any indiscretions by the diplomats that might prove of intelligence value. The SD had recruited a staff of beautiful prostitutes to staff the place, all of them under instruction to wheedle secrets from men in the throes of passion. It was also discovered that Heydrich himself was a regular patron of Salon Kitty, although the women who worked there dreaded his arrival because of his sadistic tastes: He got his thrills from torturing women. (The *Abwehr* learned that although Heydrich ordered all cameras and microphones be shut off during his visits, one night his aides forgot; the recorded result of one of Heydrich's escapades found its way to the *Abwehr.*)

The Salon Kitty operation was Heydrich's first in the foreign intelligence field, and for the moment, his only one. As Heydrich learned the hard way, the Nazis could not simply will a foreign intelligence service out of thin air. As a rigidly doctrinaire Nazi organization, the SD tried to develop SD networks around the world by posting its "pure Aryan" and politically correct men in German embassies overseas—where they stood out like elephants at a dinner party.

Still, Heydrich persisted, apparently believing that by sheer force of effort, the SD overnight could become something more than a secret police agency. Canaris monitored this effort with unease; although the SD was not demonstrating much success in the foreign intelligence field (a record of failure that continued until 1945),* he knew the ultimate objective was to replace his *Abwehr.* He also knew that just as he was collecting derogatory dossiers on Heydrich, the SD chief was busily assembling similar kinds of dossiers on Canaris. In Nazi Germany, *everybody* seemed to be collecting dossiers on actual or presumed bureaucratic opponents. No one better understood that fact than Canaris, who had secret vaults stashed with such powerful ammunition as the records of Hitler's treatment for insanity after World War I, secret financial deals by Martin Bormann and other Nazi leaders—and, of course, the truth about Heydrich's ancestry. For his part, Heydrich's dossiers revealed that Canaris secretly loathed the Nazis, and was hiding Jews in his organization to keep them out of the Gestapo's clutches. SD agents had also discovered that Canaris had friends in British intelligence, and that some of his aides had links with the anti-Nazi underground.

What made this deadly little game of dossiers all the more interesting was that Heydrich and Canaris were neighbors in an upscale Berlin suburb, and often spent evenings in each other's homes. There, Canaris would see a very different Reinhard Heydrich. Son of a musical conductor, he was a gifted violinist who could enthrall an audience with exquisite renditions. Canaris never failed to be struck by the odd contrast between Heydrich the sinister SD chief, whose very name was whispered in fear, and Heydrich the romantic violinist, his wide hips, high voice and long hands giving him an almost feminine appearance.

Officially, both men called each other friends, but neither was fooled; they were locked in a deadly struggle for the soul of German intelligence and a showdown was inevitable. The first serious clash came in 1936, when Heydrich approached Canaris to ask for a "loan" of some documents in *Abwehr* files dealing with the period in 1929 when the Germans secretly provided military training and other assistance to the Soviet Union. Canaris could guess why Heydrich wanted these documents, and his agents confirmed it: the SD chief was preparing a massive forgery to convince Stalin that his military chiefs were planning a coup.

---

* One famous exception was a walk-in: Elyesa Bazna, Albanian-born valet to the British ambassador at Ankara, approached the SD station in that Turkish city in 1943 and offered to sell top-secret documents he had managed to obtain from the ambassador's safe. Initially skeptical, the SD was finally persuaded by the sheer volume and quality of the material. They code-named Bazna CICERO and paid him $1.4 million in English pound notes. The British detected the leak in 1944 and used CICERO as an unwitting conduit for deception material to the SD. Bazna later that year stopped spying, intent on retiring for life on his money in Brazil. He planned to live in luxury—until he discovered that the pound notes the Germans paid him were all counterfeit.

Canaris wanted nothing to do with such an operation, so he refused Heydrich's request, and another black mark was entered against the *Abwehr* chief's name.

Three years later, there was an even more serious encounter. Heydrich told Canaris that the SD had been entrusted with nothing less than starting World War II. Hitler's plan was for the SD to create an "incident" on the German-Polish border that would provide the pretext for the Germans to invade Poland. Under the scheme, concentration camp inmates would be dressed in Polish army uniforms. An SD unit would attack a German radio station, broadcast a fake announcement of a Polish assault, then flee back to Germany. Meanwhile, the concentration camp inmates would be executed, their bodies left around the station to "prove" the Poles were responsible. Canaris argued furiously against the operation, to no avail. World War II began.

Whatever Canaris' misgivings, the success of the Polish operation elevated Heydrich to a new pinnacle of power. He was awarded overall supervision of Germany's entire secret police structure, including the criminal police and the Gestapo. In early 1942, he was given an assignment that dwarfed anything he had ever encountered in his career, a task that was nothing less than one of the great crimes of history: he was to arrange for the destruction of the Jews of Europe.

On a warm spring day that year, Heydrich convened a conference in a luxurious villa on the shores of Lake Wansee in a Berlin suburb. The site was chosen to remove the participants—the senior representatives of every department of government—from the pressures of their government offices and to an atmosphere more conducive to the task at hand. In the space of four hours, under Heydrich's crisp direction, they worked out the considerable challenges of a plan to round up the 11 million Jews of Europe and ship them to killing centers in Poland to be exterminated. The minutes of the conference, kept by the SD's chief executive in charge of killing Jews, Adolph Eichmann, recorded awe at Heydrich's masterful grasp of even the smallest detail. At the conclusion of the conference, with the plan for the so-called "final solution" worked out, everyone adjourned to sample a luxurious buffet lunch.

It was to be Heydrich's final contribution to the Nazi regime. A month later, in May 1942, he had returned to work at still another special assignment from Hitler, as head of the Nazi occupation of Czechoslavakia. One morning, on his way to work, he was shot to death by four Czech underground fighters.

Heydrich's end represented a classic, and somewhat ironic, intelligence failure: the SD, unaware of the underground threat, provided no security for its chief, who rode to work without bodyguards or any other form of protection. Whether it was true, as whispers hinted later, that Canaris was aware of the plan to kill Heydrich and did nothing to warn him, will never be known. Canaris, implicated later in the 1944 plot to assassinate Hitler, was arrested and executed. His dossiers on Heydrich and other Nazis were never found.

As for Heydrich, only one monument—the word is used advisedly—that actually mentions his name exists. It is located in what used to be the Czechoslovakian village of Lidice. Infuriated by the slaying of Heydrich, Hitler ordered that the village and all its 400 inhabitants be wiped off the face of the earth to serve as an example. SD killer squads murdered all the people, leveled the village to the ground, then plowed the area into a barren field. No human being ever lived there again.

But, of course, there are other, unmarked, monuments to "the man with the iron heart" all over Europe: the mass graves that contain the ashes of six million Jews. It is as the architect of their destruction that Heydrich will be remembered by history.

GABOR PETER
The Hunchback of Budapest
1898–1993

The 52-year-old American who walked out of a Budapest prison in 1956, blinking at the sunlight he had not seen for the past seven years, looked nearly twice his age. He also looked like a man who had emerged from a terrible ordeal: gaunt, his hair completely white, his eyes glazed. Indeed, Noel Field had undergone a nightmare that few ever survived, a nightmare that went under the name Gabor Peter.

When Field walked out of that prison, it represented the final chapter of a spy saga that had convulsed Eastern Europe for nearly a decade. Thousands of men and women perished in a madness that in fact was a carefully calculated gambit born in Moscow. Its chief instrument was the intelligence agent and secret police chief who had terrorized Hungary—a fearsome, misshapen man who was to become the most infamous secret police chief in all of Eastern Europe. And, ironically enough, this secret police chief, Gabor Peter, would be consumed by the very conflagration he started.

Peter represented a casting director's dream for a villain: An incredibly ugly man with a hunchback and a limp, he had a small face with a Hitler mustache. His most common expression was a sneer, often a prelude to a face contorted with pure fury. A sadist, he liked to personally administer hideous tortures, boasting that he had never failed to break anyone who fell into his clutches.

The man born as Benno Auspitz in 1898 in Hungary became a fanatical Communist during the Bolshevik revolution in Russia—to the distress of his father, a tailor, who hoped his son would follow in his footsteps. But Auspitz had become captivated by the idea of serving the cause of world revolution. In 1919, as a Communist uprising swept across the new nation of Hungary, Auspitz—by now using his Communist underground alias of Gabor Peter—was among the militants who seized power in Budapest. Proclaiming a Soviet republic under Communist revolutionary Bela Kun, the militants immediately moved to suppress all non-Communist dissent. Peter led an organization of terrorists who tracked down, then tortured and murdered Kun's opponents with a ferocity that led Hungarians to call Peter and his gang of cutthroats "the Red Terror."

Peter and his fellow militants fled to the Soviet Union following the collapse of Kun's short-lived republic in 1919. Those Hungarians who assumed that was the last they would see of Peter were in for a rude shock 26 years later when he returned to Hungary, this time in an even more bloodthirsty personna.

Peter seemed to have faded into obscurity in the Soviet Union, but appearances were deceiving: in fact, he had been recruited into the KGB, which saw potential in the ugly hunchback. After training, Peter served at a number of KGB stations around Eastern Europe, and in 1930, was given a plum assignment: agent in one of Europe's most important espionage centers, Vienna.

Peter, working with Theodor Maly, another Hungarian recruited into the KGB and also an ex-Catholic priest, focused their attention on a Zionist underground organization known as Blau Weiss. A Socialist group founded to provide recreational and other services for young Viennese Jews, it was trolled by Peter and Maly for promising KGB recruits. They discovered that although Blau Weiss was Socialist, it included a number of avowed Communists, among them the wife of the group's founder, Alice Kohlman Friedman. Known as "Litzi," Friedman had divorced her husband when they could not reconcile their respective political convictions (He was a rock-hard Socialist who despised Communists). Peter recruited the energetic and deeply committed Communist to work as a courier among various underground leftist groups the KGB had infiltrated.

This recruitment was ordinary enough in the political turmoil of 1930s Vienna, but was to prove significant for a very simple reason: Friedman's parents took in a boarder.

Friedman was living at home following her divorce. Her parents, pressed for money in the collapse of the Austrian economy in 1934, turned a spare room into cash by offering it for rent. That summer, a British student from Cambridge arrived in Vienna to study European politics. Needing a place to stay, he spotted the Kohlmans' ad in a local paper, and took the room for the summer. The day he moved into the room, he met the pretty, dark-haired Litzi Friedman, and a spark was immediately struck. Their conversations revealed a remarkable political affinity, for the Cambridge student, a member of the Communist party cell at the university, was already a committed Communist. Friedman introduced him as a likely prospect "for important party work" (meaning espionage) to Peter and Maly, and the Englishman was recruited as a low-level asset. Like Friedman, whom he was to marry later that year, he worked as a courier.

With that, **H. A. R. Philby** became an asset of the KGB. Peter had no idea that Philby would go on to become the greatest mole in history, but recruitment of the young British Communist would later enhance his reputation in the KGB. For one thing, it exempted him from the wave of anti-Semitic purges that swept through the KGB in the late 1930s, when, under Stalin's orders, virtually all Jewish agents were eliminated from Soviet intelligence. Peter also helped his cause with some pure Stalinism of his own. He had returned to the Soviet Union after a right-wing Austrian government in the late 1930s began a severe crackdown on leftist organizations, including the outlawing of the Communist party. Peter had arrived at a bad time, for Stalin's purges were decimating the KGB ranks. Besides Jews, KGB chief **Laventri Beria** was also purging foreign Communists; among the targets were the Hungarian Communists, like Peter, who had fled eastward after the failure of the 1919 uprising. Peter jumped on the bandwagon, denouncing his former Hungarian Communist friends as "Western spies." The denunciations were death warrants, for the Hungarians disappeared into the great maw of Beria's death machinery. Among the victims was Bela Kun himself; his old friend Peter denounced him as an "imperialist" who was a secret agent of British intelligence. (After a few days in the hands of Beria's goons, Kun confessed to precisely those crimes.)

By 1945, Peter was regarded by the KGB as potentially of greater value than simple intelligence agent. A man who had demonstrated a capacity for betrayal and brutality that rivaled his mentor Beria, Peter was marked for a much more important assignment: secret police chieftain. With Hungary under Soviet military domination, the KGB was actively involved in communizing the country, a task that in effect required a Hungarian Beria. Gabor Peter was to be that man.

At this stage in his life a Stalinist acolyte who often said he would unhesitatingly commit suicide if Stalin asked him to, Peter arrived in Budapest with orders to put Hungary firmly under the Communist grip. He set up an agency called AVO (later AVH), a combined foreign intelligence and internal security organization, and recruited a cadre of the most brutal Stalinist thugs he could find among the ranks of Hungarian Communists.

They went to work on Peter's first targets, the non-Communist political organizations who were part of the country's first ruling coalition. Within a year, Peter had destroyed them; politicians were kidnapped and murdered, others were bribed, and still others were threatened into silence. By 1948, Peter had turned Hungary into a one-party police state, a success that Beria cited to other Eastern European Communists as the model of how to use terror and repression to impose Communist domination.

Having established a one-party dictatorship, Peter then turned inward, carrying out a Stalin-ordered purge of Hungarian Communists. In a nightmare of terror, thousands of loyal Communists were dragged into Peter's office, there to confront the AVH chief wielding a truncheon. Some of them were old friends, but that didn't help; by the time Peter and his gang of torturers got through with them, they would confess to unimaginable crimes—such as one close friend of Peter who confessed to being a spy for Czechoslovakia since 1917, two years before Czechoslovakia even became a country.

Peter's reputation among Hungarians as "the Beria of Hungary" was well-established. His name, usually whispered in fear among his fellow countrymen, was the subject of anecdotes about this strange character. Victims who somehow had managed to survive arrest told of Peter interrupting torture sessions to sniff among the overflowing vases of flowers in his office or the window boxes outside. A lover of flowers, Peter had his office bedecked each day with freshly-cut blossoms, and it was only to these plants that he demonstrated any tenderness. For human beings, regardless of station, Peter showed nothing but savagery. For example, when Laszlo Rajk, the country's first Interior Minister, was caught up in a Stalin-ordered purge, and arrested without warning and taken before Peter, a furious Rajk demanded to see the party's First Secretary. Peter smashed him in the face, snarling, "The

First Secretary does not talk to traitors!" (Rajk, promised by Peter that his family would be protected if he confessed to being an American spy, assented, whereupon Peter killed him and the entire extended Rajk family).

By 1949, the repression machinery of Peter darkened the country like the shadow of some huge, malevolent spider. Hungarians learned to be very circumspect in their public conversations, for a network of 80,000 local informants (in a nation of only 9.5 million people) flooded Peter's office with reports on even the most innocuous utterances of ordinary citizens. Those deemed treasonous would result in an AVH arrest in the middle of the night, followed by torture, a sentence of several years in a labor camp, and, in some instances, death.

Despite this model of a Stalinist state, Stalin himself decided that Hungary—along with other Eastern European satellites of Moscow—had demonstrated insufficient Communist zeal. Obviously, there were still "counterrevolutionary elements" at work, so a new purge was ordered. Given the previous waves of purges, there was some difficulty in finding still another justification for a new one, but Peter and his fellow Eastern European secret police chiefs suddenly discovered the perfect justification. His name was Noel Field.

Described as a romantic Communist dreamer, Field was an American Quaker who became a Communist sympathizer. In 1934, when he was a 30-year-old State Department official, Field became friends with Alger Hiss, and was recruited as a KGB asset. During World War II, Field handled refugee problems and did some work for the OSS, attempting to enlist Communists for the agency. After the war, he went to work for a private refugee aid organization, but was fired in 1947 when the group discovered that Field was using its facilities to help only Communist refugees, among them Hungarian Communists. He would pay a terrible price later for his aid to those Hungarians.

Field emigrated to Prague, where he hoped to start a new career as a writer. But in 1949, he was suddenly arrested on espionage charges; a confused Field heard himself accused of being an "American master spy" who had recruited hundreds, perhaps thousands, of Eastern European Communists to destroy communism. However laughable the charge seemed, Field did not know he had become a pawn in what would become the greatest and bloodiest purge to strike Eastern Europe.

Peter was the man mainly responsible for it. He asked to be given Field for an "investigation" of "American spy activities," and in short order, Field confessed to being the key agent in a massive U.S. espionage operation that recruited virtually the top leadership of all Moscow's Eastern European satrapies, especially in Hungary. What horrors Field underwent to reach this point can only be imagined. But the result was there for all to see: hundreds, then thousands, of loyal Communists dragged into torture cellars, followed by their confessions at public show trials to being American or British spies for most of their adult lives. The Hungarian Communist leadership, along with those of other Eastern European countries, was decimated.

The effect would not be obvious for years: With its leadership destroyed in purges, the nations of Eastern Europe began to drift toward their final collapse some decades later.

Meanwhile, the "Field purge," as it became known, was to claim one last victim: Gabor Peter himself. Concluding that the purge perhaps had gone too far, Moscow now sought scapegoats. In Hungary, Peter was the chosen victim. At the KGB's orders, Peter was arrested in 1953 without charges and subjected, fittingly enough, to the same tortures he had inflicted on so many victims. He dutifully confessed to being an "agent of British and Zionist intelligence services." (This last touch was meant to underscore Stalin's new anti-Semitic purge of the KGB, justified on the grounds that Jewish agents were automatically considered to be under the control of Israeli intelligence).

But unlike most of his victims, Peter survived. He was given the relatively lenient sentence of life imprisonment and locked up in the same prison as Noel Field, one of his more prominent victims. When the Hungarian revolution of 1956 broke out, the revolutionaries released Field,* but kept Peter in prison. Peter was lucky; until suppressed by a Soviet military intervention, the revolutionaries rampaged through AVH headquarters, arresting AVH agents (some were beaten to death) and destroying part of the millions of files from the AVH's pervasive spying on ordinary Hungarian citizens.

Three years later, there came an even stranger twist to the Peter story, when he was ordered released from prison by Prime

---

* Despite his nightmarish experience, Field remained a devoted Communist. He settled in Budapest with his wife Herta (she had been imprisoned with him), and occupied his final years writing articles praising communism. He died in 1970.

Minister Janos Kadar—the very same Janos Kadar, curiously enough, whom Peter had arrested and tortured some years before during one of the first Stalin purges. For motives that remain unknown, Kadar gave Peter a minor government job. Some years later, Peter retired. Reassuming his given name of Benno Auspitz, he spent his last years humbly working as a tailor. Most people avoided the wizened, hunchbacked old tailor, aware that he was once the man who terrorized an entire country.

Peter died in 1993, and on orders of the government, his body was dumped into an unmarked grave and its location left unrecorded. It was part of an unsuccessful effort to erase forever the memory of Hungary's most infamous citizen, but the stain left by Peter on the soul of Eastern Europe remains forever.

SOME MYSTERIES . . .

HEINRICH MUELLER
A Nazi in Moscow

1900–1948 (?)

The gaunt, ravaged men who passed through the processing center had returned home at last, but before being reunited with the families they thought they would never see again, there was one last service to be performed for their country. Although exhausted, the German prisoners of war finally returning from a decade or more in Soviet prison camps that summer of 1953 took the time to sit for hours talking into tape recorders, recounting every little detail of all they had seen and experienced while their memories were still fresh.

Many of them, highly trained officers, had much technical intelligence to impart to the men of Reinhard Gehlen's Org who had been detailed to debrief the returning prisoners. This was the meat and potatoes of intelligence work, the collection of a myriad of details that later could be assembled into a coherent whole: the freight capacity of a rail line, where an important oil pipeline was located, the manufacturing process at a steel mill, and so on. All useful, but some of the officers recounted something that was downright bizarre and impossible to believe. They had seen a ghost.

Not just any ghost: They insisted, to their debriefers' open skepticism, that they had seen Heinrich Mueller, chief of the infamous *Geheime Staatspolizei* (Gestapo) from 1935 to the end of World War II, in the Soviet Union wearing a KGB colonel's uniform. Impossible, the officers were told; Mueller had died in Berlin in 1945. And even assuming that Mueller had survived the war, it hardly made sense that the KGB would enlist the chief of the Gestapo, of all people, to work in the KGB.

Yet, as other officer prisoners reported the same sighting, the Org men began to wonder. Was it possible? All the reported sightings were consistent in terms of physical description—the broad, squarish skull, the stubby figure, the pasty face with just a gash of mouth. That was Mueller all right, a man whose physical appearance was one of the more distinctive in the entire Nazi hierarchy. But there were more pressing intelligence tasks at the moment, so the mystery of Heinrich Mueller was put aside, to be revived later.

Taken at face value, it would be difficult to imagine a more astounding recruitment than the KGB managing to enlist the head of the Gestapo. It was Mueller, after all, who had destroyed the German Communist party—the most powerful and numerous outside the Soviet Union—with a ferocity that only his Russian counterpart Beria could have imagined. The German Communists, once several million strong, were hunted down like rats; they were murdered, or thrown into concentration camps, or driven into exile. By 1942, the country that was the birthplace of Karl Marx contained only a few Communists living a precarious underground existence. At the same time, Mueller's Gestapo smashed all Soviet intelligence networks in Germany, always regarded by Moscow Center as the most important intelligence cockpit in all of Western Europe.

The man who made all this happen was a cop, not a trained counterintelligence agent. Born in Munich in 1900, Mueller came from a family of typically stolid Bavarian policemen. He followed the same career path, joining the Munich Police Department in 1919. By 1929, Mueller's steady, if unspectacular, record had brought him to the middle-level position of Criminal Inspector (the equivalent of first-grade detective in an American police department). Ironically enough, in the light of later events, one of Mueller's chief concerns in the post-World War I era was a small but noisy fringe political movement, the National Socialist German Workers Party (NSDAP). Calling themselves "Nazis" from the German acronym of their movement, they were led by the brothers Gregor and Otto Strasser. The Strassers spouted a strange blend of right-wing polemics and Socialist doctrines on state ownership of all industry, but as Mueller reported to his superiors, they were being supplanted by the party's firebrand, an ex-soldier named Adolph Hitler.

In Mueller's view, Hitler and his small band of followers were a bunch of crackpots, not very different from the alphabet soup of political splinters who existed in the turmoil of post-World War I Germany. Nevertheless, he kept a close watch on the party, especially after Hitler's abortive putsch in 1923. By 1933, the year the crackpot of the Munich beer halls became chancellor, Mueller was the world's leading expert on the Nazi movement. His files—regrettably destroyed by an air raid in 1945—contained the most detailed information on the party and its officials. Mueller had compiled this information in the process of arresting many of the Nazis for various crimes, mostly brawling against political opponents in the streets.

The key to Mueller's personality was his professional detachment. At root, Mueller was apolitical; he was the classic police hound concerned only with duty. Whether he was investigating Communists or Nazis, Mueller remained unswayed by the kind of political convulsions that had torn Germany apart. He was known within the Munich police as *Der treue Heinrich*, meaning that he was the steady, incorruptible ideal of a dedicated cop who remained impervious to any influence—politics, money, or otherwise. Mueller followed orders.

For that reason, Mueller assumed he was out of a job in 1933 when the Nazis began to Nazify the German police. Mueller was not a Nazi party member—or any other political party, for that matter—and had no intention of enrolling in the NSDAP as an expediency to keep his job, as had many of his fellow cops. To his surprise, that quintessential Nazi, **Reinhard Heydrich,** asked Mueller to stay on and take charge of a new "anti-Soviet section" within the police force. With the German Communist party about to be declared illegal, Mueller would hunt down all party members. Additionally, he was informed, he would roll up all the Soviet intelligence networks believed to use German Communists as assets.

Heydrich's decision infuriated the Nazi Party's old guard, who complained that Mueller was the cop who had made their lives miserable in the Munich days. Heydrich ignored the protests, for his choice of Mueller was shrewdly thought out. To begin with, as Heydrich understood all too well, in a police state like Nazi Germany, there was a tendency for anyone connected with that machinery of repression to use the immense power for political advantage. The apolitical Mueller had no political agenda. Second, the task of eradicating communism from Germany was a job not for fanatics, but a disapassionate expert. Mueller certainly was that. As he had done with the Nazis, Mueller had built a huge information bank on the Communists. Moreover, as Heydrich was aware, Mueller had studied the methods of Soviet intelligence, and was considered among Germany's leading experts on the subject.

Armed with that knowledge, Mueller, put in charge of several dozen agents recruited from among the ranks of the Munich police, hunted down Communists throughout southern Germany with the same efficiency he had once demonstrated against the Nazis. By 1935, the Communists were virtually eliminated. This accomplishment earned Mueller a big promotion: he was named to head an entirely new division of the SD, an internal security agency called the Gestapo.

Mueller was to create in that new agency a tool of repression that would make its very name a synonym for unchecked state police power. To a large extent, the Gestapo was a reflection of Mueller himself; he recruited extensively among the ranks of German police detectives, looking for men who shared his apolitical views and blind devotion to duty. The Gestapo's approach and methods were modeled on the KGB, an agency that Mueller openly admired and often urged his men to emulate.

Within the SD, whose leadership was dominated by Nazified intellectuals ("gentlemen killers," as the *Abwehr* sneeringly called them), Mueller was not a popular figure. He had contempt for all intellectuals, and once announced, "One really ought to drive all the intellectuals into a coal mine and then blow it up." For their part, the SD leaders regarded Mueller as a Neanderthal, a typical flat-footed Munich cop whose intellectual breadth did not extend beyond beer and sausages.

This was somewhat of a caricature of the real Mueller, but there was no denying his narrow vision. A classic authoritarian, his mind was dominated by the concept of duty. If the state passed a law, as Nazi Germany did, making mere membership in the Communist party a capital crime, then Mueller was prepared to do his duty and round them up. And when the Nazis began to conquer Europe, Mueller was prepared to send his men into every corner of occupied Europe to slaughter "enemies of the state," as defined by the state. He preferred to regard himself as the implacable master of order. A man with a photographic memory who was reputed to know by name every single one of his several thousand agents, he maintained a huge card file on millions of German citizens, constantly nourished by a KGB-style network of informers he planted in every German institution. (Toward the end of the war, he regretted his inability to finish the objective of having a data card on *every* German citizen).

Mueller never made any moral judgments whatsoever; the state decided who the enemies were, and Mueller dutifully went after them. Similarly, he felt no compunction about what methods his organization used. The state told him that the enemies of the state had no rights and that *any* method was to be used to get results. Mueller was not a sadist, but he did recruit platoons of sadists to get the results he wanted in the Gestapo's infamous torture dungeons.

Known as "Gestapo Mueller" in Germany (to distinguish him from the many others with this common German surname), he appeared to be a prototypical Nazi, although few knew he was not a Nazi Party member. This fact began to cause some rumblings within the government hierarchy; did it make any sense for Nazi Germany's internal security to be headed by a non-Nazi? Accordingly, Mueller in 1939 was ordered to join the Nazi Party. The party, shockingly enough, rejected Mueller's application as "unfit" for membership. Heinrich Himmler himself had to intervene, ordering party officials to enroll Mueller forthwith—or face imprisonment in a concentration camp.

The incident further worsened relations between Mueller and the SD leadership, and their chief decided to take a closer look at the Gestapo head. Walter Schellenberg, a university-trained lawyer who had taken over the SD after the assassination of Reinhard Heydrich in 1942, did not like Mueller personally. But as a student of human nature, he also wondered about where Mueller's true loyalties lay. To an ever-suspicious Nazi ideologue like Schellenberg, Mueller's apolitical devotion to duty was a cause of concern; such a man was just as capable of following someone else's orders, if circumstances so dictated.

Schellenberg's first faint suspicions began to harden in 1942, when Mueller played a key role in the destruction of the German branch of Soviet intelligence's Red Orchestra network. A number of Red Orchestra radios had been captured, and to Schellenberg's unease, Mueller insisted on keeping some of them for purposes he did not make clear. Additionally, Schellenberg learned, Mueller had recruited a top radio expert adept in the art of *funkspiel*. Why, Schellenberg wondered, would Mueller need such an expert? The Russians were well aware that the German section of the Red Orchestra had been destroyed, so there was no possibility of a successful playback of a captured radio; obviously, Moscow Center would not believe any radio message from a network it knew to be in the Gestapo's clutches.

Schellenberg retained his own radio expert, and in 1944, he detected some unexplained signals emanating from Gestapo headquarters in Berlin eastward, toward a receiving station in Danzig. These signals, Schellenberg discovered, were in a cipher none of his experts could solve, leading him to believe that it was a Soviet one-time pad. If so, what was a radio at the Gestapo headquarters doing communicating in a probable Soviet code to Danzig in far off Poland?

There were other clues that bothered Schellenberg. In early 1944, the *Abwehr* had lost favor with Hitler, who began breaking up the agency. As a first step, he assigned its counterintelligence section to Mueller's Gestapo, which meant that Mueller now had exclusive control of all German counterintelligence operations. Coincidentally, Schellenberg discovered, counterintelligence against Soviet operations came to a halt. Mueller's official explanation was that the Germans had been so brilliantly successful in destroying Soviet networks, Moscow had in effect given up. But Schellenberg knew the Russians better than that, so he could only wonder the unthinkable: was it possible that Mueller, aware as well as anyone of the inevitability of a German defeat, had switched to the other side?

More pressing concerns forced Schellenberg to put the Mueller matter aside for the moment, and by the time he got around to it again, the war was just about over. Mueller, meanwhile, remained in Berlin until near the very end, when he suddenly disappeared. He was last seen alive on April 29, 1945, at Hitler's bunker. Subsequently, other Nazis in Berlin at the time told investigators that Mueller and an aide had tried to escape from the besieged city, but were killed by Russian troops in the attempt and were later buried in a city cemetery.

And there the mystery rested until the startling claims by returning German prisoners of war in 1953. All their stories had a common thread: sometime after their capture, they were marched through the streets of Moscow as part of a propaganda exercise by the Russians to boost civilian morale. As they marched, they noticed that among the Soviet officials watching them from a reviewing stand was a man they identified positively as Mueller.

West German intelligence tended to discount these reports, but before they could close the Mueller file, they began to hear of other strange reports concerning Mueller. One, from reliable contacts in Albania, reported that Mueller was in Albania sometime in 1953 as adviser to the Albanian secret police. That same year, there was another sighting, this one reporting Mueller working in East Germany with the East German secret police. Finally, to resolve the matter, the West Germans in 1963 decided to disinter the Mueller grave in Berlin and perform an autopsy on the body. When the grave was opened, the Germans were surprised to find three bodies in it; none of them proved to be Mueller.

So the story about Mueller's presumed death in Berlin in 1945 turned out be untrue. But what happened to him? The West Germans never did find out, although there was an occasional, tantalizing clue. In 1967, for example, two men were arrested for attempting to break into the house of Mueller's widow. An apparently ordinary enough burglary, but then police discovered that the two men were attached to the Israeli embassy and were in fact *Mossad* agents. What was *Mossad* trying to learn by breaking into Mrs. Mueller's house?

The Israelis would not say, and with that, a dark curtain settled over the case of Heinrich Mueller. Neither the Russians nor any of their Eastern European allies have ever discussed Mueller, although an East German source told the West Germans some years ago that he heard Mueller had died in 1948 in East Germany while serving as an adviser to the secret police.

The truth about what happened to Mueller after 1945 probably never will be known with certainty. Officially, he is wanted by West Germany for war crimes, so his case technically remains open. But the prospect that Mueller is still alive is quite remote; he would be over 90 years old today. That's pretty old, even for a cop with no political ambitions.

RUDOLF ROESSLER
The Enigma of Lucy

Code Name: LUCY
1897–1962

The regular monthly magazine of *Die Entsheidung*, a liberal Catholic organization in Switzerland during the 1930s, was not exactly high on the reading list of most Swiss citizens. Packed with gray columns of dense type, each issue was filled with tedious essays arguing, often obtusely, assorted political and ecclesiastical controversies. Aside from the 200-plus members of *Die Entsheidung*, nobody paid any attention to the publication.

But in 1936, the magazine suddenly became enlivened by the writings of a new contributor, a German expatriate who seemed to have an amazing and prescient grasp of events in Germany. His articles in this obscure magazine began to attract attention, for he seemed to know details printed nowhere else: political maneuverings inside the Nazi hierarchy, economic developments, and, most significant of all, specifics of Hitler's then-secret rearmament program.

The author, Rudolf Roessler, was living in exile in Lucerne, where he had fled in 1933 after being ousted from his job at a theatrical publisher for his anti-Nazi views. In terms of appearance, he looked like a typical European intellectual: small and thin, with thick spectacles, he seemed lost in thought most of the time. Quiet and introspective, he suffered from asthma, an affliction that made an already-shy man seem even more withdrawn.

However unprepossessing, this mild-mannered man would later become one of the greatest spies in history—or perhaps he

Rudolph Roessler (LUCY) arrives at a Swiss court in 1953 for his trial on espionage charges. (*AP Wide World*)

wasn't. It is this ambiguity that forms the core of the Roessler legend.

There was nothing in Roessler's background that suggested his future notoriety. He was a typical enough example of a type known as liberal German. Born in Augsburg, he enlisted in the German army at the outbreak of war in 1914, when he was 17 years old. He managed to survive four years as a combat soldier, but the experience created in him a permanent aversion to war and German militarism. A devout Catholic, Roessler resolved to dedicate his life to eliminating these twin evils.

After the war, Roessler decided to finish his schooling. He enrolled at the University of Berlin to study law, supporting himself as a journalist. He became part of a circle of similar-minded Catholic idealists, and one of them, a classmate at the University of Berlin, was to have a profound effect on Roessler's life.

Xavier Schnieper, a Swiss from a moderately wealthy family, shared Roessler's concern about the rise of the Nazis. A prominent member of *Die Entsheidung* back home, Schnieper advised his friend he had no real future in Germany, so he should emigrate to Switzerland. But Roessler decided to soldier on. In 1933, once he was fired from his job at the theatrical publisher, Roessler knew he was a marked man. Concluding he was no longer safe in Germany, he fled to Lucerne at Schnieper's suggestion and set up a small publishing house called Vita Nova to publish Catholic literature. He remained in contact, however, with some of his old similarly-minded friends in Nazi Germany, some of whom had subsumed their anti-Nazi sentiments to take jobs in various government ministries.

Roessler might have remained the owner of an obscure publishing firm, content to produce works of tortuous philosophical argument so beloved by Catholic theologians, were it not for a change in his friend Schnieper's life. In 1939, Schnieper, a reservist in the Swiss army, was called to military service, in the military intelligence branch. Schnieper told his superior, Major Hans Hausamann, about Roessler, the German expatriate who had been writing amazingly accurate articles about developments in Germany and apparently had a network of old friends in that country. Hausamann signed up Roessler as an evaluator, meaning he would analyze all intelligence reports and material from open sources about Germany, then write evaluations of what it all portended.

Roessler did not know it, but he was now part of an intricate intelligence game. Switzerland, in a hopeless strategic position that allowed it no defense against a German invasion, was determined to maintain its neutrality. To that end, Swiss intelligence was playing several ends against the middle. It cooperated, to a degree, with the Germans, but at the same time allowed extensive British and Soviet intelligence operations on its soil, with the covert understanding that neither the British nor the Russians were to make those links obvious or carry out any operations that jeopardized Swiss security. The result was an intelligence free-fire zone, with the intelligence services of a dozen nations running elaborate operations in Switzerland—all the while the Swiss pretended to know nothing of such operations, although they cooperated in some form with all of them. It was an intelligence carousel.

The largest and most active intelligence operation in Switzerland at the outbreak of World War II was a large Soviet GRU network known to the Germans as *Rote Drei* because it was actually composed of three separate rings. The most important of these rings was run by Sandor Rado, a Hungarian Communist and veteran GRU agent, whose assignment was to gather intelligence on the German military. Rado was finding it difficult to obtain such intelligence when he was secretly approached by Hausamann with an astonishing offer: the Swiss intelligence officer had a German contact with good sources in Germany who could provide top-grade material to the Soviets on German military developments. Only some of the material was of interest to the Swiss, but the rest, dealing with German military plans for Eastern Europe, was obviously of interest to the Soviets.

Rado gratefully accepted the offer, and the intelligence circus in Switzerland had now taken still another new twist. By covertly cooperating with Soviet intelligence, Hausamann had found a concealed conduit to transmit intelligence on Germany without antagonizing the Germans. Even if the Germans discovered the leak, there would be no overt connection to Swiss intelligence. Rado enlisted Roessler on a modest monthly retainer for *Rote Drei*. Seeking a code name for his new source, he settled on LUCY, because Roessler was based in Lucerne.

Roessler entered espionage immortality under that code name. Initially, however, LUCY made Moscow Center extremely nervous. For one thing, Roessler told Rado he would provide material to Soviet intelligence only on condition that he would never have to name his sources. Under ordinary circumstances, the GRU would never accept any intelligence without knowing the precise source that could be checked; otherwise, it would be too easy for the enemy to plant misleading information. The GRU decided to adopt a wait-and-see attitude for the moment, postponing a final decision on how much to trust LUCY by taking a look at his early material.

That material turned out to be very good, and it got better as Roessler began feeding an astonishingly large amount of detailed intelligence. Rado was puzzled: How was this obscure German expatriate publisher obtaining such intelligence? Roessler would not say directly, but hinted he had old friends in Germany who had now risen to high positions in the German military command structure and were providing information to a man whose political sympathies they shared. Occasionally, Roessler would mention his sources by such personal code names as INGE and WALTHER.

To Rado, an old hand at the intelligence game, none of this made any sense. Roessler's intelligence was always very current, meaning he was receiving it hot off the press, so to speak. Obviously, as an anti-Nazi expatriate, he could not travel to Germany. The mails would have been too slow, given the currency of the material, so only one explanation was possible: Roessler's sources were radioing intelligence to him. But that seemed unlikely; in the Nazi police state, where all transmitters were rigidly controlled, would high-level traitors take the risk to stay on the air for hours at a time to transmit their intelligence?

Rado had no answer for the moment, but the question was largely academic. Roessler's material kept increasing in volume and quality, and on June 17, 1941, he rushed to Rado with an intelligence blockbuster: Germany would invade the Soviet Union within a matter of days. The next day, he had an even bigger one: a complete order of battle for the invading forces, down to individual battalions. For good measure, Roessler provided the code name for the invasion (BARBAROSSA), and the precise moment when the offensive was scheduled to be launched.

As is now known, this was at least the fifth major intelligence source providing specific, detailed warning of the German invasion, all of which Stalin ignored. Rado received a waspish message from Moscow Center warning him not to pass on any further such "disinformation." But the Center's attitude changed dramatically on the morning of June 22, when the Germans struck, at the precise time and in the precise strength Roessler had revealed a few days before. At that moment, Roessler was elevated to star intelligence agent, and Rado was ordered to get from him anything he had.

Roessler obliged. In a massive stream that occurred almost daily, he provided precise intelligence regarding Hitler's orders governing strategic direction of the German forces, along with the strength, location, and size of all German units on the Eastern Front. Even more incredibly, he provided reports—which appeared to have been obtained right from *Abwehr* headquarters— on what the German intelligence service was telling Hitler about Russian positions, strength, and plans. Taken as a whole, it amounted to a breathtaking intelligence coup; the Russians not only were being told the precise strength and plans of their enemies, they also were learning of the scope and accuracy of their opponent's intelligence. Nothing like it had ever been seen before, nor has it been duplicated since.

Eager to keep this golden goose laying eggs, the Russians did not press Roessler on how he was managing to obtain such incredible intelligence. As the GRU noted, on some occasions

Roessler provided such vital tactical intelligence as German plans and axes of attack even before German units on the ground received their marching orders. What counted was that Roessler was invariably accurate. He never hedged a piece of intelligence with the words "expected" or "perhaps." If Roessler said a certain German Panzer corps would attack at 6 A.M. on a particular day at a particular place, the Russians learned they could figuratively bet the mortgage that the Panzer unit would do precisely that. Roessler also provided detailed figures on the actual (as opposed to the publicly admitted) German losses in men and equipment.

Rado and Roessler were unaware that the Russians derived an extra benefit from such detailed intelligence. They were running a large-scale deception operation via **Fritz Kauders** (MAX). Told of the German plans, the Soviet deception material could be tailored more precisely to German preconceptions.

By early 1943, as the tide of war on the Eastern Front started to turn in the Soviet Union's favor—thanks in no small part to their mysterious source in Switzerland—Roessler began to report on secret German preparations for one last, great throw of the dice in the east. Toward spring, he uncovered some further details: as soon as the weather permitted, the Germans would launch a tremendous offensive on the Southern Front, near a town called Kursk. Involving several hundred thousand troops and the bulk of the German armor, the plan was to punch through the Russian lines and then trap over a million Soviet troops in a gigantic double envelopment. Code-named Operation Zitadelle, it would, if successful, inflict a defeat from which the Soviet Union might never recover. Additionally, it would restore German military dominance after the Stalingrad disaster.

Forewarned, the Russians took elaborate measures to defend against the German thrust, while at the same time they formulated plans for a counteroffensive that would envelop the envelopers. In intelligence terms, this was a risky course, since the sole basis for believing that such a German offensive was in the offing came from one single spy. But Moscow's faith in LUCY was now total, and on that basis, the Russians gambled that he was right.

As things turned out, Roessler, as usual, was absolutely correct. The German offensive began at the time and place he said it would happen, and as a result, the Russians were waiting. They built defenses up to 70 miles in depth; bristling with hidden antitank guns and tank hunter-killer teams, they took a devastating toll of German armor. Within two weeks, the offensive was smashed, forever breaking German offensive military power on the Eastern Front. From that moment on, the Germans went on the defensive, and were never able to go on the attack again. In a war against a numerically superior foe, that meant certain defeat.

The Kursk intelligence triumph would be Roessler's last; shortly after the beaten Germans began to retreat, the Swiss suddenly moved against the *Rote Drei* networks, arresting all agents and assets. Rado avoided arrest and went into hiding, while Roessler, officially considered an asset of Swiss intelligence, was left alone. Although Roessler no longer had a means of sending his intelligence to Moscow, the fact was that his services were not really needed. Indeed, since the tide of war had turned on the Eastern Front irrevocably, there was not much further need for *Rote Drei*. Interestingly, just as the network begin to lose much of its importance, Swiss intelligence chose that moment to close it down. The Germans, aware from their radio intercepts of the existence of *Rote Drei* for quite some time, had been pressuring the Swiss for more than a year to crack down on the network.

The end of LUCY still left the great mystery unanswered: How had the shy German publisher managed to collect the most vital of German military secrets? When asked, Roessler would say only, "I didn't know who my sources were." Although it was commonly assumed this represented his determination to protect a network of German traitors who provided information to him, nearly 30 years would elapse before some vital clues emerged suggesting that Roessler may have been telling the truth.

The first clue emerged in the stacks of captured German intelligence records, which revealed that the German radio monitors carefully checked on radio traffic moving from Germany into Switzerland, known to be the location for major Allied intelligence operations. According to those records, the Germans found almost no Germany-Switzerland traffic, but a veritable flood moving from Switzerland eastward. The Germans were puzzled: Obviously, the networks in Switzerland, on the air nearly 24 hours a day, had plenty of material to transmit. Where was it coming from?

An even more significant clue emerged in the 1970s, when the first details about the British ULTRA code-breaking operation became public. Among those details was an interesting fact: early in 1941, based on their ULTRA decryptions, the British warned Stalin that Hitler was planning an invasion of the Soviet Union. That means the British were reading the German high-level military traffic by that time. Further, it is known that the British, frustrated by Stalin's refusal to believe their intelligence, set about to find some way of conveying ULTRA intelligence to the Soviet Union while concealing the source. That job was given to **Claude Dansey** of MI6, and it is in Dansey's activities and connections that further clues about LUCY emerge.

Dansey was a close friend of the head of Czechoslovakian Military Intelligence, Frantisek Moravec. In the 1930s, Moravec had carried out several significant penetrations of German intelligence, including recruitment of a German communications expert who provided the first keys to the Enigma code-breaking machine. Moravec turned over this material to Dansey, giving the initial breaks into the then-unreadable Enigma system. Following the Munich agreement in 1938, Moravec fled to London, where Dansey set him up as head of a small intelligence unit for the Czech government in exile. (In that capacity, Moravec worked with the British in organizing the assassination of **Reinhard Heydrich** in 1942.)

Moravec maintained a network of good sources who operated in German-occupied Czechoslovakia, southern France, and, most significantly in the context of the Roessler mystery, Switzerland. For some years, Moravec and Hans Hausamann of Swiss intelligence had worked as close allies, exchanging intelligence. Hausamann was also a close ally of Dansey, and when the MI6 spymaster set up his Z Organization, the Swiss began providing intelligence on the German military. That intelligence was passed to MI6 via Moravec's chief agent working in Switzerland, Karel Sedlacek, a veteran Czech agent known as "Uncle Karl."

So by the beginning of 1941, the intelligence pipeline from London to Switzerland looked something like this: Hausamann of Swiss intelligence passed material to Sedlacek, who passed it up the pipeline to his boss Moravec for Dansey. In turn, Dansey passed material of interest to the Swiss down the pipeline to Moravec, then to Sedlacek, and onward to Hausamann. The elaborateness was necessary to protect Hausamann's delicate position; at all costs, the Germans had to be convinced that he had no business with British intelligence. Indeed, to all appearances, he did not; German agents working in Switzerland kept a surveillance on Hausamann, and reported he had no contact with any known MI6 agents. They spotted Sedlacek, but all the Germans knew about him was that he was a businessman with no intelligence connections.

With such a secure pipeline, can it be concluded that Dansey used the conduit to funnel ULTRA decryptions to the Russians by way of Hausamann's source, Rudolf Roessler? Dansey, Moravec, Hausamann, and Sedlacek all died without saying, but there were two final clues which seem to clinch the case for Roessler as mere pawn in a larger game. One clue came from the Russians, and the second from Roessler himself.

When the *Rote Drei* network was rolled up in late 1943, the Russians took the loss philosophically; all networks eventually come to the end of their usefulness at some point. But they now began to wonder about the source of Roessler's remarkable intelligence. Their curiosity centered on two members of Sandor Rado's network: Rado himself, and Rado's chief radio operator, Alexander Foote, a British Communist who had been recruited for Swiss operations by **Ruth Kuczynski** in 1938. Aware of ULTRA from information provided by their assets in Britain, primarily **H. A. R. Philby** and **Anthony Blunt,** the Russians began to conclude that LUCY was in fact an elaborate British intelligence operation to feed ULTRA intelligence to the Soviet Union. Moscow Center found this very worrisome, for if the British fed genuine intelligence by this source, there was a perfectly good possibility they also used it to feed disinformation.

To get to the bottom of the problem, Moscow summoned Foote and Rado. Upon arriving in Moscow, Foote found himself immediately confronted by GRU suspicions that he had some role in transmitting "British information." Foote, who personally disliked Rado, said he knew nothing of the source of the material, and blamed Rado. In turn, Rado* claimed ignorance of the source of the LUCY material, so that was that.

Whatever questions Moscow still may have had about Roessler were eliminated in 1946 by LUCY himself. During the war,

---

* Rado, blamed for the breakup of the network, was imprisoned for 10 years in the Soviet Union. Released in 1956, he returned to his native Hungary, resumed his prewar profession of cartographer, and died in 1981, professing his unshaken belief in communism to the end. Foote, readied for a new GRU assignment in South America, defected to the British in 1947. He died of cancer in 1956, but before his death revealed he knew all along that he was transmitting ULTRA intelligence to Moscow. He also hinted that he was a double agent for MI6, recruited years before to keep an eye on Soviet networks in Switzerland.

Roessler had received about $800 a month from the Russians for his services, a handsome sum in 1940s-era dollars. He sunk every cent into his publishing house, but by the end of the war, it was failing. Desperate for money, Roessler decided to return to espionage. He contacted Karl Sedlacek, who had now switched sides and was working for the Czechoslovakian Communists. Selacek signed on Roessler to gather intelligence on American military dispositions in Germany and waited for the kind of spectacular material LUCY had once delivered to the GRU.

But there wasn't any; those presumably high-level sources who had once made LUCY an espionage legend had now disappeared, apparently. Based in Switzerland, the best Roessler could do was collect some fairly low-level material that the Czechs found unimpressive. Nevertheless, they kept him on at $400 a month, hoping for something better.

The better stuff never came. In 1952, Roessler was caught: He had been sending his intelligence to the Czechs by means of microfilm concealed in food parcels mailed to a Dusseldorf letterbox. One day, a misaddressed package was opened by the post office, which found microfilm concealed in jars of honey. Arrested in Switzerland, Roessler was sentenced to a lenient one year in prison on the grounds that he had committed no espionage against Switzerland. (It helped that his old control Hausamann quietly put in the good word to Swiss authorities.) During his trial, Roessler insisted that he was not the master spy the media had made him out to be. He admitted passing intelligence to the Soviets during the war in the name of helping to defeat Nazi Germany, but repeated, "I never knew who my sources were."

To the Russians, this chain of circumstances represented final proof that Roessler had worked as a conduit for the British. Clearly, those fabled "high sources" like INGE and WALTHER did not exist. Roessler himself refused to shed any light on the matter, and until his death from cancer in 1962, he preferred to remain a man of mystery. He continued to publish dense theological treatises, none of which offered any clues to his own motivations—except for an interesting emphasis in all the works on the question of good versus evil. Clearly, LUCY considered himself an expert on the subject.

VITALI YURCHENKO
The Spy Who Changed His Mind

Code Name: ALEX
Alias: Robert Rodman
1935–

On the morning of June 22, 1985, a group of Soviet diplomats, on a sightseeing stroll around Rome, stopped for refreshments. One of the diplomats, a 50-year-old man with a Fu Manchu mustache named Vitali Yurchenko announced he was leaving the group for a short while. "I'll join you later at the embassy," he told them. "I want to visit the Vatican museums."

But Yurchenko had no intention of seeing Michaelangelo's masterpieces. He headed straight for the American embassy, asked to see the security officer, and told him he wanted to defect to the United States. To the CIA personnel at the Rome embassy, there was no necessity for Second Secretary Yurchenko to introduce himself, for they understood instantly they had landed a very big fish indeed: Colonel Vitali Yurchenko, a senior officer of the KGB's First Directorate.

Given his background, Yurchenko was the kind of defector counterintelligence officers dream about. One of the KGB's brightest stars, Yurchenko began his career in the Soviet navy, which he joined in 1955. He demonstrated the kind of high intelligence and innovative thinking that tends to attract KGB recruiters always on the alert for bright military men, and in 1959 joined the agency. He showed a real aptitude for counterintelligence work, and by 1961 was chief operations officer for KGB units in the Soviet Black Sea Fleet, with emphasis on protecting its most advanced warships from prying Western intelligence

Vitaly Yurchenko, one of the KGB's brightest stars, entering the U.S. State Department after he defected to the U.S. for love of a woman. (*UPI/Betteman*)

agencies. In 1968, he expanded into foreign intelligence operations, and was assigned to Alexandria, Egypt, under cover of Soviet naval adviser to the Egyptian navy; his real job was to collect intelligence on the American Navy and other Western navies in the Meditteranean.

It was his next big posting, in 1975, that brought him to the attention of American intelligence. He appeared in the Washington, D.C., embassy, the KGB's most important station, as the embassy's security officer. Translated, that meant he was in charge of keeping an eye on all intelligence and diplomatic personnel at the embassy and at the same time prevent any CIA or FBI penetrations. The job put him in the KGB major leagues, and both the CIA and the FBI spent some effort studying their adversary.

The first conclusion the Americans reached was that Yurchenko was a first-class KGB counterespionage expert. Sharp and quick-witted, with a great deal of charm, he seemed to regard the world most of his waking hours with a slight sardonic smile. But, the Americans discovered, this exterior concealed a man in some inner turmoil. It was a universal problem that afflicted a certain number of men: Yurchenko, a married man with two children, was in love with another woman. To make the situation more complicated, the object of his affections was married to a Soviet diplomat.

A very interesting situation, fraught with danger: under KGB rules, even for a star like Yurchenko, such liaisons were forbidden, especially if they involved the wife of a Soviet diplomat. What made this situation even more difficult was the fact that the woman lived in Montreal, where her husband worked. Yurchenko's many trips to Montreal, at first suspected by the FBI as part of some big cross-border intelligence operation, turned out be much more prosaic than that, but they raised an interesting question: Was it possible that Yurchenko might consider defecting with his lady love to a new life in the United States?

Before anyone in the American intelligence community could figure out how such a defection might be arranged, Yurchenko himself appeared on the American doorstep. As the CIA anticipated, his first step after defecting was to request a trip to Canada. Accompanied by a CIA security detail, the spy now code-named ALEX and travelling under his new American identity of Robert Rodman arrived in Montreal for a CIA-arranged tryst with his girlfriend. It was no ordinary tryst, since Yurchenko/Rodman was to break the news to her that he had defected to the CIA, and that he wished her to abandon her husband and begin a new life with Yurchenko in America. But to Yurchenko's shock, she announced that she was willing to continue the relationship, but she had no intention of leaving her husband. And as for the idea of defecting and joining him in the United States, she flatly told him he was crazy.

The news put Yurchenko into something of a tailspin, and cast a pall over the next stage in his life, which was to sit through hours and days of debriefings while the CIA emptied his head. In that role, despite his obvious personal turmoil, Yurchenko was nothing short of sensational. Given his position, he not only knew about all ongoing KGB operations in the United States, he also knew a great deal about all other KGB operations.

As the CIA understood, it could not have hoped for a KGB source as well placed as Yurchenko. In 1980, he had completed a five-year tour in Washington, and was promoted to head Department K (counterespionage) in the First Chief Directorate, the KGB's most important division, which handled foreign intelligence operations. By early 1985, he was deputy chief of the First Department (United States and Canada) in the First Chief Directorate. In that post, he not only knew the identities of all KGB agents assigned to the Soviet embassy, he was also aware of the identities of their assets. In that latter group, Yurchenko revealed two names that were to cause severe shock throughout the entire American military and intelligence establishment.

The gravest shock was Yurchenko's revelation that the National Security Agency (NSA), the most secret component of the American intelligence empire, had been penetrated by the KGB through recruitment of a former employee. Actually, Yurchenko said, it was not really a recruitment, for the former employee had contacted the KGB at the Washington embassy in January 1980, and offered to sell whatever he knew. It turned out that the former employee, Ronald W. Pelton, knew a great deal about his ex-employer, which handles all American code-breaking and overseas electronic intercept operations. Over the next five years, until blown by Yurchenko, he was to singlehandedly destroy virtually all NSA operations involving the Soviet Union. He revealed to his KGB handlers precisely what the NSA knew about Soviet signals and cipher systems, the precise NSA technology used to detect those signals, the extent of American success in solving Soviet ciphers, and, most damaging of all, something called IVY BELLS. This deepest American intelligence secret involved an amazing technological feat: American submarines had planted sophisticated underwater devices near Soviet underseas cables that carried communications. The devices recorded all transmissions moving over those presumed secure lines, then transmitted the results to passing overhead satellites. The Russians, assuming the underseas cables were safe, made no effort to scramble or otherwise protect what was transmitted over those lines.

The next revelation caused even more shock: CIA operations in the Soviet Union had been compromised. The KGB asset in this case was another walk-in, Edward Lee Howard, who in 1983, following training for work in the agency's sensitive Moscow station, was blocked from taking the appointment when a CIA polygraph test turned up indications of drug use and petty theft. Subsequently fired from the agency, Howard contacted the Soviet embassy and offered to sell secrets about CIA operations in the Soviet Union. His information turned out to be highly damaging to the CIA: at least six CIA assets were rounded up and executed, and CIA operations came to a virtual standstill. For good measure, Howard revealed to the Soviets the names of all CIA agents working under diplomatic cover in the American embassy.

Yurchenko's revelations concerning Pelton and Howard destroyed, in one swoop, two of the most important assets the KGB ever had in the United States. During the next few weeks of his debriefing, Yurchenko was to cause even further damage. He revealed that Hans Tiedge, head of the West German counterintelligence agency, the BfV, was a long-time KGB mole, along with three other West German government officials (all of them fled to East Germany the moment they heard that Yurchenko had defected). He also revealed that the KGB had a mole inside the Royal Canadian Mounted Police Security Service.

This growing roster of severe damage to the KGB raised the question: why was Yurchenko doing all this? That question would never be satisfactorily answered. To his American handlers, Yurchenko never betrayed either of the two classic motives for defection: disgust with his nation's political system, or thwarted career ambitions. Yurchenko was a nominal Communist, but did not demonstrate any especially deep political convictions; if anything, he was apolitical. And certainly he had no career problems in the KGB, since he had already achieved lofty posts, with only promise of greater rewards and promotions ahead. In terms of the Cold War struggle, Yurchenko seemed to regard it all as a game; he laughingly told his CIA debriefers about running the KGB's "nightcrawler" operation in Washington, when KGB agents were assigned to prowl nightclubs and bars to recruit U.S. government employees who seemed too partial to drink, drugs, or sex.

The lack of real motive for defecting led at least one group of CIA officials to believe that Yurchenko was a KGB plant, assigned to infiltrate the CIA. This faction explained away Yurchenko's revelations by arguing these were probably all discards, assets whose usefulness would expire at some point anyway. The problem with the theory, of course, was that it did not explain why the KGB would forfeit so many of its greatest assets simply to bolster Yurchenko in the hopes that some day he might join the CIA and get access to high-grade intelligence.

The more likely theory was that Yurchenko, emotionally torn apart by his love affair with the diplomat's wife, had made a spur of the moment decision, however fatuous, that he and his love could somehow walk away from their awkward marital arrangements and begin a whole new life in America.

Whatever Yurchenko's real motives, the CIA proceeded to complicate things further with several serious errors. The worst mistake was then-CIA Director William Casey's decision to bolster the agency's sagging image—the Iran-Contra mess was just then exploding into public scandal—by leaking word of Yurchenko's defection. Yurchenko was appalled, and a subsequent meeting with Casey himself didn't help matters. Notorious for his New York West Side accent nearly indecipherable to anyone not born in that area, Casey befuddled Yurchenko, who was fluent in English. He was further put off by Casey's virulent anticommunism.

To worsen things, the CIA, known for its inept handling of KGB defectors, mishandled Yurchenko. Some of its agents began to condescend to him, and others openly mocked the love of his life, the diplomat's wife in Canada. Spending his time in a Virginia safe house, Yurchenko was further upset when he saw his name bandied about in television news reports. At some point, he snapped, for on the night of November 2, 1985, taken to a Washington restaurant for dinner with two CIA escorts, Yurchenko casually asked what the CIA would do if he simply got up and left the restaurant. When the flustered agents said they weren't sure, Yurchenko got up from the table and casually walked out of the restaurant, went down the street four blocks, and walked into the Soviet embassy.

What happened next represented what was undoubtedly the oddest spy soap opera in the entire history of Cold War espionage. Two days after his return, the Soviet embassy held a press conference, with Yurchenko the star. He claimed that he had been kidnapped and drugged by the CIA and forced into making statements about the KGB. He had finally "escaped" from the CIA, he said.

It was an operational disaster for the CIA, whose officials had to endure hours of being raked over the coals in closed-door sessions of congressional committees curious how the agency somehow had managed to lose one of the most valuable defectors in its history. One result of all this was a revamped American intelligence program for handling future defectors, which amounted to something like locking the stable door after the horse has bolted.

Back in Moscow, meanwhile, Yurchenko seemed to be having a wonderful time. Despite CIA leaks to the media that he had been executed once he returned to the Soviet Union, he turned out to be very much alive, happily granting interviews to reporters about the "stupid" CIA. He claimed to know nothing about Pelton or Howard*—or any other KGB asset he had blown, for that matter.

Given Yurchenko's apparently free existence in Moscow, what, then, was the truth of his appearance at the American embassy in Rome only a few months before? Only Yurchenko really knows if he was a genuine defector, but the circumstantial evidence seems quite strong that he was not a deliberate KGB plant. As for his later denials that he ever gave the CIA any significant intelligence, that assertion again is contradicted by the evidence at hand. Plant or not, the fact is that Yurchenko severely damaged the KGB; his revelation of more than a dozen of its most important overseas assets represents an intelligence disaster of the first magnitude.

These days, Yurchenko, still apparently working for the KGB, is best known within that agency for his impression of William Casey, complete with mumble. KGB officials swear it's hilarious.

---

* Confronted by FBI agents brandishing Yurchenko's revelation, Pelton confessed and was sentenced to life in prison. Then 44, he said he approached the KGB after finding it impossible to support a mistress on his $24,500 annual government salary. He got $35,000 from the KGB, a bargain for the Soviets. Howard, 41, fled to the Soviet Union, leaving behind $10,000 buried behind his house and $150,000 in a Swiss bank account. Today, he lives outside of Moscow on a KGB stipend.

NIKOLAI ARTAMANOV
The Double Agent Who Wasn't

Alias: Nicholas Shadrin
1936–1975 (?)

For the seafarers along the Swedish coast who had a healthy respect for the vagaries and furies of the Baltic Sea, the feat was extraordinary. Sailing only with a compass, the man and his wife somehow had managed to steer a small boat through stormy seas across the Baltic from Poland to Sweden.

The voyage of Soviet naval captain Nikolai Artamanov and his Polish wife Eva in June 1959, was the talk of Sweden for months. Descendants of Vikings who admire seafaring feats, the Swedes marveled how Artamanov, determined to escape from a repressive regime and find freedom in the West, contrived to obtain a boat, which he then piloted to Sweden several hundred miles away, avoiding Polish and Soviet patrol boats.

Informed of Artamanov's defection, American authorities indicated immediate interest in having him come to the United States. Their interest focused on what Artamanov might be able to tell them about the Soviet navy, then undergoing a large-scale buildup. Artamanov was moved to Washington, D.C., given a new identity as Nicholas Shadrin, and hired as a consultant to the Office of Naval Intelligence (ONI) to fill in the agency's blanks about Soviet naval technology and tactics.

On the face of it, all of this seemed a fairly ordinary Cold War defection case, with modest intelligence overtones. But it ultimately would develop into an extraordinarily complex espionage puzzle, with enough twists and turns to rival any Le Carre plot. Even decades later, only part of the full truth has emerged; the rest may never be known.

By 1960, when Artamanov was settled in the United States and busy at work with ONI, the brief flurry of world attention on his flight to freedom had subsided. The new American citizen named Nicholas Shadrin seemed like any other government employee, commuting each day from his modest Maryland home. Meanwhile, his wife was studying to qualify for an American dentistry license. But there were two agencies that had not forgotten him.

At the CIA, there were some in the agency's counterintelligence division who had a continuing interest in the case of Nikolai Artamanov. Concerned about Soviet penetration of U.S. intelligence, they had ongoing suspicions about the Soviet naval captain. To these suspicious minds, Shadrin's dramatic flight across the Baltic was less than it appeared; they had carefully checked and rechecked the route, a bit of backtracking that convinced them Shadrin's story was a lie. They began to suspect that Shadrin in fact had been planted, for what purpose at the moment seemed obscure. Perhaps, it was speculated, the KGB hoped he would rise to a high level in ONI, in a position to provide some top-grade intelligence. Meanwhile, the KGB also had a continuing interest in Shadrin. The reason for that interest is not known, but the KGB ordered its agents in the United States to find out where he was, under which new identity he was now living, and for which government agency he might be working.

No overt move was made until June 1966, when a very puzzling event took place. Then-CIA director Richard Helms, playing golf one Sunday morning at a Washington country club, got a phone call from a man named Igor Kochnov, who said he wanted to meet CIA officials for a "very important matter." Kochnov was instantly recognizable to the CIA: at the time, he was a senior KGB officer, stationed under diplomatic cover in the Soviet embassy. He was head of counterintelligence for the KGB station at the embassy, assigned the job of guarding against CIA and FBI penetration, but that was only part of his interesting background. He also happened to be the son-in-law of Yazkaternina Furtseva, the Soviet Minister of Culture, one of the most powerful figures in the entire Soviet political hierarchy (and the reputed mistress of Nikita Khrushchev). Additionally, his father-in-law was a close friend of Yuri Andropov, a future KGB chief.

All in all, an interesting character who promised to pay dividends if he could be recruited by the CIA—assuming, of course, that that was the point of his strange call to Helms. In a subsequent meeting with several CIA senior agents, Kochnov offered his services by means of a curious package deal. Essentially, Kochnov offered to become a CIA source who claimed he could provide information on KGB penetration of the agency. He said that he had been assigned by the KGB to locate Shadrin and convert him into a double agent; if the CIA would help him in this task, Kochnov said, then his stock would be boosted in the KGB, allowing him even greater access for the kind of material he could pass on to the CIA.

Taken as a whole, this was a very odd offer, but after an acrimonious internal debate, during which some CIA officials argued that Kochnov unquestionably was a KGB plant, it was decided that the CIA would accept it. Accordingly, Shadrin was approached and asked to volunteer to serve as a fake double agent. Some time later, he was approached by a KGB agent. So far so good: the KGB had taken the bait.

Given some low-grade material (known as "chicken feed" in the espionage trade) to keep the KGB's interest active, Shadrin played his role as Soviet defector who had become disillusioned with the United States and was now willing to help the Motherland, with the eventual hope of returning. Kochnov, meanwhile, working under his new CIA code name KITTY HAWK, had begun feeding out his own material to the CIA, which turned out to be equally low-grade. By October of 1966, Kochnov's tour in the United States was over, and he returned to Moscow, where he was promoted and detailed to the International Atomic Energy Agency, assigned the task of escorting (for which read keeping tabs on) Soviet delegates. For the next several years, there were only occasional brush contacts between KITTY HAWK and CIA agents in Moscow.

This intelligence minuet continued through 1971, when Shadrin was sent by the KGB to Czechoslovakia to receive special training in the operation of several high-tech spy communications devices, including a burst transmitter. The growing effort by the KGB connected with Shadrin seemed to indicate the agency's full confidence in his bona fides. That faith was further underscored in 1975, when the KGB asked Shadrin to go to Vienna for a high-level meeting with senior KGB officials. Vienna, the fulcrum point of East-West espionage, was the KGB's favorite rendezvous site for its most important meetings with its top Western assets. The CIA, sensing a breakthrough, approved the plan for Shadrin to go to Vienna.

On December 17, Shadrin, accompanied by his wife, arrived in Vienna. The following day, he met with two KGB senior officers, who told him there would be a "very important" meeting with even more senior KGB officials on the 20th. Concerned that KGB countersurveillance teams might spot any CIA attempts to keep a watch on the meeting (which would reveal that Shadrin was under CIA control), the CIA decided to let Shadrin attend the meeting alone. On the night of December 20, Shadrin was met by two KGB agents in front of a church; all three men drove off in a dark sedan. Hours went by, with no word from Shadrin. His wife sat by the telephone in their hotel room, vainly waiting for the call her husband promised to make as soon as his "brief business" was concluded.

By the time 24 hours had passed, Mrs. Shadrin was a nervous wreck. A female CIA agent came to stay with her, but attempts to calm Mrs. Shadrin were futile. Four days later, it was clear that Shadrin, wherever he was, was not coming back. He had disappeared off the face of the earth.

There was no end of theories on what might have happened. One CIA faction argued that Shardrin had been a KGB plant all along, and had now returned to Moscow once the game was over. Another faction argued that the KGB somehow had discovered his role as a double agent; he had been kidnapped and taken to the Soviet Union. KITTY HAWK was of no help; he claimed only to have actually set up the meeting and claimed to have no knowledge of what happened afterward.

And there the matter rested for the next decade. Kochnov, identified in a magazine story giving some of the bare details of the Shadrin case, was warned before publication by the CIA. He suddenly disappeared from his Moscow office and has not been seen since. In the interim, despite a number of defectors from the Soviet Union, no one had any insight into what happened to Shadrin.

That changed in 1985, when **Vitali Yurchenko** defected. Among his first revelations to the CIA was the fate of Nicholas Shadrin. According to Yurchenko, the KGB plan was to drug Shadrin and take him to Moscow, but one of the agents involved in the operation injected him with too much of the knockout drug, and Shadrin died on the spot.

On October 27, 1985, two FBI agents appeared at the door of Mrs. Shadrin and informed her that her husband, missing for the past decade, was now confirmed dead "beyond reasonable doubt." But of course there was still plenty of doubt. Three years after this supposedly final verdict, a Soviet source told the CIA that Shadrin was very much alive, having been spotted at the funeral of Admiral Sergei Gorshkov, head of the Russian navy.

So was the original Artamanov/Shadrin defection some sort of elaborate KGB operation to plant a source in American intelligence who would mislead the Americans about Soviet naval capability? Or was the CIA source mistaken about seeing Shadrin three years after his presumed death? Was Yurchenko wrong (or possibly passing along KGB disinformation) when he reported Shadrin's fate? Was Igor Kochnov, KITTY HAWK, a KGB plant?

At the moment, no resolution of these lingering mysteries is possible, for they represent the classic "wilderness of mirrors" effect of certain intelligence operations where all the lines between truth and untruth have been hopelessly blurred. But one thing does remain clear: as a result of the Shadrin case, the CIA abandoned the idea that it could play the KGB's kind of intricate double and triple agent games so popular with spy novelists. The KGB operated in a very different kind of world, where the notion of sacrificing, say, a Shadrin was routinely justified in the name of operational necessity. But in a democracy, Shadrin was a tragedy.

. . . AND A FEW CURIOSITIES

ERNEST HEMINGWAY
Papa's Crook Factory

1899–1961

However much respect he had for the abilities and talent of one of his prime assets, U.S. Marine Corps Colonel John W. Thomason Jr. of the Office of Naval Intelligence had to tell him that in this case, he was completely wrong. "No, not possible," he said to Ernest Hemingway. "There is absolutely no possibility that the Japanese Navy would be so foolish as to take on the United States Navy. That would be suicide, and the Japanese are not stupid people."

Hemingway strongly disagreed, but did not argue further. After all, Thomason was a highly decorated officer of 20 years experience, the last 10 spent in ONI. If Thomason said there was no possibility that the Japanese would attack the United States, then he was a man who presumably knew; he was the professional, while Hemingway was just an amateur spy. Still, Hemingway was bothered; everything he had heard that spring of 1941 during a trip through the Far East pointed in the direction of an imminent Japanese attack against the U.S. Navy.

The attack on Pearl Harbor some months later was to prove Hemingway right, but he never mentioned or wrote about this phase of his life. Nor did the dozens of other Americans who, like Hemingway, were recruited before World War II to serve as amateur spies for their country strictly out of patriotism. In those simpler times, they saw nothing wrong with combining professonal duties and intelligence-gathering for America's tiny espio-

In a 1947 ceremony that infuriated FBI Director J. Edgar Hoover, Ernest
Hemingway is awarded a Bronze Star by the U.S. military attache in Havana
for unspecified "meritorious war service." (*AP/Wide World*)

nage establishment.* Indeed, they amounted to America's real
intelligence capability, such as it was.

To a certain extent, Hemingway's willingness to do some
amateur spying for his country stemmed from his considerable
ego. He fancied himself a superspy, a role he began to assume
during his travels in Spain during the Civil War. Romantically
attached to the world of intrigue he encountered in the spy-in-
fested capital of Madrid, Hemingway passed on snippets of intelligence to his friends in ONI. It was low-scale stuff, but Hemingway later was to claim he had invented the term "fifth column,"
supposedly representing an enemy's invisible column of spies

---

* This disparate group ranged from journalist John Franklin Carter to financiers
Winthrop Aldrich and Nelson Rockefeller and lawyers David K. Bruce and William
Donovan (later head of the OSS). Some of the volunteer amateurs were organized
into an informal intelligence agency called The Room, headed by financier Vincent
Astor, that reported directly to President Roosevelt. Astor, a director of Western
Union, covertly provided copies of foreign embassies' coded telegrams to American
codebreakers.

moving ahead of an army's conventional four columns in march. He even wrote a play, *The Fifth Column,* whose main character, a master spy, was a thinly-veiled portrait of the playwright himself.

Later, Hemingway was asked by Thomason of ONI, an old friend, to provide whatever intelligence he might encounter during his worldwide travels. Thomason was appreciative of the intelligence his most famous asset provided, but he learned to be patient every time Hemingway came to Washington to be debriefed, for the author insisted on adding seemingly interminable analyses of what he thought the intelligence meant. Usually, Hemingway's conclusions were wrong, although there were exceptions—such as his deduction early in 1941 that the Japanese were about to strike the United States.

Hemingway was not happy to have that intelligence ignored, so he broke off contact with ONI and sulked in his Havana villa, *Finca Vigia.* Still eager to perform his patriotic duty (at age 42 he was too old for military service), he went looking for some kind of spying he could perform. He thought he had found it among the several hundred thousand Spanish refugees who had fled to the island after the end of the Spanish Civil War. As he subsequently told his friend Spruille Braden, then U.S. ambassador to Cuba, there were at least 20,000 Fascist sympathizers among those refugees, a large "fifth column" lying in wait for the signal from Berlin to rise up and take over the island. Moreover, Hemingway claimed, he had learned the Fascists were working closely with German U-boats prowling offshore.

The otherwise sophisticated Braden believed this nonsense, and enlisted Hemingway, on behalf of State Department Intelligence, to retain a network of Spanish refugees he trusted. They would ferret out the Fascists among the refugees, while at the same time Hemingway would select several of them for a daring operation to hunt down U-boats, which would involve use of Hemingway's famous 40-foot fishing boat, the *Pilar.* Hemingway recruited a network of 26 motley types that amounted to the dregs of Cuba—gunrunners, pimps, whores, bartenders, playboys, gamblers, and a few drinking buddies of the author. Paid modest sums for their trouble, they were collectively called by Hemingway "Papa's Crook Factory" after his favorite nickname.

"Papa's Crook Factory" would make no contribution to the world of espionage, but it did unwittingly play a role in an important decision by American intelligence: mainly because of Hemingway and his network, it was firmly resolved that no amateur would ever be recruited again for any important intelligence operation. Given the record of the "crook factory," there is little doubt why that decision was made.

It was not long before all of Cuba knew of the "crook factory," mainly because none of its members could stop boasting about it. Hemingway himself directed operations from atop a stool in his favorite headquarters, the Floradita Bar, and although much time was spent over *Cuba Libres* discussing various schemes, there wasn't much intelligence collection going on. As for the U-boats, Hemingway and a crew sailed out regularly aboard the *Pilar* to bring the German underseas navy to its knees, but never seemed to find any submarines. This was a disappointment to two of the crew, aging Basque jai-alai players who were assigned the task of heaving an explosive into the conning tower of a U-boat when it surfaced near the *Pilar*.

News of these shenanigans soon reached the legal attache at the U.S. embassy, FBI Special Agent Raymond G. Leddy. Under the then-existing arrangements in American intelligence, the FBI had responsibility for all espionage and counterespionage operations in Latin America, South America, and the Caribbean. Thus, Leddy was in fact chief of station for Cuba, and he was not enthused by what he saw of "Papa's Crook Factory." He was even less enthused when Hemingway one night introduced him at a diplomatic party as "Mr. Gestapo."

Leddy wasted no time informing J. Edgar Hoover, who in turn went to the State Department to get Hemingway closed down. Cuba, argued Hoover, was a very important area of intelligence interest; given its crucial postion athwart major shipping lanes, the island obviously would be a target of strong interest to the Germans. The last thing the FBI needed in Cuba was an amateur crashing around the island like a bull in a china shop. And the idea of Hemingway taking on U-boats from his fishing boat was ridiculous; how could the embassy in Havana justify giving him gas from its precious stocks for such nonsense? Hoover concluded, correctly, that Hemingway had dreamed up the whole U-boat idea merely as a way of getting rationed gas to continue his regular fishing trips with his cronies. Leddy had a boatload of agents trailing the *Pilar* during those trips; as far as the FBI agents could determine, Hemingway and his cronies were spending all their time fishing and drinking. Hoover was even more infuriated to learn that the embassy was paying Hemingway $1,000 a month to dispense to the rabble he had recruited for the "crook factory."

Hoover's protests were ignored by the State Department. Leddy reported, to Hoover's growing fury, that the *Pilar*, thanks to Braden's largesse, was now equipped with a powerful radio, a brace of .50-caliber machine guns, and a collection of small arms to do battle—or so Hemingway said—with the U-boats. Near the stern was a huge explosive device that the two old jai-alai players somehow were supposed to toss inside a U-boat conning tower, which would have been quite a feat in rolling seas, even assuming the German submarine would have conveniently surfaced a few feet from the fishing boat.

Hoover continued to protest, and finally the State Department began to waver. Braden, the ambassador in Havana, was compelled to admit that Hemingway's network had not produced one single item of useable intelligence, and the *Pilar*, for all the gallons of gas it was consuming, had not even seen a submarine, much less gotten close enough to blow it up. At last, Braden gave in: in April 1943, he ordered all support cut off for "Papa's Crook Factory."

Hemingway carried on for another few months, but his amateurs could produce nothing in the way of intelligence. With the remaining stocks of gasoline he had on hand, he took the *Pilar* out for one last cruise for the duration of the war, a long trip that turned out to involve an epic battle to land the biggest marlin Hemingway had ever seen. A few months later, offered a magazine assignment to cover the war in Europe, he closed *Finca Vigia* and threw a huge three-day party to bid farewell. The party reportedly put a severe crimp in the available supplies of liquor on the island. Pointedly, Leddy of the FBI was not invited.

History later took some strange turns in the Hemingway story. After the war, when American intelligence was transformed into a large centralized bureaucracy using professional agents, the *opera bouffe* known as "Papa's Crook Factory" underscored arguments that in a newly dangerous world, the United States could no longer afford to use amateurs in the spy game.

Hoover, noted for his long memory (and vindictiveness), never forgave Hemingway; until the novelist's suicide in 1961, he was kept under FBI surveillance, an operation that created tens of thousands of pages of reports on every aspect of his life. Later revelations of such spying operations led to new laws severely restricting the FBI's scope in this area. In the process, there was extensive public airing of the FBI's dirty linen—massive (and illegal) domestic spying operations that ultimately were to drastically revise Hoover's reputation downward.

If the lesson of the "crook factory" for American intelligence was a determination never to repeat the experience, Hemingway learned quite something else. That final voyage of the *Pilar* in 1943, including the epic battle with the giant marlin, led to the plot for his novel, *The Old Man and the Sea*, which won for Hemingway the Nobel Prize for Literature. The award was duly noted in Hemingway's FBI file without comment. Apparently, Hoover was not impressed.

GRAHAM GREENE
Our Man in Havana

Code Name: 59200
1905–1991

Trying not to look too bored, the distinguished writer sat in a classroom full of other equally bored intellectuals listening to a lecture on the intricacies of invisible inks. It was not exactly what Graham Greene hoped for, but in that dark year of 1941, he had volunteered to do whatever he could to help his country. His resolve was now being tested.

Medically disqualified from active service, the 36-year-old author at the outbreak of war had joined the Ministry of Information. He was dissatisfied with the desk job, and yearning to be more actively engaged in the war, heeded a suggestion from his sister Elisabeth, who worked for MI6, that his talents would be put to better (and more exciting) use in the agency. Assuming that the real world of MI6 was like the fictional world of his novels, Greene happily applied to the agency. It was a decision both sides would come to regret.

As was the custom those days in the old boy network that was MI6, Greene had no trouble surviving the agency's laughable security check. Despite the fact that he had been a member of the Communist party during his student days at Oxford, Greene encountered no problems with his background. What counted was his acquaintance with everyone worth knowing in the establishment, the fact that he had a sister in MI6, and, for good measure, his close personal friendship with an MI6 official named **H. A. R. Philby.**

Novelist and former MI6 agent Graham Greene. (*AP/Wide World*)

Greene was among a number of intellectuals who were re-cruited for MI6. The agency's officials tended to distrust such types, but under wartime pressure to increase the agent ranks, they were willing to bend their convictions a little bit. But they would go only so far; they decided that the intellectuals would be given a special, condensed MI6 training course instead of the regular MI6 regimen, then assigned to quiet corners of the world where they wouldn't get in the way.

Accordingly, Greene found himself in that abbreviated MI6 training course listening to an apparently endless dissertation from some elderly MI6 veteran on the esoterica of invisible inks. Like Greene, the other intellectuals—among them such glitterati as Malcolm Muggeridge—found the lecture pointless; did MI6 expect its agents to carry around jars of invisible ink to write letters to London headquarters, as though this was still the time of Mata Hari? At one point, a student asked the instructor what they should do in the event that the supply of invisible ink ran out. No problem, the instructor replied, naming a number of "temporary expedients," among which, Greene remembered later, was a disgusting formula involving human saliva and pigeon droppings.

The course completed, Greene was assigned to one of the real out of the way MI6 stations, in Freetown, Sierra Leone. To describe this tiny African nation as a sleepy outpost would be to exaggerate its general importance; as Greene discovered, Freetown had all the excitement and glamour of a turtle race. Nevertheless, it overlooked the important shipping lanes along the African coast, and thus MI6 wanted somebody there to keep an eye on any attempts by the Germans to spy on the passing convoys and convey that intelligence to lurking U-boats.

Any idea Greene may have had that his assignment would involve skullduggery in dark alleys and other such esoterica of spy novels was quickly disabused by the reality of the spy game in Freetown. Thanks to the ULTRA code-breaking operation, the British had broken the *Abwehr*'s ciphers. Therefore, they could read the messages dispatching agents to various places, along with their reports once they arrived. Greene's function was merely to arrange for the expulsion of German agents or their assets once they were detected by ULTRA.

Not a very exciting or action-packed existence, and Greene, to the annoyance of his superiors in London, began to relieve the boredom with a number of pranks. Under cover as an inspector with the British Board of Trade in Freetown, Greene filled his reports with obscure literary allusions, puns, wordplays, and occasional chunks of quotations from novels. Once, when summoned to a meeting that he was unable to attend, Greene cabled headquarters, AS THE CHIEF EUNUCH SAID, I CANNOT REPEAT CANNOT COME. As usual, Greene signed the message with his code name of 59200, but on other occasions would sign himself with the names of various characters from classic novels.

Greene's escapades drew warnings of growing sternness from MI6 headquarters, but Greene paid no attention. To the exasperation of headquarters, Greene was just one of the troublesome intellectual recruits who tended to question all orders, mock some of the more hoary of MI6 traditions, and devise assorted games and spoofs to relieve the boredom of their assignments. They drove MI6 headquarters nuts.

By 1944, when the German U-boat threat had passed and Greene had virtually nothing to do, he arranged to be transferred to the Foreign Office Intelligence Department. MI6 let him go with a sigh of relief; then in the process of shedding its troublesome intellectuals, the agency made a solemn vow never again to hire such types as agents.

Greene later was to recall his wartime MI6 service with a shudder, and he would get his revenge two decades after the war by writing the classic satire of MI6, *Our Man in Havana*. Later a brilliant film with Alec Guinness, the best-selling novel of a British vacuum cleaner salesman in Havana who is recruited by MI6 struck its British readers as hysterically funny, but MI6 wasn't laughing. In fact, the British intelligence establishment was so infuriated, there were serious plans afoot to charge Greene with offenses under Britain's Official Secrets Act. Wiser heads finally prevailed, noting that the prospect of arguing in court that the bumbling MI6 officials in the novel violated security could only convince people that such caricatures were true. Plans for any prosecution were dropped.

In subsequent years, Greene and MI6 would come to an understanding of sorts. As the older generation in MI6 passed on, their successors took a mellower view of the former MI6 agent who had made a laughingstock of the agency. Greene even developed a close friendship with one of its brightest stars (and eventual chief), Maurice Oldfield, who made it a point to say how much he enjoyed Greene's "entertainments," as the author preferred to call his novels of spies and intrigues. His favorite, Oldfield would say with a twinkle in his eye, was *Our Man in Havana*.

GIOVANNI MONTINI
The Pope as Spy

1897–1978

Like many intelligence operations, it began quietly enough. Vincent Scamporini, the chief of station for the OSS outpost in newly-liberated Rome during 1944, reported receiving a piece of intelligence that showed great promise, provided the OSS was prepared to pay its bearer $125 a month.

A pretty handsome sum in 1944 dollars, and senior OSS officials in Washington thought long and hard before finally agreeing to pay the money. The recipient, known in OSS cable traffic as VESSEL, was promising good value for the money. He claimed to have a pipeline into the highest levels of the Vatican that among other things had access to secret conversations between the Japanese representative to the Holy See and Vatican officials, including Pope Pius XII. The Japanese representative, VESSEL said, was sounding out Vatican officals on various peace formulas that Tokyo hoped would lead to some sort of negotiated peace settlement with the United States. VESSEL claimed the Japanese were seeking to avoid an American invasion of the home islands that, however costly in American lives, would destroy Japan as a modern industrialized society.

With the OSS decision to buy the VESSEL intelligence, a series of consequences were set in motion that no one involved in the operation could have anticipated. Like the ripples from a rock thrown into a pond, VESSEL set off shock waves in every direction. In no particular order, they included one of the biggest mass surrenders in history, a huge covert action program that prevented a Western European nation from becoming a Communist satellite, and the recruitment of a Pope as an asset for American intelligence.

To understand how all this came about, it is first necessary to take a look at the man who stood at the epicenter of the explosion VESSEL set off, Giovanni Battista Montini—or, as history more commonly records him, Pope Paul VI.

Born in 1897 of upper-class parents, Montini as a teenager decided on the priesthood. However, unlike most of the other Italian boys who had decided on the same calling, Montini very early on demonstrated a striking ability for organization and administration; following his ordination in 1920, he was drafted for the Vatican bureaucracy. By 1937, a meteoric career had taken him to the post of Undersecretary of State for Ordinary Affairs, a job that brought him into close contact with the reclusive and enigmatic Pope Pius XII. With Pius as an important sponsor, Montini became one of the key leaders in the Vatican hierarchy, the man who "knew all and saw all." His reach extended outside Vatican walls, for after his promotion to head the Vatican's Secretariat of State, he was the chief papal contact with a wide variety of diplomats and political leaders. Reputed to have a card index for a brain, Montini soon had a network of worldly contacts that would have been the envy of any politician. For anyone wanting to do business with the Vatican, he was the man to see. He aso acquired a reputation for his access to a tremendous variety of information, stemming in part from his contacts with politicians and diplomats and the fact that he had been assigned the job of creating the Vatican Information Service, which was in fact the Vatican's intelligence agency.

All in all, Montini represented an intelligence agency's dream recruitment: Someone with his kind of access would represent the perfect asset. There did not seem to be anything that Montini (promoted to bishop in 1944) did not know, and no one had to wonder why: his intelligence service, which collected the reports of papal representatives in every corner of the globe, was reputedly the world's best.

But Montini resisted all attempts to tap into his storehouse of knowledge. His mind was focused exclusively on the existence of the Roman Catholic Church; as the representative of a tiny city-state with no army, existing precariously in the midst of nations at war, Montini maintained an air of studied neutrality.

The representative of Adolph Hitler was accorded precisely the same attention as the representative of Franklin Roosevelt. However subtle the approach, Montini was not about to play anybody's game—not, that is, until a chain-smoking Presbyterian showed up outside the Vatican walls.

James Jesus Angleton arrived in Rome in early 1944 as the 27-year-old head of the OSS X-2 (counterespionage) branch in the Italian capital. Already marked as one of the most brilliant counterintelligence officers in the OSS, he was cadaverously thin, with huge ears and a perpetually suspicious squint that often made him look like some kind of ferret. A prodigious chain smoker reputed to go through somewhere around four packs of cigarettes a day, Angleton had an odd background for a counterintelligence officer. Born of a prominent family (his father headed National Cash Register in Italy), Angleton went to Yale, where he became the university's leading aesthete. He ran a poetry magazine that published Ezra Pound, became a close friend of T. S. Eliot, and strolled around the campus like some sort of fop. But after joining the OSS in 1942, Angleton found his real true calling in counterintelligence. By the time he arrived in Rome, the former devotee of such exotica as iambic pentameter had become immersed in the world of double agents, dead drops, and discards.

Apprised of the VESSEL operation, Angleton was immediately suspicious. As he was aware, the Vatican in intelligence terms was an impenetrable, mysterious society headed by the remote Pope Pius XII. How, then, did VESSEL manage to penetrate this closed world and discover the most sensitive conversations and deliberations? The more Angleton considered the VESSEL material, the more he became convinced that there was something seriously wrong. He concluded that VESSEL was probably deception material, possibly planted by Japanese intelligence to mislead the Americans. Or perhaps it was Russian, because several key VESSEL reports talked about how importantly the Japanese regarded the Soviet Union's role in any settlement of the war with the United States. So perhaps the Russians were feeding in material to boost their role in a postwar Asia; as the OSS already knew from other sources, the Russians were very eager to obtain major influence in the Japanese-occupied areas of Manchuria and Korea, along with Japan itself.

Despite OSS headquarters' conviction that the VESSEL material was genuine and of great significance, Angleton set about to confirm his suspicion that it was not. He moved on two fronts. One, he put some of his agents to work to uncover the source of the VESSEL material. Two, he set about to recruit a source high in the Vatican hierarchy who could confirm whether the kind of conversations as VESSEL claimed really occurred. This latter task was really tough, but Angleton succeeded in making one of the really significant intelligence recruitments of all time. His name was Giovanni Montini.

How the flap-eared OSS officer of irrefutably Presbyterian stock managed to enlist the very Catholic Bishop with the great beak of a nose that dominated a thin face remains a mystery. Neither Angleton nor Montini ever discussed it, but the result was that the American now had a nearly priceless resource. Officially, Angleton had enlisted Montini for the sole purpose of tracking down the leak inside the Vatican that was finding its way into the VESSEL reports, but as perhaps both men were well aware, that was not to be the end of the relationship.

In any event, Montini proved to be invaluable in Angleton's VESSEL investigation. After carefully examining copies of the VESSEL reports purchased by the OSS, Montini had a surprise for his case officer: there was no leak in the Vatican. VESSEL's material, Montini concluded, bore no relation to the actual content of diplomatic discussions inside the Vatican, particularly the reports relating to alleged conversations with the Japanese representative. Actually, Montini told Angleton, the man from Tokyo was floundering; beset by contradictory instructions from a divided Japanese cabinet, he was trying as best he could to cobble together some sort of a peace deal that any experienced diplomat instantly knew would be unacceptable to the Americans. As Montini himself had told the Japanese representative, the Americans could not possibly accept a peace offer that would leave the military-dominated govenment in Tokyo still in power, nor would the Americans accept the idea of Japan retaining its control over Chinese territory it had seized.

The truth now dawned: VESSEL was a complete fake—a clever one, but a fraud nevertheless. But what was the motive? Who was VESSEL really working for? The answers came when Angleton finally tracked down the instigators behind VESSEL. The key man in the deal who had first approached the OSS was a White Russian exile named Dubinin. Angleton suspected, correctly, that Dubinin, a small fish, was in fact merely a cutout for the real man (or perhaps intelligence service) behind the code name VESSEL.

As things turned out, VESSEL proved to be a lot less complicated than many had presumed. Angleton discovered that VESSEL was Virgilio Scattolini, a short, fat journalist and author whose chief claim to fame to that point was as a pornographer. Before World War I, he had won dubious notoriety as the author of a number of scorching pornographic books that became best-sellers, including his classic *Amazons of the Bidet*. Subsequently, he married a devoutly Catholic woman who convinced him to undergo a dramatic religious conversion; he began attending Mass every day, and became a lay officer in the Franciscan order. His conversion was so complete, he was hired for the staff of *L'Osservatore Romano*, the Vatican semiofficial newspaper. But in 1939, the newspaper's editor, upon learning that one his writers was in fact the infamous Virgilio Scattolini the pornographer, fired him. Scattolini then turned to fiction, stitching together accounts of what was happening inside the Vatican walls from his own knowledge of its inner workings, newspaper reports, and rumors he heard around Rome. Scattolini was so good at it, he was sought out by newspapers and wire services for "inside" news of developments in the Vatican. The war put a crimp in his little business, but the arrival of the Americans in Rome in 1943 provided new opportunities. VESSEL was the result.*

The VESSEL case made Angleton the most celebrated counterintelligence agent in the OSS (he would go on some years later to become head of the CIA's counterintelligence division), but his now-close friendship with Montini promised even greater rewards. The relationship proved invaluable in early 1945, when the German SS, using the Vatican as a middleman, negotiated with the OSS for the surrender of all Axis forces in northern Italy. The deal, under which nearly a half million Axis troops laid down their arms (in return for amnesty from war crimes for the SS officials involved), was a triumph for the OSS. It was also a triumph for Montini, who had helped broker the deal, for he had saved northern Italy's vital industries from the kind of de-

---

* And his downfall. Scattolini's exposure led to his indictment and arrest under an obscure Italian law, originally designed to deter espionage on Italian soil, that made it illegal for anyone to "commit hostile acts against a foreign government." In this case, "foreign government" was interpreted to mean the Vatican, which indeed was a sovereign entity. Scattolini was convicted and sentenced to seven months and four days in prison. Upon his release, he disappeared and was never seen again. Some reports said he became a monk.

struction that inevitably would have resulted in a full-scale military campaign.

Three years later, Montini was to play still another critical role, this one involving the very survival of Italy itself. By this time, he had been promoted to the post of Archbishop of Milan, one of the Italian church's most powerful constituencies and regarded as a stepping stone to the papacy. Moreover, Montini not only still retained his strong ties inside the Vatican, he was coincidentally head of Catholic Action, a millions-strong Catholic political action group. They represented an essential counterweight to the growing might of the Italian Communist party, which was widely expected to take power in the 1948 national elections. Such a result was unthinkable to Washington, so a large-scale covert political action operation by the CIA was set into motion. Among the operation's important case officers was Angleton, who again tapped into his friend Montini. The archbishop responded by mobilizing Catholic Action, the Vatican's considerable resources, and his extensive contacts across the Italian political spectrum to help the CIA's operation. In the end, the combination of American money, a supreme effort by Italy's non-Communist political groups, and the Vatican's considerable help turned the tide. The Communists failed to win a majority, and although they would remain a force in Italian politics for years thereafter, their high-water mark had passed.

For his part, there were a few important favors Angleton could perform to repay his debt to Montini. It was Angleton who helped arrange the reestablishment of Vatican control over the Catholic churches in southern Germany, an area within the American zone of occupation. Angleton also helped the Vatican reestablish contact with the important Catholic dioceses in western Yugoslavia. A few other, similar, arrangments helped cement the Angleton-Montini relationship. It was to result in unanticipated dividends in 1963, when the wily Vatican diplomat was chosen as Pope Paul VI. A rigid ecclesiastical conservative who enforced mandatory celibacy for the priesthood and unwavering church opposition to all forms of contraception, Montini nevertheless remained a pragmatic politician. Until his death in 1978 of a heart attack, he still had close relations with American intelligence, while at the same time began the first negotiations toward reestablishing church authority in Eastern Europe.

The precise details of what services Pope Paul VI was able to perform for American intelligence are not known, but it is a fact that 14 years after his death, one of his successors, Pope John Paul II, aided an American covert funding operation for the Polish Solidarity union. That very same Pope has now recommended Giovanni Montini for sainthood, a recommendation that, interestingly enough, does not mention VESSEL.

W. SOMERSET MAUGHAM
Our Man in Petrograd

Code Name: SOMERVILLE
1874–1965

What must have been the world's most unusual intelligence agent arrived in Petrograd (formerly St. Petersburg) in August 1917. The new revolutionary Russian government, led by the former Minister of War, Alexander Kerensky, did not quite know what to make of this odd-looking character who claimed his journey to the turmoil of Petrograd—in the middle of World War I, no less—was solely for the purpose of researching his next novel.

The Russians did not find this cover story very credible, but could not bring themselves to believe that the Englishman W. Somerset Maugham could be any kind of spy. He arrived in expensive, custom-tailored clothes, complete with spats and a walking stick. In the grimness of revolutionary Petrograd, he stood out like a diamond in a slag pile, hardly the kind of cover spies are supposed to adapt. Then too, there was the matter of his speech, marked by a pronounced stutter, along with regular coughs from his tuberculosis. To round out the portrait of unlikely spy, Maugham was an overt homosexual, prone to ogling the revolutionary sailors who had stormed the Winter Palace and overthrown the Czar.

But Maugham was a spy, dispatched by British intelligence on a mission with very high stakes and very serious consequences.

The mission to Petrograd was not Maugham's first encounter with intelligence. In 1915, he was a popular 41-year-old writer living in Switzerland who wanted to do something to help his country's war effort. Given Maugham's extensive contacts throughout the Swiss establishment and the European homosexual *demimonde*, a new British War Office entity called MI1(c)—later in the war to become MI6—recruited him to keep an eye on German agents and their assets operating in Switzerland. Maugham was successful in the assignment, and although it involved no real danger, he later embellished his experiences for the series of "Ashenden" spy stories he wrote, with himself as the thinly-disguised hero, a daring British agent.

Maugham was related to one of MI6's senior sachems, William Wiseman, head of British intelligence in the United States. Officially, Wiseman was chief of the British Purchasing Mission, but in fact he was busily engaged in running large-scale intelligence, propaganda, and counterespionage operations against German intelligence in the United States. Based in Washington, Wiseman had important connections throughout the American corporate establishment, and, more importantly, the White House via his friendship with Colonel Edward House, President Woodrow Wilson's most trusted adviser. In the absence of any effective American intelligence in that era, it was thus British intelligence that served to shape many of Wilson's perceptions.

Among them was Russia. The revolution of 1917 had complicated matters, because although the new revolutionary government under Kerensky vowed to continue Russia's participation in the war against Germany, he was coming under increasing pressure from the Bolsheviks to sign a separate peace and take Russia out of the war. "Peace and bread!" the Bolshevik slogan ran, and it was striking a deep chord in the Russian masses.

British intelligence was alarmed; with Russia out of the war, the Germans would be able to shift over a million troops from the east to the Western Front, there to fall upon the exhausted British and French. The war hung in the balance; even the arrival of American troops would not occur in time to prevent disaster. At all costs, Russia had to be kept in the war. First, however, British intelligence had to find out two things: one, the prospects of the Kerensky government surviving; and two, what was needed to keep that government in power.

It was Wiseman's idea to use Maugham for the mission. In Wiseman's calculation, Maugham's literary fame would work as ideal cover for his real mission in Petrograd. Additionally, he had some espionage experience from his work in Switzerland.

But the world of neat, ordered Switzerland was nothing like Petrograd. The city was a political madhouse. Worse, as Maugham discovered almost immediately, he had arrived too late; German intelligence had been busy and efficient. It had already arranged for Lenin and other Bolshevik leaders to be secretly transported to Russia in the famous sealed train, and had very effective propaganda operations well-entrenched. The German propaganda, which argued to the Russian masses that they had no stake in a European war that was bleeding Russia white, was having its effect. Entire Russian divisions were mutinying, and many Russian soldiers, sick of the war, were simply leaving their units and walking back home.

Only drastic action could save the Kerensky regime, Maugham reported to Wiseman. Unless the Allies were prepared to infuse the Kerensky regime with massive amounts of money to offset German intelligence's covert funding of the Bolsheviks, then the provisional revolutionary government was in imminent danger of falling. Further, Maugham reported, if the Allies wanted to keep the Russian military—or at least what was left of it—in the war, only direct military intervention would save the day.

While the Allies were deciding what to do, events overtook them. Lenin and the Bolsheviks seized power; Kerensky fled into exile, and the Russian war effort fell apart. Maugham fled Russia aboard a British destroyer dispatched to take him quickly out of harm's way.

Returning to Switzerland, Maugham, his tuberculosis worsened by the Russian climate, informed Wiseman that he was through working for British intelligence. (Folowing his recuperation, Maugham returned to writing, finally entering literary immortality before his death in 1965).

Meanwhile, Wiseman went to work on Wilson, arguing that only drastic action could "save" Russia. Wilson then agreed to a number of steps that Wiseman believed would reverse the tide of history: the landing of Allied forces in Russia, including 13,000 American troops, approval of a covert action program to disrupt the infant Bolshevik regime, and direct support for anti-Bolshevik forces in the Russian civil war that broke out at the end of World War I. All of these actions resulted in a disaster whose consequences reverberated many decades to come. All that Wilson and the Allies achieved was the undying enmity of the Bolsheviks, and it remains an intriguing exercise to wonder what would have happened if the Bolsheviks had not been made international outlaws at the very moment of their coming to power.

The man who was at center stage for these cataclysmic events—and who played no small role in them—professed to be disinterested in anything having to do with Russia. He never publicly discussed his Petrograd mission, nor did he use any of his experience in his novels. Clearly, he wanted to forget the whole thing. "My dear boy," he replied when he was once asked about it, "you cannot imagine a more *God-awful* place." He said nothing more, the good spy revealing as little as possible.

Index